"The grand trends of global history become real, Maiwald and Suerig argue, only to the extent that they become palpable to real people in real places. Microsociology is the study of how a large entity – like society – comes down to what the authors call specific 'structures of interaction.' Drawing on a wide range of key thinkers, this beautifully written and superbly organized volume invites the reader into what may become a new way of thinking. An excellent introduction to microsociology."

– *Arlie Russell Hochschild, University of California, Berkeley, USA, author of* The Managed Heart *and* Strangers in Their Own Land.

MICROSOCIOLOGY

This book offers an unprecedented, integrative account of the shape of social order on the microsocial level. Dealing with the basic dimensions of interaction, the authors examine the major factors which influence "structure" in social interaction by applying various theoretical concepts. Although the concept of "microsociology" is usually associated with symbolic interactionism, social psychology, the works of George Herbert Mead and Erving Goffman and with qualitative methodologies, this book reaches beyond interactionist theories, claiming that no single school of thought covers the different dimensions necessary for understanding the basics of microsociology. As such, the book provides something of a microsociologist's "tool kit," analyzing an array of theoretical approaches which offer the best conceptual solutions, and interpreting them in a way that is independent of their specific theoretical language. Such theoretical traditions include systems theory, conversation analysis, structuralism, the theory of knowledge and the philosophy of language.

Providing a distinct, systematic and incremental approach to the subject, this book fills an important gap in sociological literature. Written in an accessible style, and offering new insights into the area of microsociology, it will appeal to students and scholars of the social sciences and to those with interests in sociology, microsociology, interactionism and sociological theory.

Kai-Olaf Maiwald is Professor of Microsociology and Qualitative Methods at the University of Osnabrück, Germany.

Inken Suerig is Scientific Assistant for Microsociology and Qualitative Methods at the University of Osnabrück, Germany.

MICROSOCIOLOGY

A Tool Kit for Interaction Analysis

Kai-Olaf Maiwald and Inken Suerig

LONDON AND NEW YORK

First published in English 2020 by Routledge
by Routledge
2 Park Square, Milton Park, Abingdon, Oxon OX14 4RN

and by Routledge
52 Vanderbilt Avenue, New York, NY 10017

Routledge is an imprint of the Taylor & Francis Group, an informa business

Translated by Nicola Barfoot

Translation from the German language edition:
Microsociology by Kai-Olaf Maiwald / Inken Suerig the author
Copyright @ [Springer Fachmedien Wiesbaden GmbH] [2016].
All Rights Reserved.

British Library Cataloguing-in-Publication Data
A catalogue record for this book is available from the British Library

Library of Congress Cataloging-in-Publication Data
A catalog record has been requested for this book

ISBN: 978-0-367-25078-2 (hbk)
ISBN: 978-0-367-25079-9 (pbk)
ISBN: 978-0-429-28589-9 (ebk)

Typeset in Bembo
by Deanta Global Publishing Sevices, Chennai, India

CONTENTS

INTRODUCTION

Is society something big?

In our everyday use of the word "society," it seems to be something that can be localized and pointed to. We talk about "French society" or "South African society" as if they were places we could find on a map, as if "nation state" and "society" were identical. But at the same time, we know intuitively that unlike a country, society is not a specific place we can visit or travel to; and even if we were to say that we were "born into" a concrete society, we would not mean something that is defined by its state borders. So where is "society"? At other times we seem to understand society as a person, for example when we say "society is to blame," or "society needs to take action." But what – or whom – do we mean here?

If we start to search for society "on the ground," we find kindergartens, florists, conversations among friends, traffic lights, pubs, product information leaflets, official instructions, football games, postage stamps, newspapers, youth welfare offices, umbrellas, television programs, barbecues, condom dispensers, building sites, marching bands, young couples going for walks, blood donor cards, seminar rooms, Internet profiles, driver's licenses, hospitals, rubbish bins, gift vouchers. We find an odd collection of objects, places and groups. And yet it is not inconceivable that a person could, in a single day, come into contact with all these things. With a little effort, each of us could tell a story in which all the items listed above could be connected. And we could equally well tell a story in which none of them occurs, or only some of them – and many other variations.

But regardless of which story we tell: the link is human beings. Not just our existence, of course, but our actions. Any possible connection between an umbrella and an Internet profile is not determined by either the umbrella or the Internet profile. It is only when we cease to simply recount what we are seeing, and start to interpret it and make connections, that we find "society." In doing so, we have simultaneously described "society" as something that is defined by our interpretations and actions. On one level, an umbrella is a stick with a cover attached to it, and a hospital is a building with a sign saying "hospital." But we associate both the object and the word we use for it with something that goes beyond its objective materiality. Like the object, society cannot be explained without reference to actions.

These, however, are always actions in the plural. In the first instance, this has to do with the basic insight of sociology that "society" is not an actor, not even a collective actor, like a government or a company. Thus "society" cannot make decisions, and cannot be held responsible for anything, unlike governments and companies. Instead, it is something abstract, a formula with which sociology seeks to define the unity of its subject area. Few sociologists are able to do without such a formula. The need for a plural extends to the actions and contexts of action in which we encounter "society," as in the examples listed previously. In sociology, we are generally interested not in the individual actions of particular people in unique situations, but in something that goes beyond this, i.e. structures. Whatever precise definition sociologists have for this, what they are always looking for is patterns, which are reflected in particular actions. This always includes an element of repeatability: they are concerned with identifiable *modes* of action of identifiable *groups* of people in *generally describable* situations.

Since the end of the 1970s, it has become commonplace in sociology to distinguish between microsociology and macrosociology. This kind of classification of sociological research has arisen in addition to other distinctions, such as that between theory and empirical research, or distinctions based on specific subject areas: the sociology of the family, the sociology of religion, the sociology of work, etc. A key element of the distinction between "micro" and "macro" is the idea of what "structure" is in sociology, and by what methods it can be explored. Here macrosociology is usually taken to mean a research perspective which combines a focus on particular objects in society with a preference for a particular methodological approach. The idea that society and its structures are "something big" is mainly associated with this perspective: macrosociology generally concentrates on "big" social units. These can be social subsystems (such as law, the economy, or politics), or large-scale social groups or groupings (such as strata, classes, milieus, but also the socially relevant concepts of "gender" or "ethnicity"). Lastly, it is also possible to study aspects of society as a whole (social inequalities, demographic developments, generational cohorts, etc.). Empirical-macrosociological analysis generally uses standardized surveys with large numbers of cases to explore the structural features of society as a whole, or of "big" social units. This kind of analysis relies on statistically measurable correlations of characteristics, related to high levels of aggregation ("populations"). Here largely stable correlations between characteristics are regarded as "structure," e.g. the correlation between social origin and educational success. The question of how structures emerge is only investigated by differentiating between dependent and independent variables.

While many of our fellow sociologists would probably rate this characterization as an (overly) rough simplification, the understanding of microsociology as a discipline is undoubtedly even less consistent. It can, for example, be defined as research that deals with "small" social units such as family and couple relationships, small social groups, or the individual. Further typical objects of microsociology, according to this understanding, include socialization, personal identity or youth and adolescence. Obviously, these subjects can be investigated using quantitative methods, as in macrosociology. However, another understanding of microsociology is that it can be defined in terms of methodology, i.e. it can be associated with a specific aspiration to explain. The focus is then on the roots of social structures, their fundamental location. In line with this, the core idea of microsociology is that social structures (including those of society as a whole) must always have their foundations in the concrete actions of concrete individuals, and that sociological research has to take into account this level of the concreteness of social action. This does not apply solely to the structure of family relationships or small social groups. Social inequality and social status – typical macrosociological phenomena – are just as much a product of interactions as friendships or a new form of customer orientation. If social structures are real, they must become real in interactions, and they must be observable in data on social interaction. In line with this, close scrutiny of the social world – putting it under the microscope, as it were – is seen as a core aspect of empirical sociological research.

This perspective is shared by two very different approaches. The first follows on from the tradition of methodological individualism, and is, at present, mainly embodied by the different varieties of rational choice theory, with its key question of how collective phenomena can be traced back to the actions of individuals. A crucial explanatory element here is the idea of utility maximization, which is understood as an anthropological constant. In this approach, "microscopic scrutiny" is essentially limited to the level of modeling; as a rule, this is not about analyzing concrete actions, but developing models of how individual patterns of action in particular problem complexes should be imagined *in principle*. Hypotheses are then formed, operationalized and tested using the instruments of standardizing methods. We do not take this approach, however; instead we follow a second approach, which can broadly be characterized as "interactionist." According to this approach, the central units of study are not individuals (the calculations they make, the restrictions imposed on their choices of action), but interactions. And empirical analysis does not involve modeling a situation of action and then testing hypotheses, but qualitative case reconstruction on the basis of primarily "natural" data from interactions.[1]

This "natural data" can comprise not only face-to-face interactions between individuals in families, in the workplace, in organizations, in parliaments, in the public sphere, etc., but also media-based communications (newspapers, books, the Internet), or utterances by collective actors such as legislation or professional codes. Nonetheless, face-to-face interactions – as will become clear in the opening chapters – remain of major importance, because our "solitary" actions, like our media-based communications, always presuppose the experience of direct interaction. This is fundamental for both analysis and developmental logic, and will therefore be our major focus.

The primary concern of this introduction to microsociology should be understood in light of this methodological position. It is neither about the characteristics of couple or family relationships or other small social groups, nor is it about the fundamentals of a sociological theory of action. Instead, the theme is "the formation of structures in interactions." In more precise terms, our aim is to provide the conceptual tools needed to analyze processes of structure formation in interactions. The key assumption here is that what happens in interactions, what happens in our everyday and non-everyday actions in a wide range of situations, is anything but coincidental, random, or merely "individual." On the contrary, a multitude of structures can be identified, patterns that go beyond the uniqueness of the specific interaction events. These can be patterns that characterize the concrete social relationship between concrete individuals (e.g. the couple John and Jenny, the Smith family), which are representative of a type of social relationship (e.g. couple and family relationships), which show that those involved belong to a particular social milieu, and so on. These processes do not occur without any preconditions; the individuals involved do not produce them out of anywhere. On the contrary: in this book, we deal solely with those aspects that precede every concrete interaction, be they universal mechanisms (e.g. that of the formal organization of interaction) which always affect interaction, or structural parameters specific to particular societies (e.g. roles and norms), which are at least likely to affect interaction.

In the following chapters, we will present what we see as the basic "building blocks" of interaction. All of these building blocks, like sequentiality, reciprocity or social roles and norms, have been conceptualized by various theories on society and interaction; each of these concepts is quite commonly used and it is hard to do sociological analysis without them. What has been missing up until now is a microsociological "tool kit" which employs the different concepts in order to analyze the formation of structure in interaction systematically. This is what this book intends to provide. Accordingly, it deals with the *fundamentals of structure formation*, and explicitly not with the *characteristics of the structures thus formed*, e.g. social recognition (or lack of recognition), power, social inequality, status, rationality, professionalism, capitalism, etc. Structural aspects of this kind can be explored with the tools presented here. The converse does not apply.

Our concept of microsociology is, or has been, usually associated with symbolic interactionism, social psychology, the works of George Herbert Mead and Erving Goffman and qualitative methodologies. While these strands play a major role in this book, it is not confined to interactionist theories in this "classical" sense. We also draw on such diverse theoretical traditions as systems theory, conversation analysis, structuralism, the theory of knowledge and the philosophy of language. This approach may strike some readers as oddly eclectic. How is it even possible to extract concepts from their coherent theoretical framework, each with its own theoretical language, and place them in an altogether different context? Our first answer to this is that such an approach is simply necessary, because no single school of thought covers the different dimensions we deem important in order to understand the basics of microsociology. The second answer is that such an approach is not so very difficult to pursue, since we concentrate on those concepts that lend themselves to a reinterpretation in the light of interaction theory. Because of this affinity, there is no need to take into account the whole "package" of concepts a certain school of thought has to offer. What is needed, though, is a presentation that is, at least to a certain degree, independent of the specific theoretical language. So what we attempt to provide in each chapter is a genuine *re*-interpretation of this kind. Our book thus offers an unprecedented *integrative account* of the shape of social order on the microsocial level.

In another respect, too, the way we elaborate these basic concepts or building blocks chapter by chapter takes a selective approach to the relevant scholarly literature. As a rule, we will be looking at those authors who are regarded as significant within the relevant discourses. For the most part, we will refer to ideas because we see them as important and influential, but sometimes we will also discuss theories in order to highlight differences between these arguments and our own. In any case, however, this is by no means a comprehensive and comparative appraisal of the state of research. Instead, we will always offer our own independent theories as well as others, i.e. the argument presented will always make it clear "how we see things." Not just because, in view of the state of the literature, we often feel the need to present arguments more precisely (in our opinion), but also and most importantly because we see it as advantageous for an introduction to provide readers with as definite a position as possible. They can then test the cogency of this position by following up the references supplied.

The mode of presentation we have chosen differs from many other introductory texts in one further respect. Not only do we try to make complex matters comprehensible by constantly including empirical examples, if possible from everyday life, we also provide a continuous empirical point of reference, a "data source," an interaction sequence which is referred to in all the chapters, mainly in the "food for thought" section. This section contains questions which the readers can explore in relation to the material, in order to gain their own insights into the matters presented. The idea of using a single interaction sequence throughout is based on the assumption that it should in theory be possible to use *any* interaction to illustrate fundamental building blocks of structure formation in interactions. In practice, of course, some interaction sequences may be better suited to this than others. The interaction sequence to be analyzed is a scene from the movie *As Good As It Gets* by James L. Brooks. It is the story of the compulsive, egomaniacal writer of trashy novels Melvin, played by Jack Nicholson, who in the course of events gradually learns to open up to other people. In the selected scene, Melvin constantly subverts standards of social interaction that we usually take for granted, and this is why the sequence is so suitable to illustrate all those aspects dealt with in this book: Melvin's actions often strike us as strange and funny, but also appalling, and our judgments of adequacy are a good starting point for exploring what it is that is violated by his actions. The scene (minutes 1:10:33–1:12:41) takes place in a café where Melvin is a regular costumer because waitress Carol indulges his many quirks. The characters involved in the interaction are Melvin, the booking agent Frank and Carol. The plot is mainly about Frank trying to persuade Melvin to drive Simon, a mutual acquaintance who is in trouble, to Baltimore.

The best way to make use of the book's references to the film scene is not only to watch it, but also to draw up a detailed transcript, as is customary in interaction analyses. Write down everything the characters are saying, as in a movie script,[2] and add descriptions of the non-verbal interactions taking place. Once you have finished you will have about two pages of lively interaction, excellent material for applying your growing knowledge about interaction structures.

Notes

1 In this book we do not have the scope to explore the methodological side of microsociology based on interaction theory here. Nor will we deal systematically with this in subsequent chapters, although there will be hints of the "spirit" of interpretative and reconstructive research, particularly in the various empirical examples we will discuss. We refer readers here to the relevant publications from the corresponding methodological discourse.

2 As a matter of fact, the movie script of *As Good As It Gets* can be found on the Internet. If you are using the script, note that the movie's actual wording differs from the script in several respects.

1

INTERACTION

How presence becomes participation

This chapter lays the groundwork for the book by discussing and defining terms like "social action," "social relations," "communication" and "interaction." Here we draw especially on the theories of Niklas Luhmann and Erving Goffman. We use Niklas Luhmann's systems theory to establish a systematic connection between "interaction" and "society," an entry point we deem essential to understanding why sociology deals with something as (seemingly) vague and arbitrary as interaction in the first place. Luhmann, who is probably more influential in German-speaking sociology than in English-speaking sociology, is a theorist who advanced Talcott Parsons's systems theory in different respects. One important advance is a shift in the basic focus from the "actions" of individuals to "communication." For Luhmann, social systems are constituted by communications related to semantic codes that are specific to the respective system, such as "just/unjust" in the legal system. Only communications with such a "dual" reference carry weight in the system. Second, Luhmann provides a stronger concept of the unity of autonomous social systems. He not only explores several sub-systems of society (such as the economy, law or science), but distinguishes three distinct levels of system-building: interaction, organization and society. These two advances in particular make Luhmann's theory a fruitful starting point for our endeavor. However, since systems theory is a universal theory and not especially concerned with the particulars of the "interaction system" in itself, we use Erving Goffman's interaction theory to explain the "social basics" of face-to-face interaction. The important point being made in this chapter is that face-to-face interaction can be seen as the "prototype" of social relations. Based on this, we discuss the consequences of presence, co-presence, participation and collaboration, concluding that even on the most basic level of social relations, there must be a social order at work which merits in-depth scrutiny.

Microsociology, as we have established in the introduction, seeks to approach "society" via social interaction, i.e. via actions that take place between people. In the sociological sense, there is no interaction between objects (unlike chemistry, for example, where different substances can "interact" with each other), nor is there any interaction between a subject (a person) and an object (a thing), e.g. "human–computer interaction." We define interaction as the form of social action in which (at least) two acting subjects refer or relate to each other in their actions. Interaction is therefore the smallest unit of social relations, and people only have social relations with other people.

This is easier to comprehend if we bear in mind that the precondition for interaction and social relations is the capacity for social action. Here we can draw on Weber (1978 [1922]), who understands social action as intentional action which is related to one or more other (specific or non-specific) people, but does not require their concrete, instantaneous involvement. While Weber (ibid.) defines action in general as any form of human behavior to which the actor attaches a subjective meaning (i.e. the action is meaningful for the acting person himself or herself, regardless of whether this meaning is objectively ascertainable, true or right), social action is, according to its subjective meaning, focused on the behavior of others. Thus a rubbish collector acts socially when she empties the rubbish bins by the roadside; a father acts socially when he bakes a birthday cake for his daughter; a student acts socially when she proofreads a research paper for a fellow student. Acting socially, though, is not limited to doing good to others; this is where a scientific understanding diverges from an everyday understanding of "social" action. Thus the writing of a threatening letter is a social action, as is the setting of a particularly difficult examination, where it is obvious from the outset that half the students will fail. The criterion for social action, then, is the difference between self-reference and external reference, regardless of moral or ethical aspects. Thus we observe that many people have an intense "relationship" with their pet, but that the pet is not able to act socially in a subjectively meaningful way – and of course this applies even more to computers and chemical elements.

Weber (ibid.) assumes, however, that subjectively meaningful action is always (at least to a certain degree) action that can be understood by observers, insofar as it can be "adequately communicated in words" (ibid., p. 5). Here it is important, in the first instance, to note that understanding is also a subjective matter. In this context, Schütz (1967 [1932], p. 14) points out the different perspective of actors and observers as "the crucial distinction between understanding *our own experiences of the other person* and understanding the other person's experiences." We do not achieve "understanding" by completely decoding the subjective meaning of others' actions, but by being able to ascribe a meaning to these actions, independent of what is subjectively meant. The lecturer who sets an extremely difficult exam may understand this as an interesting intellectual challenge, while the students who have to sit the exam see it as an intentional and unfair imposition. Although the way the lecturer "means" her action is different from the way the students interpret it, the lecturer's action is not incomprehensible or meaningless for the students.

This example, however, should make it clear that a constant dissonance between self-understanding and understanding others – i.e. if observers always interpreted the (social) action of individuals differently from the way it is meant – is not conceivable in a human community. There is a simple reason for this: human communities are not agglomerations of actors and observers, but associations of people acting collectively. Thus when Weber observes (see previous) that understanding others has to do with something being "adequately communicable in words," the phrase might seem tautological at first glance, but it brings together three important prerequisites of joint action: the availability of "words," i.e. linguistic signs and sign systems which make things generally expressible or describable; the "adequate" use of such signs, i.e. the use of appropriate linguistic equivalents of whatever is meant to be expressed; and "communicability," that is, the possibility of making something "common" and sharing it with one another. In this line of argument, then, comprehensible action is action about which members of society can communicate in a linguistically adequate manner. And that, in turn, must mean that it is possible to rely on an "objective," shared meaning, a joint understanding. This is in fact exactly how we are socialized as members of society: not as individuals who act alone, with incommunicable motives and decision-making processes, but always, from the beginning, as people who act jointly with others, whose motives and decisions arise and are shaped and internalized in interaction with others, and are obviously open to modifications in this interaction. We will take a closer look at exactly how this works in Chapter 4 on perspective-taking. The point we want to make here is that there is something that goes beyond individual action and the observation of action, and constitutes *the* key feature of human communities: communication.

At this point we will begin by discussing the concept of communication used by Luhmann (1995 [1984]). According to this, communication is the synthesis of three selections: the specific *information* chosen from the endless possibilities of all information (what is said?); the *utterance*, i.e. the specific way this information is conveyed (how is it said?); and *understanding* as the distinction between information and utterance (what does it mean?). For example, the information that there is a traffic jam on the M1 can be communicated in the following way: "There's a traffic jam on the M1." This utterance can be understood differently from "There's yet another traffic jam on the M1," or "The traffic jam is on the M1." Thus the way the information is conveyed already contains a categorization and an interpretation: there is no information that can only be conveyed in a single, specific, unambiguous way. Thus it is not the information itself but the utterance that is understood. The utterance is the interpretation of a piece of information, and understanding is therefore the interpretation of this interpretation. The possibilities for responding to the observation "There's a traffic jam on the M1" are, on the one hand, more limited than the original selection of the information. "Bread" is certainly not a plausible response, while "Uh-huh,"

"Which section?", or "The M1 urgently needs upgrading" would all be fitting replies, showing how the utterance has been understood. As the response relates to the preceding utterance, then, we can say that the communication refers to itself. This is not about the information "in itself," but about the distinctions and interpretations which are undertaken in the communication. We also see, however, that while communication tends to narrow down topics (e.g. from the general occurrence of traffic jams to the upgrading of motorways) and thus reduce complexity, there is always more than one possible way the topic can be narrowed. This phenomenon is referred to as contingency or even, to use Luhmann's term (ibid., p. 103), "double contingency:" we can never be completely sure how the other person will choose to respond to the message, and this applies to all those involved in the communication. As there are always "action alternatives," it is never clearly predictable how others will behave. This uncertainty, however, is absorbed to a certain degree by communication, because it refers to what has already been said, and not to what is still to be said. We can only form and stabilize our expectations about the behavior of the person we are talking to on the basis of what has already been said, and structure our own behavior accordingly:

> Communication must follow on quite specifically from what has previously been said, and it must make it clear what can occur in response to this response.
>
> *(Kieserling 1999, p. 79, translated by N.B.)*

We have already noted previously that communication is the key feature of human communities. Following Luhmann (1995 [1984]), we can even argue that communication is *the* constitutive and thus structure-forming element of society. We can, of course, understand this quite simply: if we were not able to communicate (in whatever manner), we would all be isolated individual beings, incapable of collective action. But what is it exactly that communication does to make us capable of joint action? In the singular chain comprising information, utterance and understanding, we can only discern a very basic level of "collective" action in the form of a joint focus (on the utterance). But if a single act of communication – in the form of an individual conversation – turns into a communication process where other communications follow on from it, this gives rise to an unlimited number of conversations, both synchronous and asynchronous, among an unlimited number of participants, conversations which always at least have the potential to relate to other conversations. This potential has its foundations in the difference between themes and contributions; nexuses of communication, according to Luhmann (ibid., p. 155), "must be ordered by themes to which contributions can relate." This means that contributions can always be assigned to a theme (and not only to a particular person, a particular point in time, or a place where they were made); thus the theme is the overarching context which is able to connect individual acts of communication. It is therefore entirely possible for many different conversations among many different participants in different places at different times to have something in common: the theme. The more generally we understand "theme" here, the clearer it becomes that there are themes which have been, are, and will remain relevant in an especially large number of communications, for example law, education or health. Repeated references to a theme and the relevant contributions mean that certain selections are reproduced again and again in different times and places and by different people, and are made "common;" in this way expectations – not only about the specific person we are interacting with, but also about members of society in general – are consolidated. We take this to mean that social relations and therefore social systems would not be possible without the expectations consolidated (i.e. secured) in and through communication: expectations that we have of other people, and that other people have of us.

If, however, the term "communication" encompasses all this – from the three basic selections to the processual conversation and ultimately to the processes that form and reproduce society – what does the term "interaction" have to offer? In actual fact, these two terms are often used in combination or even synonymously. If we take a closer look at them, however, we can first observe that "communication" and "interaction" do not designate the same thing, in terms of the exact meaning of the words. As we have seen, communication is an exchange of information involving selection and understanding, while interaction is defined as reciprocal action. In general language use, the term "communication" has become firmly associated with the conveying of a message, and is often used with reference to communication technologies, i.e. channels of communication: telephone, letters, text messages, emails, video streaming, etc. We say, for example, that we are in "written communication" with someone, but we do not talk about "written interaction." The concept of interaction is often encountered as an adjective: for some years we have been seeing the term "interactive" more and more often in certain contexts: as "interactive television," an "interactive PDF" or even "interactive communication" (in connection with the Internet). In the first two cases "interactive" does not refer so much to the quality of reciprocal action, but more to new options for individual, instantaneous intervention in processes which previously occurred without our active involvement: for many years we were merely consumers of television programming, and had no influence on it, and a PDF file was initially conceived as a document to which no further changes could be made (e.g. highlighting, comments). As we have already noted, however, the fact that we can actively influence something does not yet mean, from a microsociological perspective, that this process constitutes interaction. When we compile our personal television schedule, or underline something in a PDF document, this is not even necessarily social action in a Weberian sense, as explained previously – unless we refer specifically to others in these activities, e.g. by including a TV documentary series which our partner likes, or underlining the passages in a colleague's PDF which we want to discuss with her later. The second example makes it clear that this is social action in anticipation of interaction, but not yet interaction itself. In contrast, the notion of "interactive communication" on the Internet, seems – strictly speaking – to presuppose that communication is by definition not interactive, and only becomes so when this quality is added to it. The underlying concept of communication here, precisely because it relates to the Internet, is technology-driven. It refers solely to technical opportunities for participating in communication, but does not thematize the quality of communication in itself, which – as we have already established – must at least involve interpersonal interaction to fulfill the basic conditions: utterance and understanding.

Communication technology is thus the key point at which we can successfully differentiate between communication and interaction. The attempt has been made to establish such a distinction from the perspective of system theory, by treating interaction not as something completely different from communication, but as a special form of it: "communication among people who are present" (Kieserling 1999). This is communication between individuals who can physically perceive each other, i.e. who are within sight and earshot of each other. According to Kieserling (ibid., p. 67, tr. by N.B.), these are communications "which also communicate the fact that this is communication among people who are present." The special emphasis here is on "presence." But before we begin to explore which aspects and factors are connected with presence and perceptibility, and why these are crucial for interaction, we should first note that the presence of other people is not just the norm, but also the "first case," in both phylogenetic and ontogenetic terms (that is, with regard to the development of both the human species and the individual). From a historical point of view, our first communications – as a species and as individuals – have occurred face-to-face. Both as the human race and as individual humans, our primary socialization has taken place in direct, immediate contact with other people. One might suppose that the explanation is simple: for most of human history, no technology was available to allow anything other than face-to-face communication. But however trite this may sound: despite the many forms of telecommunication existing today, our first contacts and our most important social relationships – and not only during our primary socialization – are not maintained by telephone, email or SMS. In phylogenetic and ontogenetic terms, a mandatory condition of our socialization is the physical presence of others. This means that we learn to understand ourselves and others by looking at them and interpreting their body language, the words they stress and their intonation (and, on an even more basic level, their smell). Historically and individually, then, the presence of other people is, as Goffman (1983, p. 2) puts it, "the primordial real thing." All other varieties of communication – from the telephone call to the SMS – can thus be described as deficient variants, because they lack certain information (e.g. facial expression, tone) which we originally have access to in order to understand and interpret the actions of another person.

The question is then whether communication – as a chain of selections of information, utterance and understanding – becomes less and less "interactive" the greater the distance between the individual selections is. This can be spatial distance, as in a phone call, or temporal distance as in email communication. When talking on the phone we "only" have to do without the use and the interpretation of gestures and facial expressions. When writing emails or text messages, two further factors come into play. First, we do not spontaneously verbalize what we are thinking, but have to take the "cognitive loop" of written expression: we write differently from the way we speak. Second, and this is also different from face-to-face communication, we cannot expect immediate responses; the people we are writing to also take different "communicative loops" than they would in direct communication. Nobody sees us carrying out this process; writing could be assumed to be self-referential action and therefore the opposite of interaction. On closer reflection, however, it is obvious that writing as a cultural technique has always been designed to convey a message, even if it is a text only intended for ourselves (a diary in which we share our thoughts with ourselves), or a text aimed at a large number of unspecified third parties, such as a newspaper article. Like communication in general, writing requires addressees, so on a purely intuitive level we could regard email exchanges and text messaging as interaction. Or to put it the other way around, it would seem counter-intuitive not to refer to a reciprocal exchange of utterances as an interaction, even if it is conducted in writing. This can also be argued without reference to intuition, however: as soon as individuals enter into any kind of exchange with others, they are aware of being perceived as expressing themselves. Even if this perceptibility does not apply directly and synchronously, it has consequences. Written exchanges may protect us from direct consequences, or deny us these consequences – an immediate hug or a slap in the face – but they do not preserve us from the consequences altogether.

The important point here is that interaction in the presence of others is the prototype on which interactions under the condition of non-presence are modeled. It can be noted here that presence is a stronger social regulator than time-delayed or spatially distanced reciprocal perception. If we imagine, for example, all the other things that can be done while talking on the phone (or while texting) – doodling, picking our nose, painting our nails, etc. – these are often things that we would tend to refrain from doing in a face-to-face conversation, "under observation," i.e. when we are aware of being visually perceived. When speaking on a mobile phone in public, on the other hand, the possibility of being perceived by third parties is the decisive factor that makes us avoid certain behaviors, even though the person we are talking to on the phone would not be aware of them.[1] Thus people within each other's presence are constantly, uninterruptedly relevant for each other – and we see this in the fact that they always adapt to one another in some form or other. But when it comes to the structure of the interaction and our expectations of it, communication among people who are present cannot differ significantly from communication among people who are not in each other's presence.

We can tell this from the fact that we not only tend to see interaction under the condition of non-presence as deficient, but that we realize this and compensate for it where possible. When we end a letter with kisses, we are very conscious that we cannot kiss the person we are writing to at the present moment. And when we insert a smiley into a text message, we are compensating for the fact that the recipient cannot see our facial expression.

Thus there are quite specific implications of presence which have a decisive influence on our communication strategies. "Presence" means being present in a certain place at a certain time. "Those present" are, in relation to this place and this time, *only* (but also *all*) those who are gathered here and now. In a system theory framework, this distinction between "present" and "absent" is crucial for the classifiability of interaction as a social system, because this code allows interaction to be clearly differentiated from its environment – in other words, the criterion of presence distinguishes interaction from *everything else* (cf. Luhmann 2013 [1997]). We use a very concrete condition, however, to determine whether someone is "present:" the fact that we can physically perceive him or her. That is, the person concerned is within sight and earshot, and sometimes even close enough to touch and smell, and these physical stimuli tell us we are not alone. And purely on the basis of this fact – that we are not alone, here and now; that we physically perceive others and are perceived by them – the other people present become relevant for us, and we for them (cf. Goffman 2010 [1966]). We cannot escape from our perceptions (unless we leave the place where we meet with others) – and conversely, we cannot escape from being perceived (unless we hide). Within the framework of what we perceive, it is visibility that is most critical, because only this is unavoidable in the presence of others: we can stay silent and thus make ourselves inaudible, but we cannot make ourselves invisible. This aspect is highlighted by the expression "face-to-face." Goffman (1983) assumes that our appearance and the first impression we make already give information about our current attitude to the situation and our current social relations, which we acknowledge in a particular way depending on the situation. It makes a difference, after all, whether we have taken care with our hair and clothing, or whether we look unkempt and grubby, whether we are "overdressed" or "underdressed," and also whether we are dark-skinned or light-skinned, in a wheelchair or walking. It also makes a difference whether we enter a room with our head held high, or try to sneak in unnoticed, whether we take a seat in the front row or go and stand at the back wall, whether we go up to others without hesitation or try to approach them inconspicuously – and so on. *What* difference all this makes can of course vary considerably from one situation to the next. In general, however, it can be observed that our appearance and our initial actions allow the other people present to categorize our immediate intentions and aims in their own minds even before anything has been said (cf. ibid.).

Thus perceptions are always interpreted, classified, and categorized: we extract information from what we are able to perceive, even when no message has intentionally been conveyed. We are accustomed to interpreting the actions of others, and we are accustomed to having others interpret our actions. Goffman (2010 [1966], p. 16) describes the consequences as follows:

> [...] when two persons are together, at least some of their world will be made up out of the fact (and consideration of the fact) that an adaptive line of action attempted by one will be either insightfully facilitated by the other or insightfully countered, or both, and that such a line of action must always be pursued in this intelligently helpful and hindering world.

The mere fact of co-presence, then, produces a state of consciousness among those involved which includes both current and potential behavior of the other person; their own current and potential behavior are therefore adapted to the presence of the other. And of course this is only possible, according to Kieserling (1999), because what is perceptible is unmistakably real, and must therefore at least be acknowledged to exist by all those present. This, then, always constitutes the minimum consensus between those present. Or in other words: our behavior in the presence of others is always determined by the presence of others, because we perceive them and perceive that we are being perceived. The precondition for the coordination of actions lies in our ability to indicate our own actions and react to such indications from others (cf. Goffman 1983).

Yet whenever other people become directly and currently relevant to us, and vice versa, there has to be a form of "social order" that regulates how those present, under the condition of the presence of others, directly and currently pursue their respective motives, intentions and goals. In "unfocused interaction," as Goffman (2010 [1966]) calls it, the relevance of the presence of others is not explicitly invoked, but is only acknowledged in the form of management of simple co-presence. We can imagine many contexts in which a universal order is adhered to, and in which this is the only exchange of information that takes place: we perceive that we are being perceived, and adhere (mostly unconsciously) to certain rules, e.g. those that apply to waiting rooms or crowded footpaths. There are social rules here (for more on this see Chapter 7) which spare those present from having to engage with each other, in order to cope with the situation. Luhmann (2013 [1997], p. 133) explains this with the "self-regulation of inter-action systems;" this "includes participants taking each other into consideration, and mutual respect for each other's roles can be expected." Thus in a waiting room, we sit on an empty chair, we do not stare at the other people present and we mind our own business (e.g. by reading the magazines that are lying around) until our name is called and we enter the consulting room. We do not have to discuss this with the other people present; we apply the appropriate rules to the situation and rely on the others doing the same. In unfocused interaction, then, we observe interaction more as mutually coordinated generalized behavior – we do not sit on a chair which is obviously occupied (e.g. if there is a handbag on it), we do not try to push in by questioning the order set by the receptionist. This of course makes it clear once again that mutual perception is never without consequences, even in unfocused interaction. Such consequences become very concrete, however, under the condition of "focused interaction" (Goffman 2010 [1966]), face-to-face encounters centered on a single-joint activity. In face-to-face interactions, the direction in which the other person is looking is already an indication of who they mean; looking at each other is, in this sense, the minimum level of mutual addressing and the most basic prerequisite for this. Focused interaction is thus not necessarily verbal interaction; it is quite obvious that we can communicate strategically with others by using gestures, facial expressions and looks. Interactants are therefore not by definition, and not constantly, speakers (cf. Goffman 1981). On the other hand, completely non-verbal interactions only occur in specific contexts, and can only be very limited in time and subject matter. For example hunters may prefer to communicate with hand signals rather than calling out to each other, to avoid scaring the game, or school pupils may give each other meaningful looks during class to exchange their views on the situation without disturbing the lesson. If, however, social interaction is primarily examined and discussed as linguistic action in a large proportion of the literature – and in this book – then this is because a large proportion of our interactions take place on the verbal level. Language not only ensures more efficient coordination between the actors, and more accurate information, but also allows us to refer to topics outside of the immediate social situation (cf. Luhmann 1995 [1984]).[2]

The more potential addressees who are present, the more concrete the form of address must be so that we feel as though it is aimed at us. The German language has a particularly illuminating expression for this: *sich angesprochen fühlen*, to feel that one is being spoken to or addressed. The focus here is on interpretation: not whether we are actually being addressed, but whether we think we are the intended recipient of a gesture or utterance. Someone who does not "feel addressed" can certainly be the addressee; but it is only the acknowledgment of this fact that makes us behave as specifically included participants in a joint activity. Focused interactions then automatically lead to the allocation of participation status in relation to the given encounter. Let us assume that two people waiting in a waiting room begin a conversation. The way this generally works (there will be more on the specifics in Chapter 2) is that they address each other and focus on each other. This joint focus on each other turns participants in the situation into participants in a conversation, and reciprocal inclusion leads to reciprocal acknowledgment as "ratified" participants (Goffman 1981). Ratified participants in an interaction then have a status in the social situation which allows them to take an active part in the communication.[3] This status may be allocated to them by a direct form of address, or they may already bring this status with them into the social situation, in a generalized form – usually by being members of the organization which provides the framework for the interaction (e.g. school pupils and teachers in class, colleagues in a team meeting). In relation to the joint activity of the conversation, all those present who are not addressed are then non-ratified participants (cf. ibid.). It is important to note, though, that they remain participants in the situation and are, as such, able to perceive those who are engrossed in the conversation and to be perceived by them. The ratified participants now have a status which permits them – by means of addressing and visual focus on the other person – to actively participate in the conversation *as a joint activity*. The non-ratified participants are therefore those people present who are witnesses to a focused interaction without being directly involved in this activity. In this sense they are spectators, observers, and overhearers (cf. ibid.; cf. Clark 1997). This participation status, in contrast to ratified participation, is not explicitly assigned by means of addressing, but is a product of momentary, situational non-addressing. This also means, however, that the status of a non-ratified participant cannot be withdrawn; we must therefore assume that even those people present who are not directly included in the focused interaction cannot be completely irrelevant for the ratified participants. Thus Herbert H. Clark (ibid.) also points out that conversations always take into account all the situationally allocated participation statuses, and not only the ratified participants: we conceive our utterances in such a way that we think those we are directly addressing will understand them, while we accept or even intend that those who are not directly addressed will, in cases of doubt, only be able to guess what we mean. We are under no obligation to make ourselves understandable towards these peripheral listeners or overhearers, and this fact influences the concrete way we phrase our utterances. What is interesting about this concept – and helpful for a microsociological approach – is that there are no non-participants in face-to-face interaction; there are only participants, who are either confirmed or not confirmed as such (cf. Suerig 2011).

Participation structures of ratification and non-ratification are not fixed. A non-ratified participant can intervene in a conversation, and assign himself or herself a ratified status, while a ratified participant can speak to someone present who is observing and listening, thereby ratifying him or her for the focused interaction. Social interaction is therefore flexible and dynamic with regard to participation status. One way this becomes apparent is the fact that mutual perceptibility under the condition of presence can undergo various modifications. At a fully occupied table, for example, a conversation involving everyone can lead into two-person conversations between individual participants (and vice versa), and the more individual conversations are taking place, the more difficult – if not impossible – it is to listen to other conversations (cf. Kieserling 1999). Concentrating on each other always necessarily involves shutting ourselves off to a certain extent from what is happening around us (otherwise we would not be able to concentrate adequately on the person we are talking to), and we often signal this to the other people present by holding conversations at a low volume, to prevent them from listening and/or to avoid disturbing other conversations or focuses of attention. The expression used by German-speaking children, "*Flüstern ist Lügen!*" ("Whispering is lying!") reminds us, however, that we cannot simply exclude ratified participants from our conversations. In the presence of third parties, actual whispering, i.e. speaking into one person's ear in a way that cannot be heard by the others, is in any case only appropriate if we are trying to avoid disturbing others. Otherwise we can easily be suspected of saying something offensive or untrue, precisely because we are deliberately keeping it from the perception of the other people present. Interestingly, this may mean that something which is explicitly not being made relevant can become relevant in the interaction.

Thus just as we can identify certain characteristics of presence and perceptibility within the interaction, and distinguish between different participation statuses, we can also distinguish different "interaction formats." Here we shall follow the categorization proposed by Goffman in "The Interaction Order" (1983). According to this system, it is possible to differentiate between five interaction units: the "ambulatory unit;" the "contact;" the "conversational encounter;" the podium performance or "platform format;" and the "celebrative social occasion" (ibid., pp. 6–7). In a sense we can say that these interaction units build on each other in an incremental or evolutionary way (evolutionary in the sense that one format can evolve into another), with the interaction between "ambulatory units" being the most basic form, and the celebratory occasion being the form of interaction that potentially includes all the other forms of interaction.

In public, people can initially appear as "ambulatory units," either singly or in groups, and as long as we are in motion, our interactions with other ambulatory units are minimal – they are usually limited to avoiding each other. On our way through the pedestrian zone or the supermarket we cut a path through the crowd; we give way to others, or others give way to us, we keep our physical distance, avoid bumping into anyone, go to the back of the queue and if we have no room to overtake we adapt our pace to match the people walking in front of us. This gives rise to a very basic order of interaction, which can be described most simply as follows: we try not to get in each other's way, or to stop each other from going about our business. To achieve this, we do have to physically perceive the others and adjust to their passing presence, but there is no need to really enter into contact with them. Goffman (ibid.) therefore initially distinguishes between ambulatory units moving around without contact, for whom the other concrete person is, as it were, only relevant as an obstacle to be avoided, and individual contact – here he includes all encounters which contain direct personal acknowledgement of another person. For it is only at the moment when we acknowledge another person as such – and this can be simply by looking at them – that the possibility of addressing arises. We cannot address someone without first having perceived them as a person. This is not about mutual exchange, even if this is always shaped by such an acknowledgment of the other person; it is about the condition under which exchange becomes possible in the first place. If an exchange, a conversation, then occurs, this is another interaction format, that of the conversational encounter. This is characterized by the limited number of participants who, deliberately and dependently on one another, participate in a joint activity. Conversational encounters can be organized symmetrically, with all participants theoretically having the same status in and the same share of the conversation, or they can follow an asymmetrical order, if there is (usually in formal, institutional contexts) a chairperson, i.e. someone who grants others the right to speak (see Chapter 2).[4] We are familiar with this from classrooms and courtrooms, for example. According to Goffman, however, conversational encounters do not have to be primarily based on spoken language; examples are games played together, shared meals, or sexual encounters. True, these kinds of joint activity do not necessarily take place in silence (and indeed perhaps rarely do so), but here it is not speaking to each other which constitutes the joint activity. A further set of interactions which can be distinguished from this large group of conversational encounters are those that take place in front of an audience; Goffman (ibid.) calls these "platform performances," in which something is presented to spectators on some sort of stage – a lecture, a play, a football game, etc. Here the spectators can be clearly differentiated from the presenters by the fact that their visual and cognitive attention is focused on what is happening on the stage: their task is to watch, and nothing else. The final interactive format identified by Goffman is the celebrative social occasion: the coming together of a particular group of individuals in circumstances which are collectively recognized. The special feature of this interaction format is that the focus is not on the joint activity, but on the mutually recognized occasion. The participation, inclusion and joint activities of the people coming together are shaped by the event. Thus a funeral has, from the outset, a different "underlying tone" from a wedding, with the event determining certain moods, as well as restricting the conditions of participation, the dress codes, and the form of the joint activities. In fact, all the previously mentioned interaction formats can also occur in this framework – simply walking past others, contact situations, conversational encounters and platform performances. However, the occasion that has brought these people together continues to be the element that connects those present and regulates their presence.

So far it has been a striking feature of both the definition of interaction and the categorization of interaction formats that the specific persons participating seem to play a less important role than the social setting in which the interaction comes about. We can note that both in Luhmann's and Goffman's conceptions of interaction (see previous), a great deal depends on the circumstances in which people encounter and interact with each other. Thus for example the specific communication at a table in a café derives some of its specificity from the fact that it takes place in a busy café, at one of many tables, and in the presence of third parties who are not directly involved in the conversation. The café as a public space determines a whole spectrum of possibilities for how the concrete interaction can proceed. For example, a waiter could appear at any time, loud laughter at one table can cause a change of subject at the next table, delicate matters are discussed in lowered voices, etc.

Because of these contingencies, techniques of social management arise, and because these contingencies are universal, we can assume that the order of interaction follows similar patterns even in quite different societies (cf. Goffman 1983). We will deal with the concrete mechanisms of ordered interaction in the next chapter.

FOOD FOR THOUGHT

Refer to your transcript of the café scene from *As Good As It Gets*. The conversation between Melvin and Frank is interrupted several times by the waitress, Carol. Find reasons why Carol is able to behave as a "ratified participant" in these sequences – over and above her role as waitress. Does she ratify herself as a participant in the conversation? Is she ratified by the other two participants?

Notes

1 Another factor, especially when writing text messages, is that this can be done in the presence of other people with whom we are interacting face-to-face – thus we can interrupt ongoing interactions to interact with people who are not present, and vice versa. There has as yet been little well-founded empirical analysis of what role those present play in interactions with those who are not present, and vice versa. Turkle (2015) assumes that texting tends to happen at the expense of direct interaction, which – unlike texting – is dependent on a synchronic joint focus.
2 This also applies, incidentally, to sign languages, which are complex language systems and not to be confused with "non-verbal communication." Sign languages are not located on the phonetic (sound) level, but otherwise fulfill every criterion for a real language.
3 Here "ratification" should be understood as a purely descriptive term designating the right to actively participate in a conversation at a given moment. This is not about a fundamental legitimation which categorically excludes certain people from the focused interaction; such categorical legitimations always precede the interaction, e.g. in the courtroom, where spectators do not have the right to participate in the questioning of the witnesses or the passing of the sentence.
4 Kieserling (1999) points out, however, that the interactive system is also particularly susceptible to confusion between prescribed interactive roles. We will discuss this in Chapter 6.

References

Goffman, Erving (1983). The Interaction Order. *American Sociological Review, 48/1*, 1–17.
Goffman, Erving (2010 [1966]). *Behavior in Public Places. Notes on the Social Organization of Gatherings*. New York: The Free Press. See especially: Introductory Definitions, pp. 13–30.
Kieserling, André (1999). *Kommunikation unter Anwesenden. Studien über Interaktionssysteme.* Frankfurt a. M., Germany: Suhrkamp. See especially: Bestimmung der Systemgrenzen, pp. 62–85.
Luhmann, Niklas (1995 [1984]). *Social Systems.* Stanford, CA: Stanford University Press. See especially: Communication and Action, pp. 137–175.
Luhmann, Niklas (2013 [1997]). *Theory of Society.* Vol. 2. Stanford, CA: Stanford University Press. See especially: Interaction and Society, pp. 131–140.

Further reading

Clark, Herbert H. (1997). Dogmas of Understanding. *Discourse Processes, 23*, 567–598.

Goffman, Erving (1966 [2010]). *Behavior in Public Places. Notes on the Social Organization of Gatherings.* New York: The Free Press. See especially: The Individual as a Unit, pp. 3–27.

Goffman, Erving (1981). *Forms of Talk.* Philadelphia, PA: University of Pennsylvania Press. See especially: Replies and Responses, pp. 5–77.

Luhmann, Niklas (1991 [1975]). *Soziologische Aufklärung 2. Aufsätze zur Theorie der Gesellschaft.* Opladen: Westdeutscher Verlag. See especially: Einfache Sozialsysteme, pp. 21–38.

Luhmann, Niklas (1995 [1984]). *Social Systems.* Stanford, CA: Stanford University Press. See especially: Double Contingency, pp. 103–136.

Schütz, Alfred (1967 [1932]). *The Phenomenology of the Social World.* Evanston, IL: Northwestern University Press.

Suerig, Inken (2011). *Students as Actors in Supporting Roles. Video Analysis of Classroom Interaction Systems as Multi-Participant Events.* Osnabrück, Germany: Hochschulschriften der Universität Osnabrück.

Turkle, Sherry (2015). *Reclaiming Conversation. The Power of Talk in a Digital Age.* New York: Penguin Press.

Weber, Max (1978 [1922]). *Economy and Society: An Outline of Interpretive Sociology.* Guenter Roth & Claus Wittich (Eds.). Berkeley, CA: University of California Press.

2

SEQUENTIALITY

How interaction is structured as a process

"Sequentiality" is about how interaction is formally organized as synchronous speaking and listening – e.g. in the form of conversation openings and closings, turn-taking, adjacent-pair sequences and repairs. This is the classic terrain of conversation analysis, as founded by Harvey Sacks, Emanuel Schegloff and Gail Jefferson in the 1970s. Their major achievement is that they were the first to subject *everyday conversations* to a systematic linguistic examination. In other words, they are concerned with the realization of language (in everyday speech, and therefore orally) as conversation, with the "grammar" that governs how we talk to one another. The rules of conversation which they identify are universal, insofar as they are not directed by cultural conventions (e.g. the norms of courtesy or principles of seniority), but by the necessities of language production under the condition of cooperation. In this sense, "sequentiality" describes the connection between the individual speech acts in a conversation, a connection created by linguistic mechanisms of mutual referencing as an expression of cooperation.

When we talk about sequentiality, we very specifically enter the linguistic level of interaction and thus the level of oral dialogues and everyday conversations. The time dimension, and with it the processual nature of action related to others, becomes especially tangible here. Linguistic action of this kind does not proceed randomly or accidentally, but follows formal structures and rules in various respects. This formal structuring is the reason why we can observe and describe social interaction as a process – and why concrete role, friendship and family relationships can acquire structure in the interaction process. Case-specific interaction and relationship structures will be a recurring theme in the following chapters.

The term "sequentiality," in connection with conversations, was coined in the 1960s and 1970s by proponents of "conversation analysis" – most prominently Harvey Sacks, Emmanuel Schegloff and Gail Jefferson.[1] Their interest mainly focused on how conversation participants ascribe meaning to each other's speech acts – a question which Garfinkel (1967) discussed in detail in his writings on ethnomethodology. Indeed, ethnomethodology and conversation analysis are often seen as closely linked to each other, since both approaches are based on the assumption that the universal (structural) mechanisms of linguistic acts are sensitive to context, that is, their realization reflects the current social situation, and the individual participants in the interaction interpret them reciprocally and in an intersubjectively comprehensible manner. The reciprocal referencing allows sequentiality to emerge as a coherent temporal succession of speech acts. What is important here, according to Deppermann (2008, p. 49, tr. by N.B.), is that temporality is "not a quality external to the conversation, but an ineluctable condition and resource for the shaping of utterances, the creation of contexts and meaning, and for the emergence of intersubjectivity." We will explore what exactly this means in the following discussion.

In the previous chapter, we already heard that mutual perceptibility generally leads to mutual responsiveness (*Ansprechbarkeit*). Before this can progress into a conversation, however, the participants in the interaction must first signal that they are actually referring to each other in their actions. This means they must also refrain from actions which would undermine the focus on the other person: as Berens (1981, p. 402, tr. by N.B.) puts it, they must "establish and maintain social and communicative relationships with and towards each other." Henne and Rehbock (1979) also describe the opening of a conversation as the phase of the dialogue in which the participants in the interaction adjust to each other as the situation requires. This type of "conversational partnership" is, as stated in the previous chapter, the smallest unit of social relationship: in a conversation we enter into a social relationship – even with complete strangers whom we will probably never see again – because we relate momentarily to each other (cf. ibid.).[2] Responsiveness can be realized in various ways here; there are ritualized forms of conversation opening such as greeting each other or checking that the other person is willing to talk ("Do you have a moment?"),[3] but there are also conversation starters which refer directly to something within the mutual horizon of perception, without any formal introduction. The important thing is that the conversation participants already address each other in the conversation opener, and refer to each other in this addressing. These two principles of interaction constitute the basic structure of every conversation, from beginning to end.

A normal conversation opener in both face-to-face and non-face-to-face conversations is a greeting, and there are a number of salutations which we use as the situation demands: from the informal "hi" or "hey" to the formal "good morning" or the regional "howdy" and "g'day", etc. If we are addressed with a greeting, we usually respond with the same salutation: a "hi" is normally met with a "hi", etc. Deviations from this rule can easily be understood as "corrections," as will be explained in detail next; while it is possible to meet an informal "hi" with an equally informal "hey," saying "hiya" in response to "good morning" marks a different take on the social relationship between the speakers. In Goffman's (1982 [1967], p. 20) words, this would be a "challenge," "calling attention to the misconduct" (which in this case consists of using a formal greeting when an informal one is called for).[4]

Thus the greeting is a standard conversation opener, but one which, under the condition of presence, does not necessarily demand any follow-up: people can greet each other in passing and simply walk on. Yet even this simple acknowledgment of presence contains an acknowledgment of mutual responsiveness, even if there is no follow-up. This is not possible in a telephone conversation, in the condition of non-presence: in a phone call, the making and receiving of the call presuppose a conversational intention which is not fulfilled by a mere greeting. We can also imagine a number of face-to-face situations in which a greeting does not seem an appropriate conversation opener – for example if the participants have already greeted each other without starting a conversation at that point, or if they have been within each other's perceptual horizon for some time, but did not greet each other to begin with. An example of the first case could be colleagues who work in the same office and who, after the first morning greeting, have each been busy with their own work. Naturally, they do not then begin each subsequent conversation – e.g. about whether to go to lunch together – by saying "hello." In the second case we could imagine patients in a waiting room or passengers in a lift – both situations in which there is no clear convention of greeting others when one enters. These are also cases where people would not start a conversation – e.g. about the long waiting times in this doctor's surgery or the poor state of the lift they are using together – with a greeting.

But regardless of which words we use to start a conversation, the first requirement of a "proper" conversation opener is a specific person to talk to: if we want to begin a conversation in a particular situation we always choose our interlocutor in advance (as in a telephone conversation), and we show this not just by speaking, but also – especially – by making eye contact. This is the only way to ensure that an utterance can actually be understood by the other person as a clear invitation to respond. We can imagine many situations in which those who are present simply say something without speaking to anyone in particular. This is especially likely if they are making a general comment on the situation, to express their indignation, annoyance or pleasure, e.g. complaining about the unfriendly service when queuing at a shop counter, commenting on the stuffy air when sitting in a crowded train compartment or remarking on the unusually punctual arrival of the bus when standing at the bus stop. In such situations, when several people are present and no one is directly addressed, the participation statuses (see Chapter 1) are unclear. Since the speaker has not "obliged" anyone to answer by addressing them directly, she must expect that no one will respond to her remark. And even in one-to-one situations, we sometimes have to check whether the speaker expects a response from us ("Are you talking to me?") if he does not look at us when speaking. Of course, this question can also serve to point out inappropriate conversational behavior, and can be understood as a reminder about the minimum requirements of a conversation: "Look at me when you're talking to me!" Regardless of the different motivations, conventions and situational limitations that affect the beginnings of conversations, then, we can state in very general terms that a conversation is characterized by reciprocal addressing, and that this is already reflected in the conversation opening. In turn, direct addressing *always* demands a response; Goffman (1982 [1967]) uses the term "obligatory involvement."

Now, this observation seems to contradict our experiences of everyday life; we can easily imagine situations in which the conversation opener is not accepted by the person being spoken to. If we look more closely, however, these situations are extremely limited, for the simple reason that not accepting a conversation opening is a violation of a universal norm (cf. ibid.); we will discuss norms and rules in detail in Chapter 7. We can tell that this is so because the person speaking to us can insist that we reply: "Hello! I'm talking to you!" or "Hey! I asked you a question!" are then typical utterances, demanding attention and a response from the other person. At the same time, both utterances also show that people can only plausibly ignore a conversation opener if they have actually not heard it – hence the insistent effort to attract their attention. Continuing to ignore the speaker, i.e. declining the conversation opener ("answering with silence") points to a manifest conflict and amounts to a conscious refusal to cooperate with the other person.

The rule, then, is that we respond when we are spoken to; we accept conversation openers and cooperate as interlocutors (cf. Berens 1981). Thus the beginning of every conversation is the start of a cooperative sequence of action, and the principle of cooperation applies even in the case of an argument or an exchange of insults: even if their aim is to offend each other, the interlocutors must cooperate. We see, then, that cooperation is a structural feature of interaction; the question of whether the participants also cooperate in the substance of the matter lies on the level of content, not structure.

On the "macro level," according to Henne and Rehbock (1979), this conversation sequence can be divided into the phases of conversation opener, conversation middle and conversation end. This general division points in the first instance to the time structure observable in the conversation; it is only when we explore the level lying below this that we can establish how the individual phases of the conversation connect and build on one another. In their groundbreaking essay, "A simplest systematics for the organization of turn-taking for conversation" (1974), Sacks, Schegloff and Jefferson offer an overview of the mechanisms of conversation organization which we wish to examine more closely here.

One elementary feature of conversations is that they are organized in "turns" or "moves": only one participant speaks at a time, and there is a recurring alternation between the different speakers and listeners in the course of the conversation. We wish to argue here that this is not a rule we have to obey to ensure that the conversation proceeds in an orderly fashion; rather, it is a rule that is actually constitutive of the conversation. We will look more closely at the difference between "regulative" and "constitutive" rules in Chapter 3. Our point here is that however unequally the talk is distributed, there is no conversation without turn-taking. That is why interactions without turn-taking are described from the outset not as conversations, but as – for example – sermons, speeches or lectures. The fact that conversations are organized in turns, with changes in speaker, is due to the need to refer to each other when conversing. People are, from a purely cognitive point of view, not able to speak and listen simultaneously; nor are we able to listen attentively to two different people at once (cf. Kieserling 1999). As trite as it sounds, it is important to note that we can only refer to what another person says if we hear what they are saying. In a conversation, then, we are potentially both speakers and listeners, and we alternate between these two roles either when our interlocutor invites us to speak ("current speaker selects next") or when we take the floor on our own initiative (self-selection). These are the two basic mechanisms of turn-taking in conversations. As mechanisms they are prone to failure, but they are also reparable, as we shall see next.

If only two people are involved in the conversation, the turn-taking in the form of "current speaker selects next" is either explicit, with the speaker directly inviting her interlocutor to speak ("What do you think?"), or implicit: she uses intonation, facial expression or a closing phrase to indicate that she has finished her utterance. In both cases, of course, she stops talking, thus compelling her interlocutor to take over the role of speaker. Usually, as we know from everyday life, such one-to-one conversations proceed fairly smoothly; there are generally no long pauses when turn-taking, and the participants switch effortlessly between the roles of speaker and listener. Furthermore, there is seldom any overlap, or only brief moments of overlap, when the speaker has not quite finished her utterance and the listener begins to speak in anticipation of the change of speaker. Of course this does not mean that we never have any trouble responding to the content of what has just been said; but even if, for example, we cannot spontaneously answer a question, we nonetheless show immediately that we know it is our turn, even if it is only by saying "um" or "well." Thus the high degree of coordination in a one-to-one conversation is not only manifested on the level of subject matter, but is already apparent in the systematic alternation between speaking and listening. Clark (1997) compares linguistic interaction to a duet: we can practice our own part to perfection, but as soon as we perform with the other person, flaws and problems suddenly appear which we would not have had on our own. The reason for this is that we have to adjust to the other person in the joint activity; we have to observe them non-stop and modify our own behavior on the basis of these observations. Speaking and listening are therefore not autonomous processes, but actions that are fundamentally dependent on each other.

Sacks, Schegloff and Jefferson (1974) are particularly interested in conversations involving more than two people. For one-to-one conversations, we can say that when one person stops talking, it is by definition the other person's turn. Even here, admittedly, the speaker has to indicate when his utterance is finished, and the listener has to interpret these indicators as such – but there can be no doubt whose turn it is next. In a conversation involving several people, however, the end of an utterance only shows that it is time for a change of speaker; it cannot automatically be clear whose turn it is, as all the listeners are potential speakers. Here the initial rule identified by Sacks, Schegloff and Jefferson is that the person who is currently speaking has the right to select the next speaker – by directly addressing someone, nodding to someone or choosing a topic which only a certain person in the group is able to talk about. This means, according to the authors, that long pauses in the conversation – which they refer to as "lapses" – can only occur if the current speaker does not select a successor. In this case one of the listeners must select himself as the speaker, that is, take the floor without having been personally invited to do so. Self-selection follows an initially simple rule: whoever starts to speak first has the right to speak. In group conversations, overlap often occurs because the current speech act already indicates that the change of speaker will take place by self-selection; the potential next speakers then compete over who will begin to speak first. If everyone talks at the same time, this means that the mechanism of "current selects next"/ self-selection has failed to work at the present moment, and that it is not clear whose turn it is. Usually, though, this is quickly clarified by those present ("You first!" – "No, you first!").

In this context, however, Kieserling (1999) points out that the larger the group is, the greater the "imposed passivity" (*Passivitätszumutung*) becomes. That is, the more potential speakers there are, the less likely it becomes that the individual will get a chance to speak and to actively shape and steer the conversation.[5] If the turn-taking is regulated purely by self-selection, the competition between the participants will be greater, often leading to an unequal distribution of talk and therefore of imposed passivity. We can imagine that this mainly occurs where the relationships between the participants are symmetrical, i.e. where there are no differences in rank and nobody has, a priori, the right to speak or to authorize others to speak – for example in a conversation between friends or colleagues of equal rank. But there are also many contexts in which self-selection as a mechanism of turn-taking is formally marked as undesirable – in any situation where either only one particular person has the right to speak (e.g. the pastor during a sermon, or the lecturer during a lecture), or only one particular person has the right to authorize others to speak (e.g. the teacher during a lesson or the host at a panel discussion). Here the interaction is standardized or formalized in a way that at least partially disables the "natural" mechanisms of conversation organization as described by Sacks, Schegloff and Jefferson (1974) (see also Luhmann 1987). And this applies not only to the right to speak, but also to speaking time. Sacks, Schegloff and Jefferson (1974) observe that the length of a conversational turn in natural, non-formalized conversations depends on many different factors, but is primarily based on sentence form, i.e. when the sentence is finished the utterance is usually finished too. Of course, sentences can vary greatly in length, and in spoken language they can be "extended" more or less endlessly, simply through intonation, regardless of syntactic rules. There is a German expression used to describe someone who talks non-stop: they speak *ohne Punkt und Komma*, i.e. "without full stops and commas." This does not mean, of course, that they speak without using punctuation – this is the preserve of written language – but that, on the level of prosody or intonation, they do not use pauses or differences in pitch and volume to mark the end of a sentence, and therefore the end of their utterance. So something that would be made up of several sentences in written language can sound like a single sentence in spoken language. In natural, non-formalized conversations, then, there are no definable rules governing speaking time; at the most, factors external to the conversation can come into play, for example if the speakers have little time for the conversation and therefore "keep it brief." In formalized interactions, on the other hand, the person granting the right to speak is also – at least implicitly – entitled to withdraw this right, on the basis of the same monopoly. Thus a teacher can interrupt a pupil and a host can interrupt a panel guest at any time; the teacher or host then assumes the right to speak herself, before granting it to another person. This, however, is purely due to the higher status of the teacher or the presenter in these interaction formats; in symmetrical interactions, the rule is to allow the other person to "finish their sentence."

This brings us to the last form of speaker change we want to discuss here: speaker change as a result of interruption. Here we can distinguish between "unintentional" and "intentional" interruption, insofar as not every interruption is intended to remove the speaker's right to talk. Long utterances in particular often contain "transition-relevance places" (ibid.), wherever a sentence appears to be finished. Thus if a person is speaking "without full-stops and commas," in a metaphorical sense, their utterance will still contain markers that the other person can interpret as a sign that they are being selected, or as an opportunity to join in by means of self-selection, even if the utterance is not yet finished from the speaker's point of view. In such a case, the speaker can explicitly point out to the interrupter that she wishes to continue speaking – "I wasn't finished" – or can simply carry on talking, which will quickly make the other person stop again, as the interruption was not intentional. If, on the other hand, we deliberately "butt in," this tends not to happen at transition-relevance places in the utterance, but in places which we think demand a direct response, one we do not want to wait with – e.g. a contradiction, a question or additional information. This means, though, that such interruptions can also be understood as "interjections:" they do not stop the utterance for good, but evoke a conversational loop, after which the original utterance can be continued ("Now where was I?"). As in the first type of interruption, the right to speak is not arbitrarily withdrawn in order to stop the other person from speaking. Deliberate interruption designed to stop the other person does occur, typically in arguments. Here the participants compete for the right to speak and the interruption can be seen as an attack, regardless of its content ("Would you just let me finish!").

This shows, firstly, that it is not possible to refer to each other without perceiving and processing the action of the other, in this case the speech act, in its entirety; we have to know what we can refer to, so we ensure that an order of speakers is observed. We can only listen attentively to one person at a time. Secondly, we also see here that changes of speaker do not usually need to be explicitly negotiated, as speech acts are formally constructed in such a way that they always contain an indication of when they are finished and require an "answer," making it clear that it is someone else's turn. From a formal point of view, a conversation only comes about if a speech act contains a marker signaling when it is another person's turn. A speech act with a monologic structure does not contain such markers. In other words, there is no indication on a linguistic level that an utterance is finished and now requires a response. There are, however, only a small number of interaction formats which are not organized dialogically: these include lectures and speeches, which – at least for their duration – do not allow for any follow-up from another person. Here listeners assume the role of "audience."

We note, then, that the coherence of a dialogue is produced "mechanically" through the presence of organized turn-taking. Every utterance which leads to someone else starting to speak involves selection and addressing of the next speaker, who then refers to this selection and addressing in her utterance. In this way, a structure of "adjacency" arises,[6] a proximity between successive utterances, with the next turn showing how the previous one has been understood – this is the "self-referentiality" of communication mentioned in Chapter 1. When we then speak of "adjacency pairs," this refers to two utterances which, when directly adjacent to each other or "taken together," make sense even (but of course not only) if they are not grammatically related to each other. For example in the sequence "I'm hungry" – "There's still some soup left," it is only obvious that the utterances are connected because they occur in direct succession, that is, as a "pair." Schegloff (2007) uses the term "nextness" as a synonym for "adjacency," but two aspects are expressed more clearly in "nextness:" the temporal level of the succession of two utterances ("next utterance"), and the requirement for a change in speaker ("next turn"). At the same time, Schegloff (ibid.) also observes that adjacency or nextness can mainly be understood "backwards," because it only becomes clear in the next utterance how the previous utterance has been understood. First, there are only very few types of utterance in which the hint of the response allows only one possibility. One example, as shown previously, is greetings (or farewells), which hardly allow any alternative responses, and usually occur in the form of "greeting – return greeting." Second, however, there are also very few potential replies that run completely counter to the possible responses indicated in an utterance; Schegloff (ibid.) refers to such responses as "counters:"

(1) A: Are you happy with me?
      B: Are *you* happy with *me*?
(2) A: Come here!
      B: *You* come *here*!

The interesting thing here is that B does refer to A's utterance, but does not pick up the response alternatives indicated in A's utterance. In these examples, then, the connection between the utterances, their "nextness," is not affected by the fact that a different possible response from the obvious or "adjacent" option is selected. On the one hand, this once again demonstrates the "contingency" of interaction mentioned in Chapter 1: we can expect that we will get an answer to a question, but we cannot absolutely count on it. On the other hand, it also shows what we *can* count on: that the person we are talking to will refer to what we say, in some way or other.

The main reason why this is possible is that the coherence of a dialogue is always partly produced on the subject level. Although the formal structure of the conversation is independent of its concrete content, it is limited by the fact that one can only ever talk about one topic at a time. Of course, we have all experienced the way a conversation can pass from one subject to another: a conversation about our holiday in Spain can transition into a discussion about the pros and cons of various airlines. This only works, however, if the connection between the two subjects is established in the speech act; failing this – as we also know from everyday life – a change of subject is explicitly proposed ("let's talk about something else"). Here too, it is necessary to ensure that all participants are able to follow this change of subject immediately and simultaneously (cf. Kieserling 1999).

Mutual references to what has already been said produce sequentiality: the temporally structured character of successive speech acts. This term describes the processual nature of the conversation: every turn in the interaction implies a selection between possible alternatives, and this selection in turn opens up a space for possible reactions. "Structure" then emerges in the linking of interaction turns, the reciprocal referencing of utterances. The meaning of each turn, i.e. each speech act, arises from its position in the sequence (cf. Schegloff & Sacks 1973).

To sum up, then, the conversational context in which we say something is crucial for mutual understanding; this concerns not only the situation, but also the context of utterance. We can conclude from this that, in direct interaction, we sequentially pursue and modify our intentions, which we express in our speech acts. This means that our utterances in interaction always refer to the development of the interaction up to this point; the utterance only makes sense in this interactional context. As researchers, we assume that such an interactional context exists; we can observe, describe, define and interpret it. As immediate participants in interaction, however, we are totally reliant on the context of the interaction. Whatever we personally want to "achieve" in the interaction with others (there will be more on this in the following chapters), we only achieve it by – on a very basic level – coordinating our actions with those of the others.

To coordinate their actions, participants in the interaction must mutually confirm that they are talking about the same thing; there has to be "common ground," a common denominator for the interaction, which is available to all the participants. A conversation is not simply a series of suitable utterances at a suitable time, but a space for the mutual construction of "knowledge," which all participants can assume that they all share. "Common ground" points to the concrete coordination of the conversation's content (cf. Clark & Brennan 1991) on the basis of shared interpretations, about which the participants inform each other, verbally and non-verbally, throughout the course of the conversation. This common ground is not fixed, but changes in the course of the conversation, is expanded and made more specific, so that, in the end, an everyday conversation between a waiter and a guest can turn into a full-blown argument. Here the "nextness" of each speech act always serves to ensure that an utterance is understood and accepted as a progressive contribution to the conversation. To understand this, we have to bear in mind that the knowledge about "what it's about" is, in itself, a component of the situation and the interaction. This not only applies to subject knowledge, i.e. the mutual sharing of factual information, but also to knowledge about the dynamics of the conversation itself. In a conversation, after all, we do more than just express ourselves verbally with reference to each other: we signal that we are listening and understanding, and we pay attention to these signals in our listeners – nodding, shrugging their shoulders, frowning, raising their eyebrows, sliding about restlessly on their chairs, etc. (cf. also the remarks on this in Chapter 11). Clark and Krych (2004) and others[7] point out that it becomes difficult for the speaker to monitor the effect of her utterance without the signals given by her interlocutor's facial expressions, and without confirmatory utterances that encourage her to continue, such as "mmm," "really," or a simple "yes." At the same time, natural speech has many different markers that make it easier for us to listen and understand, according to Clark (1997). For example, if the person we are talking to is searching for the right word, we search for it mentally as well, thus processing what has been said; or when function words (e.g., pronouns, prepositions, articles) are repeated in natural speech, this is often an indication of speakers, while speaking, making up their minds about stressing the importance of the following constituent ("I heard that from, from John"). In natural speech, something that looks like discontinuity in syntactic terms often has informational value for the listeners, helping to establish and secure common ground.

But what happens if it is not even clear what the conversation is about? Slips of the tongue, misunderstandings, insufficient information, errors: these are all phenomena which jeopardize the adjacency or, in more general terms, the common ground of interaction, the result being that we can no longer refer to each other in a mutually comprehensible manner. Such problems, however, are usually solved directly, a process for which Schegloff, Jefferson and Sacks (1977) coined the terms "repair" and "correction." As the expression "repair" indicates that something that was previously intact has suffered damage and is now being restored, we will not reduce it to individual phenomena of linguistic structure or semantics; instead we will relate it to the "common denominator" as a whole. Each repair, then, indicates that the common ground has been damaged and must now be restored. Depending on the nature of the "damage," this can occur in different ways. A slip of the tongue is remedied by saying the right word, a missing piece of information is supplied, a misunderstanding is cleared up, an error corrected. Against the background of sequentiality, however, our interest is not only in how repairs are carried out, but also in who does the repairing. This is simply because self-corrections and "other-corrections" are uttered by different participants, and thus constitute different "turns" in the conversation. There are mistakes that we notice and correct ourselves, as in the following example:

(3) A: We're meeting at half-past-six, um, half-past-seven.

But we can also be made aware of a mistake by our interlocutor – and then correct it ourselves:

(4) A: We're meeting at half-past-six.
     B: Half-past-six?
     A: Uh, no, half-past-seven.

Of course, there are also potential errors where we are not certain whether they are errors, so we give our interlocutor the opportunity to correct us:

(5) A: We're meeting at half-past-six, or was it half-past-seven?
     B: Half-past-seven.

Lastly, of course, the correction of our utterance may be both initiated and carried out by our interlocutor:

(6) A: We're meeting at half-past-six.
     B: No, we said half-past-seven.

There are indications that, in conversations, we tend to give priority to self-correction (ibid.): as listeners we prefer to wait and see whether a speaker will correct herself before undertaking the repair "in her place." Goffman (1982 [1967]) offers the explanation that it is generally awkward to correct other people, because this is potentially associated with a moment of embarrassment and affront. Giving someone the opportunity to correct themselves means allowing them to keep face; and conversely, correction by others always has the potential to embarrass someone. According to Goffman (ibid.), this can even lead us to ignore and pass over our interlocutor's mistakes and errors instead of mentioning them, to save all those involved from embarrassment. When it comes to sequentiality and common ground, however, we will assume here that erroneous utterances by participants in the interaction (be they in grammar or in content) can only be ignored if they cause no lasting harm to either. For example, there is no need to correct our interlocutor if she says "authentity" instead of "authenticity" – as long as we know what is meant (cf. Clark 1997). On the other hand, giving the wrong time for a meeting, as in the examples previous, obviously has to be corrected if the participants are not to miss each other – even if the person who is wrong about the time has just proudly announced how good she is at remembering things or how disciplined she is in managing her schedule. In this sense, the common denominator in the thing being referred to has a higher priority than avoiding the loss of face. Repairs do not always relate to things that are "obviously wrong," such as wrong information or slips of the tongue; rephrasing or elaboration can also be repairs, designed to restore mutual understanding (cf. Schegloff, Jefferson & Sacks 1977).

In summary, we can note here that repairing the common ground is, on the one hand, very much an everyday component of our interactions; on the other hand, not every mistake is corrected and not every misunderstanding is cleared up. One important reason for this is that participants, when referring to each other, also refer to background assumptions which are usually not made explicit in the conversation. We possess a large repertoire of such background assumptions, only fragments of which can be expressed in interactions; at the same time we are never fully aware of what assumptions we are drawing on when we interact. In other words, not everything that is relevant for mutual understanding is mentioned in the conversation; thus assumptions about possible responses in the concrete interaction are not made solely with regard to what is directly verbalized. This is not just because we are obliged to stay on topic; often we would not even be able to precisely identify all the things that are relevant for the current conversation. For example, in a culture which is shaped by gender dualism, we are usually not aware of our implicit assumptions about "what women are like" and "what men are like." Nonetheless, latent structures of meaning such as these influence our concrete social interactions, including those with the opposite sex. So a conversation which "should" be shaped by the different functional roles of those involved (for more on this see Chapter 6) – for example in a professional context, between a female teacher and a male social worker – is always in part a conversation between a man and woman, with all the latent background assumptions, even (or especially) if one tries to avoid this.

So far we have thought about how conversations begin and how they are structured. But another part of the conversation process is, it would seem, that it ends at some point: when we begin a conversation we are aware that it will be over at a given point in time, otherwise there would be no reason to prioritize certain topics, to keep it brief or to give detailed explanations, to leave out information or to add extra details, etc. In an endless conversation, everything would be discussed eventually, and we would be under no pressure to prioritize one thing over another.[8] On the one hand, an "endless conversation" seems unimaginable to us – unimaginably exhausting, because we would not be physically able to sustain it; unimaginably unproductive, because we have many other things to do; unimaginably boring, because we would be limited to a single stimulus. On the other hand, we all conduct a more or less large number of "endless conversations," in the sense that we maintain a more or less large number of social relationships, which go beyond the immediate conversation. Indeed, very few of the conversations we have are defined by the fact that what we do not say to each other now can never ever be said. So we could argue the opposite: the reason why we are willing and able to end conversations is that we are willing and able to have further conversations, with this person and others.

But how does a conversation end? Let us recapitulate: in the conversation opener, the participants give mutual confirmation that they accept each other as interlocutors. In the subsequent course of the conversation, the thematic focus becomes relevant – the participants discuss certain matters and exchange specific information and opinions, by referring to each other in a sequence of speech acts, giving constant intersubjective assurance of this connection. In theoretical terms, two problems arise from this: first, it is inherent in sequentiality itself as a structural feature that a conversation will continue indefinitely, because an utterance in a conversation is always a response and always demands another response. In purely theoretical terms, then, it is impossible to stop talking to one another. Second, the conversation opener has already created a momentary social relationship, which makes the partners dependent on each other in this relationship. Theoretically, the end of the conversation means the end of the social relationship. In order to end a conversation, then, we must first manage to agree, in the relevant responses, that it will come to an end. And second, we must manage to do this while acknowledging the social relationship which has been expressed in the conversation. We can see this from the fact that we do not simply get up and leave at any random point in the conversation; indeed, we do not even get up at any random point and say goodbye. Schegloff and Sacks (1973), in their essay "Opening up closings," describe the complex task of initiating the end of a conversation (complex, but not difficult – we usually cope with this easily in everyday life). In general terms, the idea is that the conversation participants indicate to each other that they do not wish to "add anything further." In other words, the interlocutor who wishes to end the conversation shows in her utterance that she herself has nothing more to add, and at the same time offers the other person the opportunity to add something. Such "pre-closings" are typically utterances such as "okay" or "right, then," in which the person whose turn it is says something, in accordance with the rules of turn-taking, but does not add any further content. It is then up to the other person to either introduce a new topic or accept the initiation of the end by not adding any further subject matter. In the latter case, we often find adjacency similar to that in greetings: a "well" or an "okay" might evoke an "okay" or a "right, then," or a comparable expression indicating that the pre-closing has been agreed upon. In situations where the initiation of the conversation end also initiates the end of mutual perception – for example on the telephone or when one of the interlocutors leaves the site of the conversation – the farewell then marks the actual end of the conversation:

(7) A: Right, then.
     B: Okay.
     A: I'll be off then.
     B: Yeah.
     A: Bye.
     B: Bye.

On the one hand, then, we can observe that the moment of actually saying "goodbye" is always preceded by an exchange in which the end of the conversation is marked as a plausible, mutually accepted next step. On the other hand, saying "goodbye" also presupposes that the participants do not expect to remain in each other's perceptual horizon.

But why do we usually not simply get up and leave? Why do we signal the beginning and end of conversations? Why do we not simply present our ideas and concerns, but instead try to refer to the person we are talking to while doing so? What is the underlying meaning of the "mechanics" of sequentiality? In order to answer these questions, we must deal more closely with the question of the social relationship expressed in the interaction. The following chapters will deal with various aspects of this question.

FOOD FOR THOUGHT

Refer to your transcript of the café scene from *As Good As It Gets*. The beginning of the conversation between Melvin and Frank is not shown. What has already happened at the point where the narrative begins? What do we learn about the events preceding the scene from Frank's first sentence: "That's why you brought me here, that's really why you brought me here?"

Would an uninvolved third person who overheard the conversation between Melvin and Frank understand what it was about? Find points in the conversation which make it clear that the two characters are referring to a "common ground" existing before the café scene. Then find points where the "common ground" is created in the present moment. How are the two things marked linguistically?

After Melvin and Frank have reached an agreement about the drive to Baltimore, Melvin closes the conversation with Frank by saying "Alright, I'll see you tomorrow." Give reasons why this would be an acceptable way of ending a conversation in other circumstances – pay attention to the choice of words and to what has previously been said.

Notes

1 The following works should be mentioned in particular: Sacks, Schegloff and Jefferson (1974); Schegloff, Jefferson and Sacks (1977); Schegloff and Sacks (1973).
2 In everyday language, then, we tend to apply the word "relationship" to constellations involving friendships, partnerships and families. From a microsociological perspective, however, we can actually expand it to include any type of interpersonal cooperation. We will discuss this in detail in the chapter on reciprocity.
3 Schegloff (2007) describes such conversational loops as "pre-expansions:" they do not serve to introduce any actual "topic of conversation," but to signal that one wishes to talk about or suggest something, and wants to make sure that the other person will accept this invitation.
4 Of course this does not necessarily mean that the "challenger" is "right" with his or her take on the social relationship at hand. For example, when a student meets the teacher's "good morning" with "hiya," it is clearly an act of defiance towards the prevailing social norms of the classroom and an instance of "misconduct" in itself.
5 Goffman (1982 [1967]), on the other hand, expresses this as follows: the more participants are present, the less the social event depends on a single person, so individuals can exchange their views in subordinate side interactions which have nothing to do with the main event. A typical example is a school lesson.
6 Adjacency pairs are then two successive utterances made by two different speakers, of which the second utterance is *conditionally* pre-structured by the first. Adjacency pairs are therefore only those sequences of utterances which are normatively regulated in such a way that the interactants do not have to instantaneously decide how to respond to one another (cf. Schegloff 2007).
7 E.g. Bavelas, Coates and Johnson (2000); Clark and Brennan (1991); Clark and Carlson (1982).
8 If we sometimes observe that we "run out of things to talk about" in certain conversations, we do not mean that all topics have already been discussed – that would be completely impossible. What we mean is that there are no further topics to which we and our interlocutor currently accord a similar degree of relevance.

References

Clark, Herbert H. (1997). Dogmas of Understanding. *Discourse Processes, 23*, 567–598.
Sacks, Harvey, Schegloff, Emanuel A., & Jefferson, Gail (1974). A Simplest Systematics for the Organization of Turn-Taking for Conversation. *Language, 50*, 696–735.
Schegloff, Emanuel A. (2007). *Sequence Organization in Interaction. A Primer in Conversation Analysis*. Vol. 1. Cambridge etc.: Cambridge University Press. See especially: The Adjacency Pair as the Unit for Sequence Construction, pp. 13–21.
Schegloff, Emanuel A., & Sacks, Harvey (1973). Opening up Closings. *Semiotica, 8*, 289–327.

Further reading

Bavelas, Janet, Coates, Linda, & Johnson, Trudy (2000). Listeners as Co-Narrators. *Journal of Personality and Social Psychology, 79/6*, 941–952.
Berens, Franz-Josef (1981). Dialogeröffnung in Telefongesprächen. Handlungen und Handlungsschemata der Herstellung sozialer und kommunikativer Beziehungen. In Peter Schröder & Hugo Steger (Eds.), *Dialogforschung* (pp. 402–407). Düsseldorf, Germany: Schwann.

Clark, Herbert H., & Brennan, Susan E. (1991). Grounding in Communication. In Lauren B. Resnick, John M. Levine & Stephanie D. Teasley (Eds.), *Perspectives on Socially Shared Cognition* (pp. 127–149). Pittsburgh, PA: University of Pittsburgh.

Clark, Herbert H., & Carlson, Thomas B. (1982). Hearers and Speech Acts. *Language, 58/2*, 332–373.

Clark, Herbert H., & Krych, Meredyth A. (2004). Speaking While Monitoring Addressees for Understanding. *Journal of Memory and Language, 50*, 62–81.

Deppermann, Arnulf (2008). *Gespräche analysieren. Eine Einführung.* Wiesbaden, Germany: Springer VS.

Garfinkel, Harold (1967). *Studies in Ethnomethodology.* Englewood Cliffs, NJ: Prentice-Hall.

Goffman, Erving (1982 [1967]). *Interaction Ritual. Essays on Face-to-Face Behavior.* New York: Pantheon Books. See especially: On Face-Work, pp. 5–45; Alienation from interaction, pp. 113–136.

Henne, Helmut, & Rehbock, Helmut (1979). *Einführung in die Gesprächsanalyse.* Berlin, Germany: de Gruyter.

Kieserling, André (1999). *Kommunikation unter Anwesenden. Studien über Interaktionssysteme.* Frankfurt a. M., Germany: Suhrkamp. See especially: Differenzierte und undifferenzierte Sozialsysteme, pp. 32–61.

Luhmann, Niklas (1987). The Evolutionary Differentiation between Society and Interaction. In Jeffrey C. Alexander, Bernhard Giesen, Richard Münch & Neil J. Smelser (Eds.), *The Micro-Macro Link* (pp. 112–131). Berkeley, CA: University of California Press.

Schegloff, Emanuel A. (2002). Beginnings in the Telephone. In James E. Katz & Mark Aakhus (Eds.), *Perpetual Contact: Mobile Communication, Private Talk, Public Performance* (pp. 284–300). Cambridge: Cambridge University Press.

Schegloff, Emanuel A., Jefferson, Gail, & Sacks, Harvey (1977). The Preference for Self-Correction in the Organization of Repair in Conversation. *Language, 53*, 361–382.

3

INSTITUTIONS

What we take for granted in social action

The "linguistic" view of interaction is not limited to describing the mechanisms of conversation production at a particular moment, but also deals with the important question of what language contributes to mutual understanding, beyond what is actually said. One philosopher of language who has explored this question in many relevant works is John Searle. In his reflections on linguistic "institutions," Searle's starting point is the observation that, in many cases, the things we denote and describe with words, as a matter of course, only become the things that we mean as a result of the terms themselves. Usually, the linguistic designation gives the person, object or matter designated a meaning which cannot be deduced from the person, object or matter "in itself." And often the linguistic designation even creates something that would not exist without the term and the associated meaning. It is therefore crucial for social interaction that there be generally recognized rules and generally recognized meanings which we refer to with language, without the need to explicitly name them.

In the previous two chapters, we dealt with fundamental *formal* qualities and mechanisms of interaction. Among other things, we discussed how one becomes involved in communication in the first place, and how interaction is temporally structured. The question of "how" will now be followed by the question of "what." Again, our approach will focus on the fundamentals, examining how we are to understand the *content* of our interactive turns. In this content, we refer to friendship, family, property, convivial evenings, opera performances, jobs, soccer; in short, we refer to things that have only been produced by human communities. And the manner in which we refer to them linguistically also differs fundamentally from communication in the animal kingdom. How can these differences be defined in theoretical terms? What is the nature of the "fabric" that makes up our interactions? In an attempt to find an answer, we will have recourse to one of the basic concepts of sociology: the "institution" or "institutionalization." We use it, however, in a broader sense than usual. We want to describe the content of interaction in general as "institutional facts."

> We live in a sea of human institutional facts. Much of this is invisible to us. Just as it is hard for the fish to see the water in which they swim, so it is hard for us to see the institutionality in which we swim.
>
> *(Searle 2010, p. 90)*

These are the sentences with which the philosopher of language John R. Searle introduces a book chapter concerned with the same subject we will be dealing with here. The omnipresent and inconspicuous character of these facts becomes apparent when he depicts a typical scene from everyday life, italicizing the kinds of facts which particularly interest him – and also us at this point:

> I get up in the morning in a house jointly *owned* by me and my *wife*. I drive to do my *job* on the *campus* in a car that is *registered* to both of us, and I can drive *legally* only because I am the holder of a *valid California driver's license*. On the way, I *illegally* answer a cell phone call from an old *friend*. Once I am in my *office* the weight of institutional reality increases. I am in the *Philosophy Department* of the *University of California* in *Berkeley*. I am surrounded by *students*, *colleagues*, and *university employees*. I teach *university courses* and make various *assignments* to my *students*.
>
> *(ibid.)*

Searle extends this description further, but even these first examples should be enough to give us an intuitive sense of what this is about. It also becomes clear that a very broad concept of "institution" is being used here – one that includes things as diverse as marriage, private property, university courses, and friendship. We might well ask what is *not* an institution: are "house," "car," or "cell phone" not also social concepts or objects? In a sense they are, if they are regarded as linguistic institutional facts. We will come back to this later. Here we have to bear in mind that this is about reference: it is about what kind of objects we *refer to* with linguistic expressions. And ultimately, in the case of houses, cars or cell phones, these are physical or physically describable things. In contrast, the objects Searle italicizes are, in a way, not actually objects in the ordinary sense at all: we cannot see, feel or smell them. We can see a building and say "That's the University of California," but what we really see is a (university) building, not the university. Or we can point to a group of people and say "Those are students," but what makes them students is not really something we can see or measure (their age, weight, blood group, etc.).

In spite of this limitation to non-linguistic facts, we still have a very broad concept of institution here. When sociologists use this expression, it is mainly in a narrower sense. For example, they often mean something that is also covered by another concept, that of the organization, as in the expression "trust in institutions." This designates social units that go beyond individuals and small groups (and which the individual trusts to function smoothly): the Catholic Church, parliament, the justice system, the police, the trade unions. This does not refer to any groups of people as such. The laity and the clergy, the members of parliament, the legal professionals are part of an institution, but do not define it. Nor are concrete organizations – a specific club, trade union, party, etc. – generally referred to as institutions.[1] This is more about abstract institutions which are somehow part of a community, and which are seen as necessary for its functioning, its preservation, its particular appearance. In this sense, we can also speak of the family as an institution. A different conception is advocated by Douglas (1986) in her book *How Institutions Think*: here institutions are interpretive complexes for understanding the world, which are characteristic of a particular culture and therefore also decisively influence the worldview and the thinking of the individual members of society.

In general, however, the sociological concept of "institutions" largely coincides with the way the term is used in everyday language. If, for example, we say "Jack's an institution in the village," then the expression implies at least two things. First, he must stand for something, i.e. he must have a function, in the broadest sense. He might, for example, be the landlord of the local pub, who knows about everything that goes on in the village; the person everyone goes to if they want to hear the latest news. And second, everyone knows him and knows about this function. Things are very similar in sociology. Sociology takes institutions to mean social bodies which play a prominent role in society and are generally recognized. This applies to the Catholic Church, parliament, the justice system, the postal service, the employment agency, etc.; it does not, however, apply to university courses, students or assignments. The reason why Searle nonetheless counts these and many other things as institutional facts is that he sees the aspect of general recognition as crucial. The key factor is that these things play a role in society; whether the role is *prominent* is of secondary importance.

This aspect of general recognition takes center stage in sociology too, when we say that something is "institutionalized." What is meant is that a specific claim, status, area of responsibility, expectation, etc. becomes firmly established in a historical process, or in short, that something is *valid*. Thus sociology arrives at a similarly broad concept of institution. We want to further investigate this aspect in the following section, examining the connection between social objects and general validity. We thus treat "institution" as *the* key sociological term, that is, the thing that shows social facts to be an independent reality, a "reality sui generis," as Durkheim (1982) programmatically called it. In other words, institutions are objective – because generally valid – structures of meaning.

A prominent theory dealing with institutions in the context of their emergence was proposed by Berger and Luckmann (1967). Following Gehlen (1956) in particular, Berger and Luckmann essentially see institutions as (clusters of) solutions to problems, which have been pre-established within society and relieve individuals of the burden of decision-making in certain situations. Here the emergence of institutions is linked to specific decision-making situations. The starting point is actions that are frequently repeated, and have thus proven themselves as solutions for dealing with the natural and social environment. These actions, according to the authors, tend to be treated as a model or pattern by the actors; they become "habitualized," i.e. individual routines or habits are formed. Even on this first level of institutionalization, there is an element of disburdenment, which can also help to explain the process of habitualization: the advantage of reproducing tried and tested courses of action, as if following a pattern, is that one does not have to redefine the situation and start afresh every time, weighing up and trying out the alternatives.

As we have seen, however, institutions are not individual, but supra-individual matters. According to Berger and Luckmann (ibid.), this initially requires a second level of institutionalization: the mutual typification (see also Chapter 9) of habitualized action by the actors. Not only is the action itself understood as a pattern ("an action of type X"), but so are the actors themselves ("actors of type Y"). For example, a certain way of dealing with clay becomes "pottery," and the person who carries out these actions is a "potter." Such typifications become common property, they become part of the general store of knowledge. Or in any case, they do so under the condition that the actions in question are relevant for the people involved, in their shared situation. The models are then available to the members of society as tried and tested courses of action.

On this second level, the institutions are still very much bound to their situation of origin; they are still recognizable as models of proven solutions to problems, which have been found by actors. However, the fully developed "institutional world" is characterized by a considerable degree of "objectivity." In other words, the institutions confront the members of society as a given reality – like a second nature. The authors ascribe this to a third, crucial level of institutionalization: the socialization of the patterns. It is only when the patterns are handed down to the next generation that they lose their situation-bound character and become generalized norms – for the parents as well as the younger generation: "The 'There we go again' now becomes 'This is how these things are done'" (Berger & Luckmann 1967, p. 59). What was originally an active grappling with particular problems becomes, at the end of this kind of process of institutionalization, a normative pattern, which the members of society are expected to follow. For those socialized in this way, the problem-solving character of the institution is no longer part of their living experience. At the same time, it can still be discerned from the perspective of third-party observers such as sociologists.

There is something to be said for the idea that institutions are pre-established solutions to problems which members of society regularly encounter and have to cope with, saving them from having to expend energy finding a solution themselves. A familiar situation is that of entering an empty seminar room at the beginning of the semester and having to choose where to sit. To do so, we have to apply the categories available to us, weigh them up and make a decision. The next time we will tend to take the same seat – if the conditions and criteria are the same, in any case. Why? To save ourselves the trouble of going through another decision-making process. And it is possible to imagine similar processes for a number of social institutions: "give way to the right," "the person entering the room says hello first," "go to the back of the queue" – all these can be understood as solutions to typical problems. The model can also be imagined on a larger scale: political institutions are solutions to the problem of collective (and binding) decision-making, laws are solutions to regularly recurring conflicts, religions are solutions to individual questions about the meaning of life.

But this concept has its limits. On the one hand, not all institutions can be understood as solutions to *pre-existing* problems. For Berger and Luckmann (ibid.), the starting point is always problems dealing with the natural or social environment, problems that are somehow "objectively" given. But as we will see, there are institutions that cause problems in the first place, i.e. from an analytical perspective, the problems are inconceivable without institutions. On the other hand, this concept pays too little attention to what identifies institutions *as institutions*. This question is hidden in the problem of transmission. Because what happens here is more than the imposition of symbolic form and separation from the context of living experience. From the beginning, this is treated as if it were not a body of experience that was being handed down, but collective knowledge. Not "my/ our experience becomes your knowledge;" instead, right from the start, it is "our knowledge" or "the way we do it." But what is it that marks this "collectivity?" In other words: how are we to visualize the social *validity* of institutions?

This is the point at which we return to Searle. The theory which he developed over many decades (e.g. Searle 1969, 1995, 2010) combines a number of merits. It offers a general concept which also includes the narrower sociological understanding of institutions; a concept that not only describes what is to be understood by institutions, but also explains their structure, including their importance for structure formation in interactions. In the process, the relationship between institutional facts and language is also clarified. And finally, the theory provides the social sciences with an elegant model for defining their subject area.

Searle's perspective – as may already have become clear – is different from that of Berger and Luckmann. While the latter, with a sociological preconception of social institutions, basically ask how these can arise out of individual actions and gradually acquire an "objectified" status for the members of society, Searle asks on a more fundamental level what actually constitutes the subject area of the social sciences as opposed to that of the natural sciences. What characterizes social facts in contrast to natural facts? The critical question here is whether the facts are independent of the observer (Searle 1995). This applies to the "brute facts" of the natural world, e.g. "There's snow on the summit of Kilimanjaro," or "The hydrogen atom has an electron." Even if facts of this kind are conceived and given linguistic expression by "observers," we have to assume that the things conceived and expressed in this way would not cease to exist even if there were no longer any human observers. This is different for institutional facts such as "this is a ten euro note." Independent of the observer, there is only a piece of paper. It only becomes money through a kind of agreement between the observers – through the fact that we see the piece of paper as money. The same, incidentally, applies to university courses, students and assignments: they too only become facts because we consider them as such. What does this mean, in more precise terms?

The first prerequisite for institutions is the assignment of status functions. What is meant by this is an ability that fundamentally distinguishes human sociality from subhuman sociality: humans can ascribe functions to things or people which these things or people cannot fulfill solely on the basis of their inherent physical characteristics. This can be readily illustrated with the example of the ten euro note. Certainly, this piece of paper has some characteristics that make it suitable as money, or at least more so than other pieces of paper.[2] But obviously, the function of a generally valid means of payment is not the result of these characteristics, as any currency reform can demonstrate. Or if we take a letter: one aspect of the status function of the letter is that it is only destined for the receiver. But again, this does not result solely from the characteristic of the closed envelope, which, after all, offers the contents only limited physical protection. What is crucial is the general recognition of the status function. This stops us even from reading completely unprotected messages such as postcards if they are not addressed to us.

The example Searle (2010) uses to illustrate the difference between functions arising from physical characteristics and ascribed status functions is as follows. Imagine a wall around a village. It primarily constitutes a physical barrier to keep out animals or enemies. Over the course of time, the wall falls into disrepair, until only one row of stones is left. It is conceivable, however, that the inhabitants will continue to recognize this row of stones as something that it no longer physically embodies: a "border." Now the only crucial factor here is general recognition. The basic model of the assignment of status functions, which is contained in all institutions, is expressed in the following formula by Searle: in context C (in this case the village), the status function Y (in this case a border) is ascribed to an object X (in this case the row of stones).[3]

It is important to see that this has consequences for action. The assigned status functions are not "mere symbols," but generally possess what Searle calls "deontic powers" (Searle 2010). That is, there are rights, obligations, requirements, etc. associated with them. By creating institutions, we make a (practical) difference in social life. And the meaning of a concrete institution consists of the specific deontic powers associated with it. For example, in the case of the boundary of the imaginary village, marked with a row of stones, it is possible to imagine that within the boundary one is obliged to offer solidarity and assistance to everyone, and one is entitled to receive such support oneself, but that no such obligation exists outside the boundary. In the real social world, the status function of citizen includes the right to vote, the status function of "friend" includes the duty of loyalty, and the status function of "office" includes the restriction that no private parties may be held here.

Talk of deontic *power* is not to be understood metaphorically. Institutions are accompanied by binding requirements for action, which are independent of our subjective inclinations and wishes.[4] They are, as it were, the direct consequence of the prevailing status functions themselves. We do not have to first take ownership of them, test our attitude towards them, turn them into the motivation for our actions, etc. before they can develop their interaction-structuring power – because they do this of their own accord. If the assigned status function exists, then so do the rights, etc. that are connected with it, regardless of the stance we take. So if the status function of the citizen includes the right to take part in elections, and the obligation to pay taxes, then citizens *have* the right to take part in elections and *are* obliged to pay taxes, regardless of whether they care about the former or like the latter. Here the source of the deontic power is not a legal sanction, even if many institutional facts do have such sanctions available to them, but the validity of the ascribed status function itself. If the status function of a good friend includes a certain degree of loyalty and solidarity, then I, as a good friend, *am* obliged to provide these. And if the status function of the office includes not holding private parties here, then I *am* subject to this restriction.

This is not the same thing as "conformity." If status functions are accompanied by deontic power, this does not mean that we always, in every case, fulfill such rights, obligations or requirements. We can certainly contravene them. But first, not every violation of rights and obligations implies a questioning of their validity. A theft is, as a rule, simultaneously an infringement of another person's right to property, and an acknowledgment of the institution of private property, as the thief wishes to make the stolen goods her own property. And a bigamist will not expect the second or third woman he has married to marry (or have married) a second or third man. Second, in view of the "sea of institutional facts" in which we are swimming, the violation of institutional requirements is always the exception. Although we may violate rights and obligations that are associated with particular institutions, even as we do so we will automatically recognize other institutions. Even if we feel that private property or the exclusivity requirement of marriage do not apply "to us," we will nonetheless, in our actions, not call into question the validity of the institutions "driver's license," "job," "office" or "president," etc., including the deontic power associated with them. Third, any infringement or violation of rights and obligations requires justification, while conforming to them does not. Indeed we can conduct a thought experiment in which this is the test criterion: if we doubt whether a status function is really valid, we can ask which courses of action related to it require justification, and which do not. Take the question of whether paid employment for women has now become institutionalized. This would mean that the status function of "full member of society" (Y) in modern Western societies (C), which is ascribed to women (X), also includes the obligation to have an occupation and to carry out paid work. In order to determine this, we would have to ask which action requires justification: in the present day, is an adult woman who is not in paid employment required to justify this (e.g. by saying "If I went to work instead of looking after the household and children, my whole income would be spent on after-school care and domestic help anyway"), or is it necessary to justify going out to work (e.g. by saying "I work because my husband's income isn't enough for us at the moment")?

The deontic power associated with the ascription "X counts as Y in context C" is not a "norm" (see Chapter 7), even if normative expectations or requirements are often associated with institutions. The obligation to pay taxes is legally – and thus normatively – sanctioned, one can say that friends have to stick together, and there are rules about what one is and is not allowed to do in the office. But the mode of action is more fundamental. Norms relate to the deontic power of status functions, but the converse does not apply; thus deontic power does not result from normative provisions or requirements. We will try to make this even clearer in the following discussion. For now, it should suffice to say that the fundamental importance of institutional requirements for action can be seen in the fact that only some of them have found their way into normative demands. A large part of what makes a citizen, a good friend, or an office remains implicit – but this in no way detracts from its influence.

In all this, we obviously have to bear in mind that the deontic requirements of institutions can be not only fulfilled or contravened, but also criticized. Of course, there is institutional change, and in large part, the starting point for this change is critical scrutiny of institutions.[5] Subsequently, entirely new status functions may be created, the scope of existing status functions may be expanded or restricted, or the rights and obligations associated with the deontic power may be changed. We do not need to go into this here. It is, however, important to emphasize that the "imperative" nature of institutions is shown by the fact that criticism also necessarily includes acknowledgment of the validity of the status function assignment that is being criticized. If it were not valid, there would be no need to abolish it. And the success of the criticism of specific institutions depends on whether, in the context of social struggles, the changes in the formula "X counts as Y in context C" come to be generally recognized.

This aspect of reciprocal agreement, acceptance or general recognition is therefore of critical importance for the whole concept of institutional facts. How is this to be understood? It might be supposed that this was about making a kind of value judgment, taking a yes-or-no stance on a claim to validity which is being laid. In the same way that we can criticize institutions, we could potentially declare ourselves to be in agreement with them. And if the majority of the population supports the assignment of a concrete status function, has it then not found general recognition? Interestingly, this is actually *not* the case. Of course, we can declare that we agree with institutions such as marriage, private property, parliamentarianism or driver's licenses. And in terms of social integration, it is undoubtedly important that the crucial political and legal institutions are supported by as large a proportion of the population as possible. But this is not what we mean by recognition. In the concept proposed here, recognition is not a question of degree, and it is not a matter of "approval" or "endorsement." Instead, we should imagine the validity of a status function ascription as more like that of a rule of play; recognition happens when we play by the rules.

In this context, it is important to distinguish between two basic types of rule, constitutive and regulative rules, a distinction already introduced by Searle (1969) in the context of his speech act theory. While regulative rules (such as road traffic regulations) regulate an already existing practice, constitutive rules (such as those of chess) generate the practice they regulate. Regulative rules suggest *that* we should do certain things, and *how* we should do them, e.g. "Red means stop/ green means go," "Do as you would be done by," "Don't talk to strangers." Constitutive rules, on the other hand, always tell us *what* certain things *are* as well: "A goal is scored when the ball has completely crossed the goal line," "The first-born son inherits the farm."

This distinction has major implications, but is not easily grasped. Giddens (1984, p. 20) also has his difficulties with it. He argues that the "etymological clumsiness" of the concept of the regulative rule indicates that there is something suspect about this distinction ("After all, the word 'regulative' already implies 'rule'"). In his view, these are not so much two different types of rule as two aspects that all rules display: they have both "sanctioning" and "defining" aspects. For example, a rule that all workers must clock in at eight o'clock in the morning would be part of the definition of a concept of industrial bureaucracy. Giddens thus assumes that the distinction between "regulative" and "constitutive" can be set aside. The disadvantage from a microsociological perspective is that he misses the crucial point, and cannot make use of it in his social theory. Because of course, all sorts of rules can tell us something *about* social practice; they help us to understand it, and we can use them to develop our sociological concepts. But this is not the point of the distinction. It is, rather, about the different ways of *taking effect within* social practice. And in this respect, the two types of the rule are fundamentally different.

To clarify the distinction we will – as in other accounts – begin with an example from the field of games and sports: the rules of soccer. So which rules here are constitutive, and produce the practice of soccer in the first place? To start off with, it is necessary to define more closely which practice we want to consider: street soccer, indoor soccer or tournament soccer on the field? Let us take the latter. Next, we have to give up the idea that "constitutive" means that these rules are mainly fundamental for the *appearance* of the sport; this would bring together a large number of heterogeneous elements, from the offside rule or the permitted size of the field to the convention that tournament soccer is not played in swimming trunks. The crucial question is, rather, whether a social practice (of the game) does actually *come about*.

Here is a thought experiment: imagine two teams, one of them playing as if one particular set of rules prevailed, and the other as if another set of rules were in place. The two teams meet on a general-purpose field of the kind found in schoolyards, i.e. the external preparations for different team games (markings, baskets, goals, etc.) are present. What happens? If team A was, according to its own unshakeable conviction, playing soccer, while team B was equally firmly convinced that it was playing basketball, not a single cooperative move would occur. As soon as the players from team A kicked the ball, those from team B would stop playing in consternation, and would protest, etc. And as soon as the players from team B threw the ball to each other, team A would protest. The crucial point is immediately obvious: it would not work. No joint practice could come about, at least not in the sense of a game. It is constitutive rules that are crucial here.

Conversely, when different opinions about the validity of a rule mean that a cooperative social practice cannot come about, we can see this as an indication that this rule is a constitutive one. Take, for example, the offside rule in soccer: imagine two teams, of which one plays in accordance with the offside rule, the other not. What would happen? Unlike the first example, the game would last for a while. But with the first offside situation, the game would effectively be over, because one team would see this as a regular (or irregular) play, and the other not. Even if this is only a rule that relates to certain situations in the game, it means that a basis for cooperation in the game is fundamentally lacking.

This test also allows us to see that the rules of tactical formation, which are of major importance for the appearance of the game, are not constitutive rules, but regulative ones. They govern what a soccer game is (according to current tournament rules), by organizing the teams according to criteria of effectiveness. This can be done by establishing nuanced rules for the allocation of roles (defense, midfield, attack; back four or sweeper, classical attack or attacking midfield, etc.). But it can also be done by essentially following the basic rule of "staying close to the ball," as sometimes seems to be the case in games for the under 7s. It undoubtedly makes sense to follow some rule to organize the team's playing technique. What is crucial, however, is that this is unimportant for the cooperative practice of the game as such. When two teams who have chosen different versions of the rules in this respect meet on the field, the outcome may not be a satisfying game to watch or – from one team's point of view – an effective one. It is, however, a social practice which is in principle successful: it finishes after 90 minutes, and in the end, either 1 team has won or the match is drawn.

These examples can also serve to show, once again, that the recognition of constitutive rules is not a question of degree or of assent. Either the rules are the basis of my (our) action or they are not, and then it is a different game. It is also unimportant for actual practice whether I think the offside rule is good or bad. What is crucial is that it is valid and that I confirm its validity in my actions.

I do this even when I shoot a goal from offside and then accept that this goal is disallowed. And when I accept the decision, even though I do not believe that it was offside, then I am confirming another constitutive rule – that the referee's decision is final in all cases.

Games and sports, however, are special forms of practice outside of everyday life. What is the situation in "real" social life? What are the constitutive rules of everyday interaction? This question is harder to answer than in the case of the rules of play, for at least two reasons (and this is probably why the latter are often chosen as examples). On the one hand, a larger array of institutional facts play a part in everyday interactions, and many of these facts are not specific to the concrete interaction. For instance, "private property" is not only relevant for business relationships, but also when a friend buys a beer for another friend, or when a neighbor gives another neighbor a bucket of plums. There are systems of constitutive rules linked with all these institutional facts. We really do live in a "sea of institutional facts." This makes things very complex. It must be clear, then, that the answer to the question can only ever refer to an extract of the interaction under consideration. On the other hand, the constitutive rules that structure everyday interaction are usually not codified. There is no official set of rules to give us orientation and support. In practice, we mainly follow these rules in the same way we follow the rules of language, that is, without really "knowing" them, and without being able to state what the rules we are following actually look like. This is the "invisibility" Searle talks about in the quote at the beginning of this chapter. It is not simply that we do not notice the institutional facts as such because they are so omnipresent and because we take them for granted. It is also that we can only understand them in this way because the way they influence us is, in the vast majority of cases, "latent." We follow the rules without consciously having them at our disposal. And yet, to stay with the example of language, we "know" exactly whether a sentence in our first language is "right," i.e. grammatically correct, or not. It is the same in interactions: we usually know what is "right" (i.e. appropriate to the situation and the status functions relevant in it), and what is not.[6] What this means for the description of constitutive rules in concrete interactions is that we must *make them explicit*; we must try to bring to light the things that are hidden in our tacit knowledge of the rules, and that structure our judgments about what is appropriate. In concrete terms, we must try to spell out the meaning of the institutional facts by identifying the things that "belong to" these facts as a consequence of deontic power.

Let us take the simple example of an interaction between a customer and a shop assistant in a bakery. Here we will disregard the linguistic or communicative institutional facts (the constitutive rules of interaction opening, turn-taking, reciprocity, etc.), as well as the non-linguistic facts – such as "money," "private property" or "contract" – which are relevant in a number of different types of interaction. Nor will we investigate the significance that the status functions "woman" and "man" might have here. (The fact that these aspects could certainly be among the things negotiated here gives us an idea of how complex things are in the real world when it comes to constitutive rules.) So what is left? Plenty of things. For a start, "bakery" itself is undoubtedly an institutional fact, as this status function is not exhaustively defined by the physical features of the building in which it is found. One can imagine very different forms of a building that might be considered as a "bakery"; the only thing they would have in common is that they would have to contain an oven somewhere.[7] What else is involved? A bakery is not simply a place in which baked goods are produced; they must also be sold here. One element of "selling" is that, in principle, any person can enter this place and, under the condition of payment, can purchase corresponding goods. This addressing of strangers is marked by a notice or sign which is legible from outside. Another aspect of "bakery" – as with any sales business – is, of necessity, interaction (at least) in the framework of the complementary roles of seller/buyer.[8] Another requirement is that we as buyers must be informed in some way or other about the products available and given the opportunity to examine the goods. For this, there are rules specific to each type of product (displaying of goods on shelves, lists; visual inspection, touch/smell, samples, etc.). There are also rules for how the goods are made available to us, and how the financial transaction is organized (service at the counter, self-service; payment to the salesperson, differentiation between salesperson and cashier, etc.). This then also includes the rules of pricing (fixed prices, haggling, etc.).

This list can certainly make no claim to completeness, but will suffice for now. All the things listed here are seemingly mundane. Yet it is important to see that these are rules that determine how we act; courses of action that we mostly take automatically, but whose binding character becomes clear when we imagine diverging courses of action. Thus if we were faced with a building that plainly offered baked goods, but did not have a shop sign, we would be uncertain what it was. Our uncertainty would increase if there were people standing at the door whom we would identify as "bouncers." The shop assistant, for her part, would undoubtedly be disconcerted if, instead of saying "Three rolls, please," we asked, "Do you feel like selling me three rolls?". And she would probably react with indignation if we were to casually go around behind the counter, examine the rolls one by one, and put them into a bag ourselves. As these deviations from constitutive rules show, institutional facts are associated with expectations in a more than merely cognitive sense. This is what Searle means by "deontic power": we have "a right" to certain behaviors, and this "right" is based on the institutional facts themselves.[9] They are part of the "game" which is associated with them. Conversely, the deviations mentioned are characterized by the fact that a different "game" is being played, in opposition to the existing institutional facts, as it were. Since these "games" refer to other institutional facts and the relevant constitutive rules, we are able to identify them. In the case of the above-mentioned deviations, this would be: the "game" of an exchange not between strangers, but between acquaintances; the "game" of associating the service with a particular milieu; the "game" of a close social relationship; the "game" of self-service.

The fact is that if we are swimming in a "sea of institutional facts," this also means that we cannot get out. Institutional facts are our "element," the way we act in interactions is always shaped by them, and it is these facts that first give "meaning" to our actions and to the situations in which we interact. The constitutive rules belonging to them guide our actions. We are subject to their deontic power, in the sense that we have no choice but to refer to them, even in the case of divergent action or criticism. Here the constitutive rules of the form of interaction in question come to be universally accepted as the ineluctable basis for action in general. This does not mean, however, that they are valid everywhere and at all times. The extent of their validity can vary: there are institutions that are only valid in a particular milieu or in a particular family; what is crucial, however, is that they are seen as generally valid within this context.[10]

At the beginning of this section we said that Searle distinguishes institutional facts from natural ones by suggesting that the former are relative to the observer, the latter not. Now if, as we have tried to show with reference to Searle's work, institutional facts are to be understood as social facts par excellence – in other words, if they are what makes up the subject area of the social sciences – then this distinction has uncomfortable consequences for these areas of scholarly endeavor. This is because one could fundamentally question whether they are capable of "objectivity." For if the subject area of the social sciences is fundamentally characterized by relativity to the observer, that means that ontologically, i.e. in terms of its "way of being," it is – unlike the world of the natural sciences – not "objective" but "subjective." Does this mean that the social sciences are not "real" sciences? Do we have to retain the old Anglo-Saxon distinction between "science" and the "humanities?"

In Searle's theoretical edifice, this "threat" is defused, in the first instance, with the observation that ontological subjectivity is not the same as "epistemic" (knowledge-related) subjectivity. The fact that an object is relative to the observer does not necessarily mean that no truth-apt statements can be linked with it. Social facts – as institutional facts – are not relative to the observer in the same way as feelings of happiness or pain, about which one can only make subjective judgments ("I'm very happy," "I'm in great pain"). Instead, they allow epistemic objectivity; they allow truth-apt statements. The critical factor here is the general validity of the constitutive rules underlying them. Recourse to these rules is crucial for the truth-aptness of empirical analyses in the social sciences. This applies not only to sentences such as "John F. Kennedy was the 35th president of the United States of America" or "This is a bakery." Particularly in interaction analyses, we must constantly refer to the constitutive rules of institutional facts, in order to determine the meaning of the actions we are confronted with in our data material. We need to know what a bakery, a shop assistant, an order, money, property, etc. is in order to be able to conduct a concrete interaction in a bakery in everyday practice and to subject this interaction to sociological analysis. And by drawing on generally valid rules, we lay the foundation stone, as it were, for the truth-aptness of our assertions.

But even more importantly – and this brings us to our last point in this chapter – we also have to know what a greeting and a farewell are, and what speech acts mean (e.g. "Please," "Thank you" or "Do you drive?"), in order to react appropriately in everyday practice, or to produce an adequate sociological analysis of what these actions mean in concrete interactions. The social world does not consist solely of (non-linguistic) institutional facts, but also of linguistic facts. Not only must these also be understood as institutional facts, they actually have a special significance for the social world, because this world is linguistically constituted.[11] This is not to say that collective action and cooperation cannot also take place on a pre-linguistic level (cf. Tomasello 2008). But a world full of institutional facts in the sense discussed here is unimaginable without language.[12] Here Searle (2010) ascribes particular importance to a special type of speech act: the declaration. Declarations are those utterances which serve to create a social practice that did not previously exist (in this form). For example: "I now declare you man and wife," "I now declare the Olympic Games to be opened" or "I now christen you Harry." Without these utterances, the couple would not be married, the Olympic Games would not begin and the boy would not be called Harry. These special performative phrases ("I now declare," etc.) make this reality-generating force especially apparent, but they are not crucial. The registrar could also say "You are now man and wife," the head of state could say "The Olympic Games are opened" and the priest could say "Your name is Harry." The distinctive feature of these speech acts is that they simultaneously describe and bring about a situation. In this respect, they resemble the ascriptions of status functions or the underlying constitutive rules. They have the same logical form: "X counts as Y in context C." Searle's assumption is that non-linguistic institutional facts of this special kind require linguistic representation. Sometimes this is explicitly the case, as some institutional facts are produced by declarative acts: the republic is declared, the president is deposed, a minister is sworn in, a company is founded. But even where this is not the case, the creation and preservation of institutional facts are always linked to the representation of a declarative act. This can be illustrated as follows: whenever we refer to institutional facts in our actions, that is, whenever we "use the vocabulary of the status functions" (Searle 2010, p. 104), we implicitly make use of their declaration. When we say "This is a bakery" or "As my friend, you're obviously invited," this also always implies "We collectively recognize that this is a bakery" or "We collectively recognize that you are my friend." Every linguistic utilization of non-linguistic institutions in interactions can thus be understood as a reinforcement of their status functions. Every speech act helps to assert the validity of the constitutive rules, and this claim to validity is confirmed in interaction – except in those cases when it is criticized.

For us, the most important thing to note in the present context is that linguistic facts are already institutional facts themselves. Speech acts of assertion or promise, for example, are based on constitutive rules, which stipulate that an utterance (X) counts as an assertion or a promise (Y) in the context of a given language (C). They also have a deontology, just like non-linguistic facts: by promising or asserting something, we commit ourselves to something, namely the keeping of the promise, or the truth of our assertion. One could also say that performing the speech acts *imposes this commitment* on us – since the deontic power of constitutive rules of language, just like that of (non-linguistic) institutional facts, functions independent of our will. We cannot escape from the commitments that are associated with our speech acts by claiming that we did not really mean our promises, and did not really believe in our assertions. Insincerity and lies only "work" if the people we are speaking to, or indeed all those involved, regard sincerity and belief as crucial conditions of our speech acts. We are therefore obliged to provide justifications if we do not keep our promises, or if our assertions do not match reality.

It is not only promises, assertions, requests, thank-yous, apologies, etc. that have deontic power, but also their content and the specific manner in which the types of speech act are realized. At every moment, at every point of interaction, language use is accompanied by an abundance of institutional commitments. They are the implications of our acts, which impose obligations on us – and on our interaction partners, who must react to our speech acts in specific ways. And they are therefore no more and no less than the meaning of these acts. The meaning of the utterance "Three regular rolls, please" consists in the fact that it refers to a particular context of utterance (in which the sale or at least the distribution of bread rolls is pre-established), it raises certain expectations about us (we really do want the rolls; we have money to pay for them) and it commits us and our interlocutor to subsequent actions (taking the rolls, packing them, stating the price, paying). Here the meaning of utterances, including all the linguistic and non-linguistic institutions evoked, is generated by the underlying constitutive rules.

As we will discuss later (especially in Chapter 12), these commitments do not have "one-to-one" implications for action: they do not tell us what exactly we have to do in practical terms, and they do not turn us into robots. We can also say "Three regular rolls, please" to our partner at the breakfast table; the salesperson in the bakery could respond to our request by saying: "We don't have those any more" or "Sorry, they're all gone. Would you like some of the poppyseed ones?;" we could take the rolls and run out of the shop without paying. But whatever significance these courses of action might have in any specific case, this significance always depends on what the utterance they refer to means – according to generally accepted rules. And our particular situational courses of action are also understood in the light of their general meaning. In our actions, we create facts, to which we are then committed, and to which our interaction partners must refer. The manner in which we do this in practice – in other words, the way we operate in the sea of institutional facts – depends on our decisions (and those of our interaction partners). But what they mean is not determined by us; it is determined by the institutional world in which we operate.

FOOD FOR THOUGHT

Refer to your transcript of the café scene from *As Good As It Gets*. "Café,"
"waitress" and "customer" are certainly non-linguistic institutions in the sense
understood here. But what about "road user" or "pedestrian"?

Try to analyze the deontology of Melvin's speech act "Think white and get
serious!" What are the conditions for the fulfillment of this utterance? What
situation(s) does it refer to? What facts does it create?

Notes

1 There are, however, exceptions. If, for example, we follow Goffman (1968 [1961])
  and speak of a "total institution," this can certainly refer to a specific psychiatric facil-
  ity or a specific prison.
2 One of these characteristics is that it is, from a technical point of view, not really
  made of paper.
3 This example is only intended to illustrate physical qualities of things and the assignment of status functions. Searle is neither arguing that status functions have generally
  been derived from physical characteristics, nor is this meant to suggest (as in the ideas
  of Berger and Luckmann) that institutions fundamentally have their origins in the
  living experience of individuals.
4 The philosophical term "deontic" or "deontology" refers to this element of obligation.
5 We cannot explore this point in depth here. However, one thing that can ignite criticism is a lack of clarity about what the requirements associated with the institutions
  are. There are always unclear cases, too: what are the boundaries of civic obligations?
  Where does the duty of loyalty in friendships end? What private matters can I legitimately deal with in the office?
6 In the debate in philosophy and the social sciences, this kind of non-conscious knowledge has come to be known as "tacit knowledge" (cf. Polanyi 1974).
7 "Building" and "oven" point to the fact that artifacts are also part of the social world.
  We do not have the scope here to explore this interesting category of things any further. Note, however, that Searle (2010) does not count them among the institutional
  facts. In his example, which we quoted at the beginning of this chapter, "house,"
  "car" and "cell phone" are not highlighted. The reason for this could be seen to lie
  in the fact that they fulfil their status function on the basis of their inherent physical characteristics. Unlike the painted piece of wood which a child refers to as "my
  phone," a cell phone is in general an object whose physical characteristics make it a
  cell phone. At the same time one could say that it participates in the social world, in
  the sense that these physical characteristics could not have come about without the
  assignment of status functions.
8 This even applies to the extreme cases of vending machines or online trading: here
  the seller is the vending machine or the website with its programmed structure.
9 Garfinkel (1967) discovered the (in this specific sense) "normative" implications of
  institutional facts in his famous "breaching" experiments.
10 For the distinction between the generality of constitutive rules and the extent of their
  validity, see Oevermann (1986).
11 An initial indicator of the more fundamental importance of language can perhaps be
  expressed as follows: language *is* not already institutionalized or does not *become* institutionalized, because speaking a common language always includes the condition of
  being institutionalized.

12 Indeed Searle (2010) believes that the creation of non-linguistic institutional facts is the necessary consequence of human language. This is a strong hypothesis, but not one we will explore here; instead we will merely attempt, in the following section, to briefly check the plausibility of the weaker assumption that language is the precondition for the creation of non-linguistic institutional facts.

References

Berger, Peter, & Luckmann, Thomas (1967). *The Social Construction of Reality: A Treatise in the Sociology of Knowledge*. New York: Anchor Books. See especially: Chapter II.1, Institutionalization, pp. 47–91.

Searle, John R. (2010). *Making the Social World: The Structure of Human Civilization*. Oxford, UK: Oxford University Press. See especially: Chapter 1, The Purpose of this Book, pp. 3–24; Chapter 5, The General Theory of Institutions and Institutional Facts: Language and Social Reality, pp. 90–122.

Further reading

Douglas, Mary (1986). *How Institutions Think*. Syracuse, NY: Syracuse University Press.

Durkheim, Emile (1982 [1895]). *The Rules of Sociological Method*. New York: The Free Press.

Garfinkel, Harold (1967). *Studies in Ethnomethodology*. Englewood Cliffs, NJ: Prentice-Hall.

Gehlen, Arnold (1956). *Urmensch und Spätkultur*. Bonn, Germany: Athenäum.

Giddens, Anthony (1984). *The Constitution of Society: Outline of the Theory of Structuration*. Berkeley, CA: University of California Press.

Goffman, Erving (1968 [1961]). *Asylums. Essays on the Social Situation of Mental Patients and Other Inmates*. London: Penguin Books.

Maiwald, Kai-Olaf (2013). Der mikroskopische Blick. Rekonstruktion in der Objektiven Hermeneutik. *Sozialer Sinn, 2013/2*, 185–206.

Oevermann, Ulrich (1986). Kontroversen über sinnverstehende Soziologie. Einige wiederkehrende Probleme und Mißverständnisse in der Rezeption der, objektiven Hermeneutik. In Stefan Aufenanger & Margit Lenssen (Eds.), *Handlung und Sinnstruktur. Bedeutung und Anwendung der objektiven Hermeneutik* (pp. 19–83). Munich, Germany: Kindt.

Polanyi, Michael (1974). *Personal Knowledge: Towards a Post-Critical Philosophy*. Chicago, IL: University of Chicago Press.

Searle, John R. (1969). *Speech Acts. An Essay in the Philosophy of Language*. Cambridge, UK: Cambridge University Press.

Searle, John R. (1995). *The Construction of Social Reality*. New York: The Free Press.

Tomasello, Michael (2008). *Origins of Human Communication*. Cambridge, MA: The MIT Press.

4

RECIPROCITY

How social relations emerge from joint action

Reciprocity as a structural feature of interaction seems self-explanatory at first glance, if we intuitively assume that interaction is always, somehow or other, mutual. This does not just apply to the specific interchange, however, but also to the assumptions we have about the current and future behavior of the people we are interacting with. Thus reciprocity in a sociological sense means more than just mutuality in the current exchange; instead, it is about the obligation to reciprocity as a basic prerequisite of cooperation. This can be demonstrated particularly well by looking at the seminal work on the "gift" by the French sociologist and ethnologist Marcel Mauss, who studied the exchange of gifts in archaic societies. He is not solely concerned with the question of why presents must be reciprocated, but with the appropriate form and time for this to happen, and with the mutual obligations that arise between the interactants, over time, as a result of this. For our observation of interaction structures, a particularly important point here is that the assumption of reciprocity underlies every interaction, not just the exchange of gifts.

In the preceding chapters, we have seen that communication and interaction show an underlying cooperative structure. We cannot *not* react to an utterance addressed to us: if we have understood the utterance, everything we do is a reaction to it, and is understood as such by the addressee. The opening and closing of interactions is a reciprocal matter: the questioner can demand an answer, and we cannot simply leave a conversation when we have had enough of it, but must first reach agreement on this. The first turn makes a second turn necessary. If this does not occur, there is either a communication problem (lack of knowledge of the language, psychopathology) – or a conflict. But what if the second turn is a "no?" We may be forced to communicate, but we are not obliged to continue the interaction beyond a bare minimum. It would obviously be simplistic to conclude that because the basis of communication is cooperative, there is no alternative to collaboration. We can refuse offers of cooperation, for whatever reasons. And we are capable of a number of hostile actions which contravene the cooperative basis of interaction.

However, the fact that people enter into (and end) social relations as a matter of course relies on the presence of a basic attitude of cooperation. We do not ask "Friend or foe?" at every encounter. It is only in exceptional circumstances – which are then no longer everyday situations – that we wonder whether the person we are speaking to may be hostile towards us. If we consider international relations, however, we can see that this is not to be taken for granted. In the relationship between certain states at least, the question "Do we cooperate or not?" is a permanent item on the agenda. Within a society, this is not the case. But what is it that ensures we are fundamentally disposed towards cooperation here? How is the willingness to cooperate pre-established in such a way that we can decline certain offers of cooperation in a manner that is at least "civil," that is, inherently cooperative? (For example: "Would you like to try some?" – "No, thank you.") The answer is: by means of reciprocity, which is expressed in a certain form of exchange.

Today, when we think of "exchange," the first thing we visualize is probably something like an exchange platform, where collectors and other private individuals offer items they wish to part with, and receive other items or money from like-minded people in exchange. This is either done via the intermediary of Internet platforms and newspapers, or face-to-face at charity bazaars and fairs for stamp collectors or model-making enthusiasts. Other examples of exchange that might occur to us are swapping places in a restaurant, swapping tennis racquets in a friendly match, or sometimes even swapping families for a reality TV show. But abstract things are also "exchanged": opinions, experiences, information. However varied relations of exchange may be, they are always based on the same simple pattern. We give away something we can do without and receive something else, something that is useful to us.

Even if we do not usually describe it in this way (the term "stock exchange" is an exception), all our everyday and non-everyday market transactions are, in principle, exchange processes of this kind. From supermarket shopping to buying a house, we give away things (money or groceries) in order to receive other things (groceries, houses or money), which we think we do not have enough of. What is crucial, in each case, is that the things that are actually exchanged mean different things to the exchange partners. In the terminology of Karl Marx, we can say that the crucial thing is the difference in the "use values" of the objects: we see the object received in the exchange as having a greater utility than the one we have given away. Thus I exchange my labor for money, which has a greater utility for me, in the sense that I can use it to purchase a whole range of consumer goods (food, entertainment, higher status, etc.). The use value of a Spider-Man trading card is comparatively low if I already have three of them, so I am willing to exchange it for a picture of Iron Man, which I do not yet have. This is the reason why I enter into a relationship with my exchange partner (or relationships with several possible exchange partners). The relationship between market participants is then essentially limited to the exchange, which is based on a contract-like agreement specifying the modalities of exchange. Furthermore, the exchange usually has the form of a direct exchange of service and payment. This also applies to longer-term relations of exchange, for example, rental arrangements. All this seems quite mundane and obvious to us, as it concerns basic aspects of the exchange of goods and services. These economic transactions are of fundamental importance for societies which produce "surplus product," i.e. goods that can be exchanged. This applies particularly to modern, capitalist societies. However, we do not wish to consider economic exchange in any further detail here. The point of discussing economic exchange is to help us envisage the pattern of other kinds of exchange processes.

There are, in fact, forms of exchange that are quite differently structured. In them, the *difference in the use value* of the exchanged objects is not of key importance. In keeping with this, the primary concern is not the *utility* that the object received has for each exchange partner. The exchange is *not only a direct one*: sometimes a feature of the exchange is that we only receive something later on, and possibly from someone other than the person we have given something to. Finally, the *relationship* is *not only a means* to an end; rather, the relationship is an end in itself, and the *exchange is always, in part, a means to this end*.

Exchanges that can be characterized in this way are phenomena such as Christmas and birthday presents, the bucket of plums we take to our neighbor, the dinner invitation and the flowers brought by the dinner guests, the door which is held open for us and which we then hold open for the next person. Such transactions are not accorded any great prominence in the self-image of modern societies. They are seen as marginal, as peculiarities. Yet in the following section, we will demonstrate that they are actually, in a certain respect, more fundamental for "society" than the economic relations of exchange – because the former need to take place before the latter can be established.

On closer examination, the smoothness with which economic transactions are generally carried out does require an explanation. We take it for granted that we will receive the bread rolls we want if we put the corresponding money on the counter – and vice versa. If this does not happen, we are at least very astonished, and probably even angry. But why? It would only be to our own advantage to put down less money for the bread rolls, or to fill the bag with yesterday's plum tart, which nobody wants to buy any more, instead of the bread rolls. And to be quite sure that the exchange will proceed according to our wishes, the exchanged commodities should actually be handed over simultaneously – otherwise one party might take off with the bread rolls or the other with the money. We are familiar with such scenarios from films: enemy nations exchange spies, kidnappers and the families of their victims exchange hostages for ransoms, but nobody wants to make the first move, because there is no confidence that the countermove will follow. This does not apply, however, to the contractual transactions of everyday life, be they small or large, unspoken or written. In the case of larger sums of money or private transactions, we may worry about whether it will all be "above board," but as a rule we assume that transactions will happen smoothly. The question of why this is so, or of what forms the basis for compliance with contracts, is linked with many debates in philosophy, law and the social sciences, for example with regard to the significance of sanctions, or of trust on the part of the exchange partners. Here we favor an interpretation which was most prominently advocated by Emile Durkheim: contractual agreements of any kind – and thus economic exchange processes – are always based on preconditions of a non-contractual nature (cf. Durkheim 1992 [1957], 2014 [1893]). The contract itself cannot guarantee compliance, and referring to sanctions for non-compliance with contracts only displaces the problem – assuming one sees these sanctions as being based on a contractual agreement themselves. After all, what ensures the validity of this agreement? In short, what is at stake here is the social foundations of cooperation. In this respect, exchange processes that differ from economic transactions – in the manner described previously – play a central role. What we are talking about here is the exchange of gifts.

How do we explain those processes that can be referred to as the exchange of gifts? Why do we exchange gifts? Why do we give something to others without expecting a direct return – let alone one that directly corresponds to the "exchange value" of our gift? In everyday psychology we might speak of "altruism," but of course this is unsatisfying from a sociological perspective, since it is a moral category: at best, it highlights a certain orientation, but disregards the structure of the interaction. And yet it is precisely this structure that is meant when we talk about "exchange," even in those cases in which we do not associate any direct purpose with our transactions. Peter M. Blau (2005) speaks of a "social exchange,"[1] which he distinguishes from economic exchange processes. However, he holds the view that even social exchange is still linked with the desire to maximize individual benefit, an orientation that is characteristic of human nature (with the emphasis on "nature"). According to this, then, there is an overriding or subliminal purpose to which the exchange of gifts is subordinated: we want to enter into contact with people if we expect to derive benefit from this contact. In this line of argument, social exchange serves to facilitate such contacts, as it leads to a diffuse obligation to return the favor in the future. According to Blau (ibid.), then, it is advantageous to voluntarily do things for others, as the others are then obliged to reciprocate. On the positive side, this theory does clearly identify one characteristic of the exchange of gifts: unlike economic transactions, such exchanges contain neither a firm agreement nor any specified services. Instead, there is an obligation to reciprocate which is diffuse in content and has no defined time frame, and it is precisely this obligation that turns these actions into exchanges. However, there are several drawbacks to Blau's conception: the element of obligation is not explained, but merely presupposed; it remains unclear why the (overriding) benefit is concealed at all; and lastly – but this will become even clearer in the following discussion – it is not by any means certain (nor is it crucial) that the gift really includes any personal advantage for the receiver.

Let us first consider the element of the obligation to reciprocity, which is at the center of the theory of Gouldner (1960). In his analysis, he considers various exchange processes: the economic exchange of equivalents, the exchange of gifts, but also asymmetrical exchange processes reflecting relations of power. In his opinion, the obligation to give something in return for a gift is not (solely) the result of economic advantages or constraints of labor division. Instead, he suggests we should assume that there is an overriding, general moral obligation to repay services, which is linked with the "history of previous interaction" (ibid., p. 171) and reflects a general norm of reciprocity. Gouldner argues that this social norm, which mainly stipulates that we should acknowledge and support those who have helped us, is universal and is found in all the known cultures. With his concept of the "norm of reciprocity," Gouldner is attempting to offer a genuinely sociological explanation: norms are not quasi-natural orientations like the desire to maximize individual benefit, but central elements of "society" (for more on this see Chapter 7). Furthermore, the explanation is intuitive in terms of everyday reality – after all, we know any number of legal formulae and aphorisms that express this norm: "pacta sunt servanda,"[2] "do ut des,"[3] "one hand washes the other," "I scratch your back, you scratch mine." When the butcher gives a small child a slice of sausage, the parents often prompt the child with: "What do you say?" Undoubtedly, then, there are norms of reciprocity (in the plural). We are aware of our obligation to reciprocate (this is what the butcher is counting on) – or at least to say thank you. The problem with this theory, however, is that it identifies obligation as a *consequence* of socialization; norms reflect the fact that reciprocity is firmly established in exchange transactions in society. Here, however, it seems to make sense to regard the exchange of gifts as a *mechanism* of socialization itself.

This is the path taken, most notably, by the ethnologists and cultural anthropologists Marcel Mauss and Claude Lévi-Strauss. For them, the processes termed "exchange of gifts" are not only the expression of a social bond between those carrying out the exchange, but are interactions that give rise to such a bond in the first place.[4] Of crucial importance here is the famous essay *The Gift* (Mauss 1990 [1923/24]). Here Mauss compares a wealth of rites, practices, and interpretations of exchange processes among tribal societies from all regions of the world – from the Native American *potlatch*, in which the protagonists try to outdo each other with reciprocal gifts or by the ceremonial destruction of valuable things such as copper platters and blankets, to the Melanesian *kula* system, in which tribes voyage across the sea and exchange valuable objects, mainly necklaces and bracelets, with each other. The common feature of all these practices is that they do not fit into the pattern of economic exchange processes of modern societies, as described previously: although valuable objects may be involved, their utility is not the center of attention. The value of the things is sometimes played down, in some cases the recipients of the gifts are not seen as their owners, and sometimes the things are even destroyed. In the *potlatch*, the gift is not a benefit that is granted (cf. Blau 2005), but a challenge to the recipients, who must try to outdo the givers with their subsequent "return gift." A direct gift in return (of equivalent goods) is not envisaged, as it would contradict the logic of these exchange processes, which form part of long-term social relationships.

We can see that a direct repayment contravenes the logic of the gift by considering a simple example from the present day. Imagine you had a garden with fruit trees, and at harvest time you took a bucket of plums to your neighbor; you would feel quite affronted if she were to give you something in exchange at the door – a piece of cake or money. It would be quite different if, instead, she were to invite you in for a coffee and then offer you a piece of cake. Why? Because the coffee drinking is not related to the plums, but is a gift of its own kind. One would not say "Come on in, you can have coffee and cake in exchange for the plums," but something like "Come on in, would you like a coffee?" This is then an invitation (and thus a gift) which we can either accept or not accept.

Mauss (1990 [1923/24]) does not regard the rites and practices of gift exchange which he examines as ethnological curiosities, but as an elementary and universal component of social integration, at least for these forms of society. This is already clear from the fact that they cannot be considered in isolation; they are not, as in modern societies, part of a function system known as "the economy," but encompass all social institutions: religious, legal and economic. They are, according to Mauss, "total" social phenomena. It would make no sense to describe them with the dual terms egoism/altruism, because these practices can always be put to "egoistic" uses as well, for example to acquire social status and power. But at the same time, this is not the key to their structure. Instead, their most prominent feature is the establishment of a social bond: the exchange of gifts ties individuals and social groups into a relationship in which those involved are simultaneously, and in the long term, both creditors and debtors. The gift obliges the receiver to give something in return, which then creates a new obligation.

For Mauss (ibid.), the crucial question now is how the obligation to give something in return arises; what power must be inherent in the object given for it to have this effect. Unlike Gouldner, however (see previous), he not only concentrates on the position of the person who receives the gift, but considers the exchange of gifts as a complex of interactions. An explanation of reciprocity based on social norms then becomes obsolete, for the simple reason that this interaction complex posits a contradictory link between free will and obligation. To begin with, however, Mauss (ibid.) only distinguishes three kinds of obligation in the exchange of gifts: the obligation to give, the obligation to receive, and the obligation to reciprocate. In fact, there appear to be normative parameters in all respects in the societies examined by him. There is a threat of losing status and recognition: in certain situations, the failure to show generosity, to accept a gift, or to reciprocate graciously leads to a loss of face. We must bear in mind, however, that dividing the complex of interaction into three separate interaction turns – for this is ultimately what it amounts to – has always implied an element of free will. This is particularly true of the first turn, giving. The point in time, the nature of the gift and its addressees are apparently never altogether predetermined by ritual, and are thus subject to the initiative of the givers. If the acceptance of the gift is also a separate interaction turn, then the givers are not setting in motion an automatism, but exposing themselves to risk. It is the independent significance of this turn (accepting the gift) that makes the difference between this and the modern economic transaction – where this turn simply does not exist – especially clear. In the context of a contractual agreement on the exchange of objects or services which are equivalent but have different use values, the only thing that potentially makes sense is rejection (if the object does not correspond to the agreement), but not acceptance as a separate act. In the logic of the exchange of gifts, in contrast, the decision about acceptance/ rejection means that the first turn (giving) is understood as "voluntary," i.e. as a gift. Of course, rejection is an affront to the givers, who have exposed themselves to risk, but this is something that can happen within the logic of the exchange of gifts – as Mauss himself notes, this decision is not unusual, for example in the *potlatch*. And the third interaction turn, reciprocation, also leaves room for the initiative of the givers, precisely because the time and the nature of the return gift are not fully predetermined. This is what makes it a gift, and not the repayment of a debt.

According to Mauss, then, the exchange of gifts can be understood as a fundamental mechanism of social integration, which creates a willingness to cooperate by allowing participants to enter, long-term, into a relationship in which they are simultaneously creditors and debtors. The question then is how this binding, socially integrative force works. For Mauss, the crucial factor here is the *thing* given, or more precisely, the connection between the person and the object of exchange. He observes that in tribal societies, objects are seen as animated, in a sense, and they derive this animation from a close relationship between them and their owners. Here Mauss refers particularly to the Maori concept of *hau*, which designates the soul of an object and relates it to the person who owns it. However, he also finds ideas of a lasting connection between individuals and the things they own in other cultures. For him this explains the binding power of the gift exchange:

> In this system of ideas one clearly and logically realizes that one must give back to another person what is really part and parcel of his nature and substance.
>
> *(Mauss 1990 [1923/24], p. 16)*

He argues that it is in fact positively dangerous to retain the things accepted, because if I keep another person's *hau* long-term I give him power over me. This interpretation, however, is not only incompatible with certain forms of generalized exchange, in which the recipient does not give something to the giver, but to a third person. It also contradicts the logic of the establishment of a lasting bond, because if I give *back* a specific thing to the "actual" owner, then this gift no longer has any element of obligation. It can therefore be regarded more as a loan; if the object borrowed is returned undamaged, the cycle of exchange is closed, and no future obligations are created.

The criticism made by Lévi-Strauss (1987 [1978]) takes an even more basic starting point. He sees Mauss's explanation as too rationalistic, but above all as unnecessary. He argues that it is wrong to divide up cycles of exchange into individual elements, then search for some "emotional-mystical cement" (ibid., p. 58) that holds them together. Instead, he says, they should be seen as a system of relations, functioning like symbolic thought, indeed like language. This argument is not easy to follow. One possible bridge is offered by a study which seems, at first glance, poorly suited to this task. Theodore Caplow, a sociologist whose research actually focused more on macrosociology, carried out a large-scale analysis of the social structure of an American town. One of the aspects he surveyed and analyzed was the way the inhabitants celebrated Christmas (Caplow 1984). Here he discovered a number of rules that can more or less be understood as rules of gift exchange, for example "the tree rule" (families must have a tree, singles or couples without children do not have to), "the wrapping rule" (Christmas presents must be wrapped before being exchanged), "the scaling rules" (the nature and above all the value of the present is based on the relationship between those involved in the exchange, and their position in this relationship [asymmetries]), "the gift selection rules" (the emotional value of the relationship is reflected in the nature and value of the presents) and – of course – "the reciprocity rule" (the participants in a family gift system must give all the other participants at least one Christmas present per year).

As a researcher concerned with social structures, Caplow was accustomed to using complex methods of calculation to discover statistical connections. What most astonished him here was the near-total degree of conformity to these rules: almost the entire population of the town covered by the study followed them. How, he wondered, could this be possible? No sanctions were attached to these rules, so conformity could not be understood as the result of mechanisms of social control. Furthermore, the actors were in most cases not even aware that these rules existed. How could they nonetheless follow them, and with such consistency? Against this background, Caplow astutely concluded that we should imagine these rules of Christmas gift exchange to function in the same way as language. While the rules of language are largely concealed from us, we nonetheless follow them:

> Gift exchange, in effect, is a language that employs objects instead of words as its lexical elements. In this perspective, every culture […] has a language of prestation to express important interpersonal relationships on special occasions, just as it has a verbal language to create and manage meaning for other purposes.

(Caplow 1984, p. 1320)

Perhaps this is what Lévi-Strauss had in mind: we do not need to seek a "deeper reason," an "ultimate force" that sustains the exchange of gifts as a system of mutual obligations. The rules of reciprocity "work" in exactly the same way as the other rules of shared symbolic systems.

This analogy with language is convincing, but has its limitations. For both Mauss (see previous) and Lévi-Strauss (see previous) are not solely concerned with cultural, but also with practical integration. Mauss makes this very clear at the end of his essay:

> Societies have progressed in so far as they themselves, their subgroups, and lastly, the individuals in them, have succeeded in stabilizing relationships, giving, receiving, and finally, giving in return. To trade [in an economic sense], the first condition was to be able to lay aside the spear. From then onwards they succeeded in exchanging goods and persons, no longer only between clans, but between tribes and nations, and, above all, between individuals. Only then did people learn how to create mutual interests, giving mutual satisfaction, and in the end, to defend them without having to resort to arms.
>
> *(Mauss 1990 [1923/24], p. 105)*

And Lévi-Strauss (1969, p. 58) also emphasizes a "fundamental situation" in which it is still open whether a relationship will be characterized by enmity or friendship. The aim is to establish a social bond; to gain security. This is made possible by the rules of reciprocity in the exchange of gifts. The purposeless exchange of things is, in his view, *the* form of cooperation that enables further cooperation. This is precisely what we mean by "creating a willingness to cooperate."

In this respect it is advantageous that the things exchanged are not merely symbols. Because – philosophically speaking – "being for others" (Quadflieg 2014, p. 186) is materialized in things. Or to put it in somewhat simpler – and perhaps somewhat simplistic – terms: the things we give offer a permanent representation of the fact that we *do* things for the other person (and – if the gift is accepted – *have done* such things), for no specific purpose. This is essential for reciprocity: it is not about sequentiality or adjacency, but about a particular *filling* of this formal structure, without which follow-on interactions would not be possible. The first move or turn consists in doing something for the other person "on our own initiative." Economically speaking, we have to make an advance payment, give credit. As in Lévi-Strauss's (1969) famous example of a custom he observed in cheap restaurants in the south of France: when two strangers sit opposite each other at a narrow table, each with a small bottle of wine which is included in the price of the dish of the day, each pours some of her own wine into the other's glass. The situation, according to Lévi-Strauss, bears some resemblance to the "fundamental situation" (see previous), as the close spatial proximity generates a certain anxiety about what inconvenience the encounter might bring. This uncertainty is then removed by the exchange of the wine. Here too, the person who takes the initiative is exposing herself to risk, as the offer of cooperation can also be refused; the other person can give less or can outdo her. If, however, she reciprocates in like manner, then coexistence becomes cooperation.

> Further, the acceptance of this offer sanctions another offer, for conversation. In this way a whole range of trivial social ties are established by a series of alternating oscillations, in which offering gives one a right, and receiving makes one obligated, and always beyond what has been given or accepted.
>
> *(Lévi-Strauss 1969, p. 57)*

If we state that the exchange of gifts, the logic of purposeless reciprocity, stands at the beginning of cooperative relationships, we could object that this mainly applies to archaic tribal societies, or, in general, societies with a low degree of social integration, whose units – as in the previous quote from Mauss – are only just moving towards each other. In fact, modern Western societies are socially integrated to such an extent that their individual units are relieved of the burden of having to establish cooperative relationships by exchanging gifts. The elements that are probably of crucial importance here are the formation of a political community and the attendant institutions in the context of the nation state, the establishment of a state monopoly on power, the rule of law, and the institutionalization of participation in the political process. This disburdening framework is particularly apparent in the figure of the "stranger," which cannot exist in this form in tribal societies (cf. Oevermann 1983). What is meant here is strangers in public spaces: the people we encounter in the streets, in soccer stadiums and museums, in department stores and universities. We do not have to build up a cooperative relationship with each of these people by exchanging gifts. We are no longer in the situation of the societies studied by Mauss and Lévi-Strauss, who only had the alternative of friendship or enmity: "one trusts completely or one mistrusts completely" (Mauss 1990 [1923/24], p. 81). In this respect, "strangers" constitute the "middle ground," the state of neutrality, which is unknown to tribal societies. This means we can conduct economic transactions with such "strangers" without any special precautions.

But this is only a framework. It seems that even in modern societies we are not able to dispense with purposeless reciprocity altogether. We have already mentioned, in passing, various phenomena of gift exchange, and the list can easily be extended.[5] There are, of course, the many institutionalized occasions for giving gifts: Christmas, Easter, Valentine's Day, Mother's Day, Father's Day, birthdays, anniversaries, the start of a new job or the last day at an old job, presents brought back and postcards sent when on holiday. Of course, the parties we throw, the meals we invite people to, the rounds of drinks we buy, are also phenomena of gift exchange. There are luxury goods that virtually demand to be shared with others, such as champagne and fine wines.[6] And in the concrete practices of gift-giving, there are many aspects that emphasize the element of purposelessness, making it explicit that this is not about the utility of the objects exchanged. We can give each other the same present at Christmas, and yet this is still a fully valid exchange of gifts. We like to give things that have no (particular) use value per se; there are entire retail chains selling "gift items" of this kind. Similarly, the cut flowers which guests present to their host are a transient luxury. And the wrapping paper that turns "useful" or "sensible" things into gifts is, a priori, destined for destruction. Any number of examples can be found, including occasions of collective wastefulness: the fireworks on New Year's Eve, the sweets and flowers thrown into the crowd at Germany's Karneval parades, the "champagne bath" following a Formula 1 race.

If "small gifts preserve friendship," as a German saying goes, then this applies to the area of close personal relationships in general. Couple and family relationships are society's key sites of gift exchange. Couple relationships, therefore, depend not only on cooperating as a collective (cf. Maiwald 2013); the emotional tie must also be maintained long-term by mutual gifts, in which one partner acknowledges the other in his or her individuality, and in his or her particular structure of needs (cf. Honneth 1996). These can be individual presents or physical demonstrations of affection, but also unspectacular everyday services, which signify something "extra" in contrast to the usual division of labor in the couple relationship. Such "gifts" can establish the foundation for a "rich economy of gratitude" (cf. Hochschild 1989). Furthermore, gifts that express love can be reciprocated with emotional attention (cf. Nelson 2004, 2011); the interaction itself then constitutes a source of loving attention (cf. Maiwald 2007).

But the exchange of gifts in modern societies is not limited to exceptional occasions and special social relationships. It appears that elements of gift exchange are virtually indispensable for creating a willingness to cooperate in relationships between individuals and collectives. Even if these gifts are unspectacular, they are still found in every opening of a face-to-face interaction; in this respect, the exchange of actions of greeting can be understood as purposeless reciprocity (cf. Oevermann 1983; cf. Bergmann 1994). Every greeting is an offer of cooperation, with which those giving the greeting expose themselves to risk, because the recipients of the greeting can theoretically reject the offer, they can refuse to shake hands or simply walk on. If, however, we accept the offer and return the greeting, this opens up a cooperative space which the participants can fill with follow-on interactions – or not, as the case may be.

But what turns the action of greeting into a gift? It really depends very much on what we actually do. If we say "hello" with no expression on our face, it is very hard to find anything about this that could be understood as a gift. But as a rule, we do not do this. The tone of our "hello" is different from the tone we would use on the phone when we think we may have been cut off. And we will "give a smile" to the addressee, that is, we will use facial expression to indicate that we are pleased about the presence of the other person, even if we do not know them. And what do we do when we use "classic" greetings? We wish our interlocutors well-being, in a generalized form ("Good day"), or God's blessing (the German greeting "Grüß Gott"); we take an interest in their state of health ("How are you?") – and we do all this without knowing whether these specific people are actually worthy of this. In short: we give credit; we invest an element of personal attention in the interaction before this has been justified by the actual course of the interaction.

Such an "investment" is not absolutely essential, in a functional sense, or at least not in social relations shaped by specific roles (see Chapter 6). This also applies to other courses of action that take the form of gift exchanges in our everyday business contacts. By saying "I'd like" and "please," we act as though the service provided by the bakery sales assistant were a gift, the fulfillment of our wish; by thanking him for the change, we act as though this were not to be taken for granted. Yet obviously it is. The situational framework of the bakery as a place of business, the roles of buyer and seller which we naturally assume here, the logic of contractual agreement which then governs our actions, all of these things mean that a "minimal interaction" such as "Three rolls!" – "One fifty!" (bread rolls are given, money is given) would theoretically be possible. But we act differently – why? Perhaps simply because the forms we use here make it clear that the economic relationship is just a special case of social relationship, and because we sense that it is always embedded in a relationship of a different kind, a relationship that guarantees cooperation, even beyond the specific transaction.

FOOD FOR THOUGHT

Refer to your transcript of the café scene from *As Good As It Gets*. After Melvin has refused to accept Carol's thank-you note, he turns to Frank with the question: "Shouldn't that be a good thing? Telling somebody, no thanks required?" What do we usually mean when we say "no thanks required"? Could this be phrased differently, or better? And why should it be "a good thing"? Can this be explained with reference to the "exchange of gifts"? Now consider the actual exchange between Melvin and Carol which precedes this remark. Is "no thanks required" really what is expressed here? Or is Melvin violating rules of reciprocity when he rejects Carol's letter? Give reasons for your answer.

Notes

1 This designation can already be considered unfortunate, because it implies that economic exchanges are not per se social.
2 Lat.: "Agreements must be kept."
3 Lat.: "I give that you might give."

4 It is this fundamental meaning that has led to a renewed interest in "reciprocity" and in the work of Marcel Mauss in recent years. Cf. Adloff and Mau (2005); Moebius (2006); Hillebrandt (2009), and Dirk Quadflieg's analysis of Marcel Hénaff's theses on the exchange of gifts and social integration, published in *WestEnd: Neue Zeitschrift für Sozialforschung*, 7 (2010), issue 1.
5 See also the numerous examples in Lévi-Strauss (1969).
6 If sparkling wine is the classic drink for collective celebrations, then there is something objectively tragic about the miniature bottle.

References

Gouldner, Alvin W. (1960). The Norm of Reciprocity. A Preliminary Statement. *American Sociological Revue, 25/2*, 161–178.
Lévi-Strauss, Claude (1969 [1949]). *The Elementary Structures of Kinship*. Boston, MA: Beacon Press. See especially: Chapter V, The Principle of Reciprocity.
Lévi-Strauss, Claude (1987 [1950]). *Introduction to the Work of Marcel Mauss*. London, UK: Routledge & Kegan Paul.
Mauss, Marcel (1990 [1923/24]). *The Gift: The Form and Reason for Exchange in Archaic Societies*. London/New York: Routledge.

Further reading

Adloff, Frank, & Mau, Steffen (Eds.) (2005). *Vom Geben und Nehmen. Zur Soziologie der Reziprozität*. Frankfurt a. M., Germany: Campus.
Bergmann, Jörg R. (1994). Kleine Lebenszeichen. Über Form, Funktion und Aktualität von Grußbotschaften im Alltag. In Walter M. Sprondel (Ed.), *Die Objektivität der Ordnungen und ihre kommunikative Konstruktion* (pp. 192–225). Frankfurt a. M., Germany: Suhrkamp.
Blau, Peter M. (2005 [1968]). Sozialer Austausch. In Frank Adloff & Steffen Mau (Eds.), *Vom Geben und Nehmen. Zur Soziologie der Reziprozität* (pp. 125–137). Frankfurt a. M., Germany: Campus.
Caplow, Theodore (1984). Rule Enforcement without Visible Means: Christmas Gift Giving in Middletown. *American Journal of Sociology, 89/6*, 1306–1323.
Durkheim, Emile (1992 [1957]). *Professional Ethics and Civil Morals*. Bryan S. Turner (Ed.). London/New York: Routledge. See especially: Morals of Contractual Relations, pp. 184–195.
Durkheim, Emile (2014 [1893]). *The Division of Labor in Society*. New York: The Free Press. See especially: Organic Solidarity and Contractual Solidarity, pp. 158–181.
Hansen, Karen V. (2004). The Asking Rules of Reciprocity in Networks of Care for Children. *Qualitative Sociology, 27/4*, 421–437.
Hillebrandt, Frank (2009). *Praktiken des Tauschens. Zur Soziologie symbolischer Formen der Reziprozität*. Wiesbaden, Germany: Springer VS.
Hochschild, Arlie R. (1989). The Economy of Gratitude. In David D. Franks & E. Doyle McCarthy (Eds.), *The Sociology of Emotions: Original Essays and Research Papers* (pp. 95–113). New York: JAI Press.
Honneth, Axel (1996). *The Struggle for Recognition. The Moral Grammar of Social Conflicts*. Cambridge, UK: Polity Press.
Maiwald, Kai-Olaf (2007). Die Liebe und der häusliche Alltag. Überlegungen zu Anerkennungsstrukturen in Paarbeziehungen. In Christine Wimbauer, Annette Henninger & Markus Gottwald (Eds.), *Die Gesellschaft als "institutionalisierte Anerkennungsordnung" –*

Anerkennung und Ungleichheit in Paarbeziehungen, Arbeitsorganisationen und Sozialstaat (pp. 69–95). Opladen and Farmington Hills: Barbara Budrich.

Maiwald, Kai-Olaf (2013). Solidarität in Paarbeziehungen. Eine Fallrekonstruktion. In Dorothea Christa Krüger, Holger Herma & Anja Schierbaum (Eds.), *Familie(n) heute – Entwicklungen, Kontroversen, Prognosen* (pp. 324–342). Weinheim and Munich, Germany: Juventa.

Moebius, Stephan (2006). Die Gabe – ein neues Paradigma der Soziologie? Eine kritische Betrachtung der M.A.U.S.S.-Gruppe. *Berliner Journal für Soziologie, 16/3*, 355–370.

Nelson, Margaret K. (2004). Reciprocity and Romance. *Qualitative Sociology, 27/4*, 439–459.

Nelson, Margaret K. (2011). Love and Gratitude. Single Mothers Talk about Men's Contributions to the Second Shift. In Anita Ilta Garey & Karen V. Hansen (Eds.), *At the Heart of Work and Family. Engaging the Ideas of Arlie Hochschild* (pp. 100–111). New Brunswick, NJ: Rutgers University Press.

Oevermann, Ulrich (1983). Zur Sache: Die Bedeutung von Adornos methodologischem Selbstverständnis für die Begründung einer materialen soziologischen Strukturanalyse. In Ludwig von Friedeburg & Jürgen Habermas (Eds.), *Adorno-Konferenz 1983* (pp. 234–292). Frankfurt a. M., Germany: Suhrkamp.

Quadflieg, Dirk (2014). *"Vom Geist der Sache". Zur Dialektik der Verdinglichung nach Hegel und Mauss* (Unpublished habilitation thesis). Frankfurt a. M, Germany.

5

TAKING THE PERSPECTIVE OF OTHERS

Who we are as far as others are concerned

Adopting the perspective of others is another important structural feature of social interaction, and the sociologist who developed the pioneering theoretical foundations for this is George Herbert Mead. In his principal work, *Mind, Self and Society*, Mead focuses on the socialization of individuals into members of society; he sees personality development and the formation of identity as necessarily connected to social interaction and participation in society. His reflections on role learning in play and competition are especially pertinent. When it comes to perspective-taking, Mead is concerned with similar questions of how we learn to interact appropriately (i.e. successfully) with other members of society. The central elements here are language and speaking as a medium of self-observation and observation of others. In this chapter, we undertake a detailed analysis of his complex reflections on this subject.

In the last chapter, we saw how the basic principle of cooperation can be envisaged, and how it is possible to create this basis interactively. To be able to participate appropriately in cooperative processes, however, we have to be in a position to take the perspective or position of our exchange partner. How are we to know, otherwise, what gift it would make sense to give in what situation, and what gift is likely to be accepted and reciprocated? If we imagine taking someone else's perspective, the first thing that occurs to us may be what we associate with the term "empathy": seeing the world through another person's eyes, putting ourselves in their shoes, projecting ourselves into them, putting ourselves in their place. In everyday language, all of these expressions refer to the way we manage to gain an understanding of another person's actions, when these actions seem strange or incomprehensible to us, or when our interlocutor is in an emotional state that we do not share at the time. Empathy is therefore often understood as sympathy or compassion, and always has a moral connotation.

In the microsociological sense, however, taking another person's perspective does not mean feeling sympathy or showing understanding for them. The fact is that humans do not use this ability constantly. There are many situations in which we do not make any effort to be understanding (e.g. of the long queue in the supermarket), and we deal with many people without putting ourselves into their position, and without trying to experience their joys or dilemmas (e.g. when we expect someone to fulfill their tasks, regardless of how they are feeling at the present moment). But this does not mean that we do not take these people into consideration *somehow* when interacting with them. In order to understand how this works, we will use an example of an interaction that is anything but empathetic, borrowed from Goffman (1981, p. 124). It is a newspaper clipping, reporting on an event from 1973; the main protagonist is the then president of the United States, Richard Nixon.

> After a bill-signing ceremony in the Oval Office, the President stood up from his desk and in a teasing voice said to UPI's Helen Thomas: 'Helen, are you still wearing slacks? Do you prefer them actually? Every time I see girls in slacks it reminds me of China.' Miss Thomas, somewhat abashed, told the President that Chinese women were moving toward Western dress. 'This is not said in an uncomplimentary way, but slacks can do something for some people and some it can't.' He hastened to add, 'but I think you do very well. Turn around.' As Nixon, Attorney General Elliott L. Richardson, FBI Director Clarence Kelley and other high-ranking law enforcement officials smiling [*sic*], Miss Thomas did a pirouette for the President.[1]

Today we would generally criticize Nixon's behavior as sexual harassment.[2] The female journalist is addressed in a sexualized manner that has nothing to do with her professional role, in front of a male audience. She not only has to put up with remarks about her clothing, but also judgments about her attractiveness, and in the end she is well and truly "put on show." What we are looking at here is not empathy, then, but an incident that severely demeans a female journalist. And yet even these aggressive acts, which objectively constitute an assault, still operate under the conditions of taking into account the perspective of others, as we will show in the following discussion. Here we understand perspective-taking as a structural feature of interaction, i.e. as an essential foundation of every interaction, a task that is always performed, regardless of one's interlocutor and his or her specific situation, and which is, in this sense, not guided by moral considerations. Instead, it forms the very basis for every "advanced" empathy. The question that will concern us in this chapter, then, is this: how is the other person's perspective brought to bear in interaction?

A pioneer in reflections of this kind is George Herbert Mead. In works such as *Mind, Self and Society* (1992 [1934]),[3] Mead explores how the human psyche functions, and what it is that enables humans to behave as social beings. Mead sees himself as a "social behaviorist," in other words he classes himself as belonging to a school of thought oriented towards the natural sciences, which seeks to explain human behavior as patterns of stimulus and reaction. Today this theoretical tendency is only accepted with reservations and with considerable modifications. This does not, however, detract from Mead's pioneering work on the phenomenon of perspective-taking.[4] In fact – as will become clear below – Mead does not pursue a reductionist explanatory strategy, and does not seek to explain social phenomena in terms of natural science. On the contrary, he is determined to define the difference between animal and human communication as precisely as possible.

The social behavior that mainly interests Mead is linguistic behavior, because our linguistic behavior is the behavior we can most easily observe in ourselves: we do not see ourselves acting, or only do so to a limited extent, but we do hear ourselves when we speak. For Mead, this means that speaking with others always – in purely physical terms – includes the possibility of self-observation. But unlike the "vocal gesture" in animals, this possibility is only realized in human communication. The basic assumption is that, when speaking, we always address both ourselves and the others. To use concepts from behavioral theory, our speech act thus constitutes not only a stimulus for our interlocutor, but also for ourselves. At the same time, self-addressing is the condition for consciousness, for thought. Mead (1992 [1934]; 1964) repeats this assumption frequently in his work, in different variations. Here are a few key passages:

> That is, we can hear ourselves talking, and the import of what we say is the same to ourselves that it is to others.
>
> *(1992 [1934], p. 62)*

> We are unconsciously putting ourselves in the place of others and acting as others act. [...] We are, especially through the use of the vocal gestures, continually arousing in ourselves those responses which we call out in other persons, so that we are taking the attitudes of the other persons into our own conduct.
>
> *(ibid., p. 69)*

> When we speak of the meaning of what we are doing we are making the response itself that we are on the point of carrying out a stimulus to our action.
>
> *(ibid., p. 72)*

> Where the response of the other person is called out and becomes a stimulus to control his action, then he has the meaning of the other person's act

in his own experience. That is the general mechanism of what we term 'thought,' for in order that thought may exist there must be symbols, vocal gestures generally, which arouse in the individual himself the response which he is calling out in the other.

(ibid., p. 73)

It is not until an image arises of the response, which the gesture of one form will bring out in another, that a consciousness of meaning can attach to his own gesture. The meaning can appear only in imaging the consequence of the gesture.

(Mead 1964, p. 111)

In the process of communication the individual is an other before he is a self. It is in addressing himself in the role of an other that his self arises in experience.

(ibid., p. 312)

The initial argument seems intuitively plausible: when we speak, we ourselves perceive this communicative act in a very similar way to the addressees of the speech. When we say "Turn around," this utterance strikes us as "available" in a different way from the communicative act of a gesture. In any case it would be less plausible to say, in the case of a wink, that we were also winking to ourselves. A vocal utterance "hangs in the air," as it were; a gesture is more "targeted." But it is not easy to understand what the consequence of this difference should be. Moreover, Mead obviously sees the possibility of self-observation when speaking as part of a complex interrelationship between coordination and control, meaning and consciousness. Let us try to explore this interrelationship little by little. Our first step will be to ask how we can possibly trigger the same stimulus, the same inclination to act in ourselves as in the person we are talking to. This is about the fundamental characteristics of human language.

People sort out the impressions they receive from their environment and the observations they make by distinguishing them from one another and labeling them. As a result, our concrete observations and experiences are abstracted into a symbol, a "word," which represents the observation. The word is not identical to the object, but it evokes associations with the object, fact or feeling thus designated, and vice versa. While, however, every aspect of human reality is theoretically distinguishable from every other aspect, and can, therefore, be named, the linguistic abstraction of observations also serves to summarize and categorize them: no two leaves on a tree look alike, and yet we do not have a separate word for every leaf on every tree. Obviously this does not mean that we would be unable to distinguish the individual leaves from one another by linguistic means – for example we could certainly differentiate between "this leaf" and "that leaf," between the "oak leaf I use as a bookmark" or the "red-speckled maple leaf

I decorated the table with." Of course, the person in question is at liberty to give a name to the specific oak leaf she uses as a bookmark – "kro," for example – but in conversation with others she would not be able to use this name. Utterances such as "With my kro, I always know what page of the book I'm on," or "I've lost my kro, have you seen it anywhere by any chance?" remain incomprehensible until the interlocutor has been informed of what "kro" is – and this only works if reference is made to *shared* linguistic symbols. In Mead's terminology, then, only those linguistic symbols that others also understand are "significant." This word is to be taken literally here: these are symbols that "signify" something. Thus "kro" may signify something for one person, but it is not significant in the sense that it would be obvious to all members of the language community what is meant by it, or what it stands for.

What Mead is concerned with here is not simply understanding in the sense that all members of a language community use the same words and attribute the same meaning to them. This is only the basic precondition for what the "significant symbol" actually does. Like Searle (see Chapter 3), Mead assumes that it structures interaction by providing an objective structure of meaning, which has consequences for the concrete actions of those involved. And so, to remain with our opening example, we must assume that what Nixon says has the same meaning for him and for Thomas (and also for us). In other words, both of them understand "Are you still wearing slacks?" as a question implying, among other things, a comparatively intimate relationship context, and both see "Turn around" as a request implying that the speaker is in some way entitled to make it. But unlike Searle, Mead sees the reaction of the other person as playing a key role in the interaction. It is only in the response of others to what we are saying that the meaning of what we are saying becomes manifest.

Before we deal with the meaning of our interlocutors' reactions, however, our second step will be to clarify what could be meant by Mead's assertion that, when speaking, we trigger the same stimulus in ourselves as in the other person. After all, this can hardly be a direct stimulus. When Nixon says "Turn around," he is hardly likely to experience this as a direct call to action meant for himself, as he would then have to somehow suppress a corresponding reaction on his own part, or resist the inclination to turn around himself. Thus it would appear that Mead had something in mind which he could not adequately express with the terminology of social behaviorism. Here we follow the interpretation of Schneider (2002). According to Schneider, what Mead means in this context is that the acoustic perception of what we say to others goes hand in hand with "self-addressing," in the sense that we address ourselves by hearing what we are saying. This must, however, be taken to imply that when speaking to others we are constantly envisaging what reaction we will elicit in them. This then enables us to anticipate how the other person will react to our utterance – that is, in the same way, we would react if this utterance were directed at us. The meaning of our speech act is then, in the moment of speaking, represented in ourselves as a predictable behavioral tendency in the other person.

This can be illustrated with a further example: if person A asks person B to close the window, this does not mean that person A has a "tendency" to close the window herself. Instead person A, in this situation, takes the perspective of person B when speaking, in the sense that she, *as person B*, would close the window after such a request – if this were not the case she would not make the request. We can imagine various scenarios that plausibly explain why person A does not close the window herself, but asks person B to do so. For example, person B could be standing directly beside the window, and person A at the other end of the room, so it is more economical if B closes the window and A does not have to come over especially to do so. Or person B is the one who has opened the window in the first place, so it is her responsibility to close it again. Person A could also have a higher status than person B, and therefore be authorized to give her orders – for example, if A is a teacher and B a pupil. In all these cases, however, the idea is that person A takes the position of person B into consideration when speaking. And she would not urge person B to close the window if she did not assume that person B would comply with this request. By anticipating a particular response, we have in a sense already defined what an appropriate reaction to our utterance is.

In what way might Richard Nixon have considered Helen Thomas's position when urging her to "Turn around"? He could have expected that she, as a journalist – and a woman – would obey a request from the president of the United States – and a man – even if it obviously oversteps the parameters of his general and situational powers (as Searle (1969) would say: the framework of the deontic power of the institution he embodies). It would also be conceivable that – on the basis of his acquaintance with her – Nixon puts himself in Thomas's specific position and thus anticipates a critical utterance in the name of women's equality. In any case, however, Nixon will have expected that his utterance would put him – in Thomas's position – in a very unpleasant situation. This is the objectively aggressive aspect of the scene.

To accurately assess the significance of this aspect of perspective-taking, it is important to bear in mind that this is about more than mere anticipation of the behavior that is to be expected. Such anticipation must be assumed to exist prior to the actual utterance. Without it, we would be unable to form any sentence plans and realize them when speaking. The crucial difference consists in the fact that what was intended and thus still hypothetical, as it were, becomes real when it is spoken. We then hear what we are actually doing, or more precisely, what we have done. Perspective-taking, then, refers to an element of reflexivity that is inserted into the interaction itself, a reflexivity that functions as a "stimulus," insofar as it confronts us with the communicative consequences of what we are expressing. Addressing ourselves as well as the other person can thus be understood to mean that we *always focus on the perspective of our interlocutor when speaking, and reflect on the effect our utterances would have on ourselves if we were in the other person's place.*

We know from our own everyday experience that taking the perspective of others cannot always be a conscious process; compared to the quantity of our daily social interactions, we actually only rarely find ourselves in the situation of having to consciously reflect on how we would react to ourselves in the other person's position. Furthermore, we are already aware (see Chapter 1) that interaction under the condition of presence offers little scope for detailed reflection, in contrast to letter-writing, for example, when we have time to hone our phrases and to think about how we can best express something (with the least potential for misunderstanding). Thus "reflexivity" should be distinguished from "reflection" as a conscious process. Mead's statements on this – as shown by the previous quotes – are not consistent. On the one hand, he says that we unconsciously put ourselves in the position of others; on the other hand he associates perspective-taking with an awareness of the meaning of utterances. This contradiction can be resolved by positing that the perspective of the person we are interacting with is "present" for us when we speak. We, therefore, have the option of referring to our speech acts. This is what is meant when Mead (1992 [1934], p. 73), in the passage quoted previous, speaks of a "stimulus to control [our] action." This reflexivity, as a potential for continuous self-observation, is empirically revealed not only in situations where the realization of what we are saying triggers explicit reflections ("Oh no, what did I just say!?"), but above all in the many changed sentence plans and self-corrections which we undertake, often while we are speaking, when we notice that what we are saying does not match what we want to express. Even Nixon's interaction with the journalist contains an element of self-correction of this kind: "This is not said in an uncomplimentary way."

It is probably not an exaggeration, then, to say that taking into account the perspective of others when speaking puts us in a position to know what we are doing. We do not speak "at random"; we do not test meanings or nuances of meaning by a process of trial and error. Rather, the meaning of what we are actually saying is "present" for us, because when we are speaking we anticipate how we would act in the place of our interaction partner. Taking the perspective of others includes reflexivity, in the sense that the meaning of our utterances is available to us as we speak (in the sense of "awareness"). But it is not just those actually speaking who validate the perspective of the addressee in the interaction. We do not only correct ourselves; in direct interaction, we are also immediately presented with the reaction of our interlocutor. In communication among people present, our utterances are directly exposed to reflection by others; if, for example, we use a vulgar word, the reaction of the other person shows whether he or she views this word as appropriate or inappropriate, and in the latter case our subsequent self-correction (e.g. an apology) seems to be a direct reaction to this reaction. This brings us back to the question of the part played by the other person's response. But what we can already note at this point is that whatever the reaction is, we would not be able to assess its meaning if we had not already considered it when speaking ourselves. Taking another perspective makes us capable of a "relationship discussion." The expected reaction here is the background against which we appraise the actual reaction of the person we are interacting with. We see it as "appropriate" (and take it for granted) if it more or less meets our expectations, but if it deviates from these expectations it can lead us to undertake a correction or an "attempt at repair," or to voice criticism – depending on whether we view the reaction as appropriate or inappropriate, in the light of the understanding that underlies our speech act.[5]

As we have seen, Mead regards the reaction of our interaction partner to our utterances as playing a fundamental role. It is only through this response, he argues, that their meaning becomes manifest. Our third step now must be to clarify what exactly might be meant by this. In this context it makes sense to refer to symbolic interactionism, because this is the core idea of this school of thought, which was strongly influenced by Mead. Herbert Blumer (1986 [1969]), a student of Mead's, constructs a concept based on the notion that meaning arises and is modified *in interaction*. He thus rejects ideas that locate the meaning of objects – in a broad sense including natural and social things – either in the objects themselves or in the mental states of individuals. Instead he rightly emphasizes the inherent importance of what we would call "structures of meaning." Furthermore, he dismisses the assumption that interaction consists solely in the application of pre-established meanings. He argues instead that meanings are selected, tested, rejected, re-formed and transformed by the actors, in the light of the situation in which they find themselves and with regard to the direction of their actions. In general, Blumer regards interaction as the source from which meanings arise. This mainly occurs – and here he utilizes the figure of perspective-taking – when people interpret the actions of their interlocutor and thus put themselves in his or her position. And like Mead, he understands "interpretation" not as an act of exegesis that follows an action, but as an effort to comprehend that accompanies action.

But in order to understand in what way meanings can actually arise or – to borrow a turn of phrase frequently used by proponents of symbolic interactionism – be "negotiated" in interactions, differentiations are necessary. Let us take Nixon's request to "Turn around" as an example. Is it conceivable that there is any doubt about the general meaning of this utterance in the interaction? In theory, yes: it would certainly be possible to imagine that there is a lack of clarity in this respect. Thomas could, for example, respond with the question: "Is there someone standing behind me?", or: "Do you mean a half turn or a full turn?" Generally, however, we can assume – as do Searle and Mead – that grammatically correct utterances are understood in the same way by members of the same language community. Utterances such as "Turn around" are, as we saw in Chapter 3, institutional facts, whose meaning is generated by constitutive rules, which have general validity. In this sense, their meaning is actually "pre-established," that is, it is valid or applicable before any concrete interaction. But this does not mean that the reaction of those addressed in this way does not play a part. As we have seen, institutional facts can certainly be criticized in the interaction. This also applies to linguistic institutional facts. Thus a young woman could respond to being called "Miss" by saying "Don't call me Miss," and such reactions could potentially lead to this word disappearing from the active English vocabulary – as has happened with the word "Fräulein" in German. Conversely, the situational "acceptance" of institutional facts, as understood by Searle, can also be seen as reviving (or "refreshing") their validity. Thomas's "pirouette" is certainly just such a confirmation of the general meaning of "Turn around." However, this would also have been confirmed if – as is conceivable – she had responded with "Mr. President, with all due respect, I will not do that." And yet this reaction would mean something quite different.

This brings us to the reflection that something else can be meant by the "negotiation of meanings" – something more obvious. What is crucial for the interaction is not (only) what an utterance *generally* means, but what it means *in this particular interaction* and *for the specific relationship of the interaction partners*. "Turn around," for example, would mean something quite different if these words were spoken by a good friend of Thomas, if they were out shopping together and Thomas was trying on a pair of trousers in a fitting room. From a friend, in this specific situation, this would be an unproblematic, appropriate utterance, since the aim here is to try on and appraise items of clothing, and this context entitles the friend to utter a request of this kind. Doing a pirouette in response would then not only demonstrate that Thomas had understood the meaning of "Turn around," but more importantly it would show that this request was appropriate, in the context of their social relationship and the specific situation. In short, the reaction turns the request into part of the two friends' cooperative activity. In contrast, President Nixon's request is inappropriate, from the perspective of an observer: it corresponds neither to the powers of a president of the US nor to the circumstances of the specific situation. And yet Thomas makes it appropriate, and this is why her reaction in the Oval Office gains a fateful quality. By actually complying with the request, without criticism, she "confirms" Nixon's utterance as appropriate. By behaving in this way, she acknowledges his perspective on her position, and demonstrates that: "Our social relationship is of such a kind that you can say that to me." If she had had the great courage required to refuse the request, and perhaps the quick-wittedness to find a less abrupt turn of phrase than that suggested by us – she would have imposed a different shape on her relationship with President Nixon.[6]

This is what we are concerned with here: by interacting, we shape our relationships with our interaction partners. We do this by having recourse to generally valid structures of meaning. But what we say always also has a specific meaning for the specific social relationship in which we find ourselves. And precisely because we know what "Turn around" – or any other speech act – means in general, we also know what it can mean in the specific situation and for the specific social relationship. In this respect, the reaction of our interaction partners plays a crucial role. Here talk of a "negotiation of meanings" seems particularly apposite. In interactions, we constantly stake claims about the shaping of relationships, and our interaction partners respond to these claims in their reactions. Whether this is their intention or not, the things that our interlocutors do in response to our utterances have the effect of testing, rejecting, re-forming or transforming the meanings of our utterances with respect to the relationship. For us, on the other hand, the reaction is a direct reflection on what we have said, and thus a "test" of our perspective-taking.

What we propose, then, is to distinguish more clearly than Mead and Blumer between two fundamental types or levels of meaning of speech acts. In keeping with this distinction, the role of the other person's reactions must also be framed in different theoretical terms. This role consists not only in the acceptance or rejection of *general structures of meaning*, but also, more importantly, in the negotiation of *interaction-related structures of meaning*, that is, of those implications that our actions have for a specific social relationship in a specific situation. So we can say that relationship structures are in fact "made" in interaction. This distinction now also enables us to develop a more nuanced understanding of what is achieved by taking the perspective of others. If we consider the interplay between perspective-taking while speaking on the one hand, and the reaction of our interlocutors as a reflection on what has been said on the other hand, it becomes clear that perspective-taking is always dependent on the *specific relationship* with our interaction partners. In some situations, the "person" in the phrase "this is how I would react in that person's place" can have a general, impersonal touch. This is the case when we interact with relatively anonymous interaction partners in social relationships that are very much structured by a social role (see Chapter 6) – for example as a guest in a café, interacting with a waiter. When we say "An espresso, please," it is relatively unimportant what sort of a café it is and who is serving us. What matters is the extent to which the utterance is appropriate to the role relationship. This is different in those interactions that connect to previous interactions and are likely to be followed by future interactions, such as those with our work colleagues, and especially those that take place in the framework of friendship and family relationships. The specific "history of interaction" (cf. Luhmann 1976) then feeds into the perspective-taking (and thus into my utterances): "If I were Jill, this is how I would react in the context of our relationship." And the appropriateness of my utterances can be measured by their connectivity (i.e., their potential to be processed further in the interaction history) in this specific social relationship.

So far we have treated the reflexivity that is associated with perspective-taking when speaking as a "one-way street." The initial utterance of a speaker has been treated as a given, so to speak, and the accompanying reflexivity, as well as the reflection resulting from the listeners' reactions, has only been considered with reference to this. We must bear in mind, though, that the reactions of our interaction partners are also relevant with regard to the subsequent course of the interaction history and thus the relationship, as suggested previously. This is because the manner in which what *has been* said by the speaker is interactively negotiated also has effects on what *will be* said in future, and therefore what perspective will be taken. After the journalist's reaction, for example, President Nixon will bear in mind in future interactions with her that he "can say that sort of thing to her," and will follow this up with other (verbal) assaults. If Thomas had reacted differently, then the perspective-taking of the president in subsequent interactions would at least have to contain an element of conflict – which the journalist could then refer to in her reaction (along the lines of "I made it quite clear to you … ").

The effect of the reactions of our interaction partners is an especially important aspect of early childhood socialization. Language acquisition and the formation and ongoing development of relationships depend on perspective-taking being especially receptive to input from the reactions of the relevant interaction partners. Martin Dornes (1993) illustrates this with the interaction between a toddler and his father, in which the child not only looks in the direction the father is pointing in, but subsequently checks by looking back at his father's face again that he was actually looking in the direction intended (at whatever the father was pointing to). In the first instance, according to Dornes, this reflects the need to jointly see the same thing, and to jointly pay attention to the object in question. In early childhood, children take their cues, particularly in their affective responses, from their parents. Imagine, for example, a toddler going for a walk, who sees a snake lying in the grass and runs up to it, full of curiosity, to take a closer look. Suddenly she hears her father call out in alarm: "Watch out!". She stops, turns around to her father, and sees the frightened expression on his face, which she then interprets as the appropriate reaction to the situation. She models her own reaction on this, and will now tend to react with fear rather than curiosity. This kind of "affect attunement" must in turn go through a feedback loop of reassurance or confirmation; if the child shrinks back from the snake, the father might, for example, give an explanation about the potential dangers posed by snakes, and thus confirm that the child's feelings are appropriate. Here the child is not learning from experience that snakes are dangerous (the snake is simply lying in the grass and not moving), but that the sight of a snake inspires fear. She learns this by adopting her father's fearful perspective towards her own fearless behavior.

We can understand this as the "original form" of perspective-taking, which is not yet concerned with linguistic behavior, but with affective behavior. This shows that right from the start we unconsciously assume that other people – or at least our parents and then later, by extension, members of our own language community – are subject to the same cognitive processes as us, so our interpretation of the other person's perspective is transferable and, as it were, universally valid. Perspective-taking is therefore the crucial principle that allows *intersubjectivity*: the shared assessment of a situation by various individuals.

Michael Tomasello (2008), who researches the gestural communication of primates (including humans), speaks in this context of "shared intentionality," which generates joint action, or in other words, cooperation. When we inform our interaction partners about something, we are simultaneously informing them that we want to inform them about something; the other person's acknowledgement of the information is always in part an acknowledgement of our need to give information. Searle (1969) similarly assumes that the global meaning or purpose of our speech acts consists in *being understood*. By directing the attention of our interlocutor to a particular matter, or suggesting a certain course of behavior to her, we are making it clear that we regard the matter or the behavior as important for her; and conversely, she also assumes that the matter we are bringing to her attention is relevant and important to her. In the Meadian sense, then, she is taking our perspective – and thus laying the foundations for cooperation. Here Tomasello discerns a genuine, mutual tendency of humans to trust each other to share a fundamental motivation to cooperate. Goffman (1982 [1967]) goes even further; he not only assumes a basic motive of cooperation, but also a universal willingness to *accept each other*. How is this to be understood, and what does it have to do with taking the perspective of others?

According to Goffman (ibid., p. 5), our behavior in social interaction always serves to claim a positive social value for ourselves. We can imagine that this kind of "positive social value" might comprise all manner of things, depending on the occasion and the situation: in lively, light-hearted company it is a positive social value to be funny and entertaining; in a serious personal conversation it is more important to be able to listen well and ask appropriate questions; in a political debate we are judged positively if we express our arguments clearly and make our position understandable for others; and on formal occasions it is "socially valuable" to observe rules of politeness and conduct cultivated conversations. According to Goffman, however, claiming a positive social value in this manner only succeeds if the others also assume, a priori, that this is the intention we are pursuing with our behavior. In this sense, the important thing is not that the other guests at the New Year's Eve party really find our jokes funny; instead what matters is that the addressees of our jokes assume that our intention is to be funny, and acknowledge this intention in a positive way, even if our jokes largely miss the mark. Our "face," the face that we show others and want to "save," thus depends very much on our behavior in interactions and on other people's assumptions about this behavior, about which we in turn make assumptions and so on. What is compelling about Goffman's argument, as stated previously, is that when interacting we tend not to question the face that our interlocutor shows us, but to accept it: we smile at the joke, even if it was not really funny, and thus confirm the positive social value the other person is claiming for himself. Now one could assume that we do this "as a matter of courtesy" only; or one might suppose that those involved in the interaction were wary of confrontation, perhaps because the cause was too minor, or because people generally prefer to avoid conflict. All these explanations, however, only describe symptoms of the underlying perspective-taking. Let us recall once again the mechanism of the process: "How would what I am saying to person B affect me if I were in person B's position?" If we now include in this equation the "positive social value" which all the participants in the interaction claim for themselves and assume for the other person, then the previously mentioned politeness and conflict avoidance in interactions are a reflection of the fact that we ourselves want to avoid any questioning of our positive social value. What then matters is not whether we confront someone (with a shortcoming, a mistake, a misdemeanor etc.), but whether we are willing to risk the consequent loss of face on their part. This also makes it clear that perspective-taking, a willingness to cooperate, intersubjectivity and mutual acceptance, as structural characteristics of social interaction, do not necessarily lead to an absence of confrontation and conflict. It is, however, precisely these structural features of interactions that allow us to avoid confrontation and conflict in the first place – and to realize when we are not doing so.

FOOD FOR THOUGHT

Refer to your transcript of the café scene from *As Good As It Gets*. The character of Melvin is certainly not a person gifted with empathy. But does this also apply to his ability to adopt another person's perspective? Use the end of the conversation and especially the utterance "Uh, let's not drag this out, we don't enjoy one another *that* much" to show the difference between empathy and perspective-taking.

Notes

1 Here we are using only an extract from the newspaper clipping, which Goffman himself does not consider under the aspect of perspective-taking, but as an example of what he calls a change of "footing" in interactions. Essentially this is a matter of changes in the framing of interactions (see Chapter 8) in the interaction itself.
2 Even in 1973 it was regarded as worthy of a newspaper item – suggesting that the event was recognized as something out of the ordinary. However, the nature of the reporting – for example, the fact that Miss Thomas's clothing is described – also allows a reading that is "complicit" with the president's chauvinist behavior.
3 It should be noted that Mead did not write this book himself; it is a collection of notes and transcripts from his lectures by his students.
4 Note that Mead (ibid.) himself does not use the term "perspective-taking," but speaks of "role-taking," which we will not adopt in this book, as we use the term "role" in a much narrower sociological sense (see Chapter 6) than Mead.
5 And sometimes we expect the critical reaction of the others, because we have become aware of the inappropriateness of our utterance even as we speak.
6 The action of disrespect is probably particularly serious for the person who is disrespected if she participates in it with her own action. Conversely, it may be supposed that this is what constitutes the real triumph of Nixon's aggressive act: Thomas confirms him in a (male) claim to power which goes beyond his office.

References

Mead, George Herbert (1987 [1964]). *Selected Writings*. Andrew J. Reck (Ed.). Chicago, IL: The University of Chicago Press. See especially: What social objects must psychology presuppose?, pp. 105–113; Social Consciousness and the Consciousness of Meaning, pp. 123–133.

Mead, George Herbert (1992 [1934]). *Mind, Self and Society from the Standpoint of a Social Behaviourist*. Charles W. Morris (Ed.). Chicago, IL: The University of Chicago Press. See especially: The Vocal Gesture and the Significant Symbol, pp. 61–68; Thought, Communication and the Significant Symbol, pp. 68–75; Meaning, pp. 75–82.

Further reading

Blumer, Herbert (1998 [1969]). *Symbolic interactionism. Perspective and Method*. Berkeley, CA: University of California Press. See especially: The methodological position of symbolic interactionism, pp. 1–60.

Dornes, Martin (1993). *Der kompetente Säugling. Die präverbale Entwicklung des Menschen*. Frankfurt a. M., Germany: Fischer Verlag. See especially: Intersubjektivität und Affektivität, pp. 152–163.

Goffman, Erving (1981). *Forms of Talk*. Philadelphia, PA: University of Pennsylvania Press.

Goffman, Erving (1982 [1967]). *Interaction Ritual. Essays on Face-to-Face Behavior*. New York: Pantheon Books. See especially: On Face Work, pp. 5–45.

Habermas, Jürgen (1981). *Theorie des kommunikativen Handelns. Bd. 2: Zur Kritik der funktionalistischen Vernunft*. Frankfurt a. M., Germany: Suhrkamp. See especially: Zur kommunikationstheoretischen Grundlegung der Sozialwissenschaften, pp. 11–68.

Joas, Hans (2000 [1980]). *Praktische Intersubjektivität. Die Entwicklung des Werkes von G. H. Mead*. Frankfurt a. M., Germany: Suhrkamp. See especially: Die Entstehung des Konzepts symbolvermittelter Interaktion, pp. 91–119.

Luhmann, Niklas (1976). Einfache Sozialsysteme. In Manfred Auwärter, Edit Kirsch & Klaus Schröter (Eds.), *Seminar: Kommunikation, Interaktion, Identität* (pp. 3–34). Frankfurt a. M., Germany: Suhrkamp.

Schneider, Wolfgang Ludwig (2002). *Grundlagen der soziologischen Theorie. Band 1: Weber – Parsons – Mead – Schütz*. Wiesbaden, Germany: Westdeutscher Verlag. See especially: Handlungen als Derivate der Interaktion: George H. Mead, pp. 180–233.

Searle, John R. (1969). *Speech Acts. An Essay in the Philosophy of Language*. Cambridge, UK: Cambridge University Press. See especially: Expressions, meanings and speech acts, pp. 22–53.

Tomasello, Michael (2008). *Origins of Human Communication*. Cambridge, MA: The MIT Press. See especially: Human Cooperative Communication, pp. 57–108.

6

SOCIAL ROLES

What we are to each other

In this chapter, we are interested in social roles in their significance for social interaction. We focus on Talcott Parsons's structuralist approach, because it conceives of social roles as *social relations* right from the outset – a fact that is often overlooked in the reception of Parsons's role theory. This distinguishes the ideas of Parsons, but also those of Niklas Luhmann and Erving Goffman (which we also refer to) from other relevant role theories, in which the social role is mainly used to describe the relationship between individual and society (in the form of position and status). At present the concept of roles is primarily used in gender studies, though here it is not so much the object of theoretical interest, but instead serves to highlight diffuse power relations.

With the title "Social roles: What we are to each other" we are narrowing our perspective on the phenomenon in this chapter right from the start, by viewing "roles" as categories of social relationship that are operative in interaction. This perspective is actually also adopted[1] in classic role theory,[2] but it is not central for the definition of role here: roles are declared to be "social," yet are, in the conventional classifications, conceived in egological terms. Common designations such as "situational role," "positional role" and "status role" (cf. Dahrendorf 1973 [1964]; Linton 1947) describe the individual in his/ her egological position in the coordinate system of social differentiation; we, on the other hand, viewing the social role as a category operative in interaction, conceive it a priori in dialogical terms. Seen in this way, it is not the social role that requires a role partner ("*because* I am a supermarket cashier, I have customers"), but it is the respective role partners who demand a definition of their currently relevant social relationship ("my role as a supermarket cashier turns my role partners into customers").

Not all the relationships that I have in the "field" of my work position as a supermarket cashier are actually relationships I have *as* a supermarket cashier: to my colleagues I am a colleague, and to my manager I am a member of staff, and these roles naturally make quite different demands on me than my job. We can begin then, with the observation that roles are always complementary (cf. Luhmann 2013 [1997]) – "cashier-colleague" does not exist as a complementary role pair, and nor does "cashier-manager." Thus there is no social role that is not determined by way of the social role of the role partner: in order to be a patient, I need a doctor as a role partner; to be a son I need a father or a mother; to be a shopper I need a shop assistant; to be a friend I need a friend, etc. A doctor without a patient is simply a person with a license to practice medicine, and a patient without a doctor is merely a sick person. It is only in interaction, then, that the social category becomes a social role, which we adopt and to which we adapt our behavior. The advantage of such a perspective, which concentrates on the role complementarity of social relationships, and not on the role behavior of individuals, is that we do not necessarily have to allocate social roles to every social situation – and its disadvantage is that we cannot do so, and that the social role is therefore only of limited usefulness as an explanatory model for the relationship between individual and society.

The explanatory potential of the social role for this relationship is, however, the starting point for sociological discourses on theory from the 1950s to the 1980s, in which social roles are a central theme. Studying social roles gives insight into a crucial interface – some would say *the* crucial interface – between individual and society: the social role as an expression of functional differentiation, allowing individuals to be socialized into functioning members of society (see esp. Dahrendorf 1973 [1964]; Parsons 1962 [1951]; see also Berger & Luckmann 1967). Thus social roles can be understood as an important ordering principle of society; it might be said that one of the things making social order possible is that tasks, functions, activities, rights and duties are allocated to the members of society by way of the roles they occupy. A social role, then, according to the minimum consensus of social scientists, is a cluster of generalized, anonymized behavioral expectations,[3] which arise from these tasks, functions, activities, rights and duties. From the perspective of "society," the individual is then a cluster of generalized roles which he or she occupies successively in the different social spheres in which he or she operates. Through predefined and pre-interpreted expectations, our roles "commit" us to certain tasks and behaviors in the framework of the different positions we occupy in social contexts. It should be noted, though, that while this is the minimum consensus, the discussion of roles in sociological theory has largely come to a standstill since the 1980s or earlier. The term is still used, since we cannot get by without it, but the explanatory potential of social roles for social relations has not been fully explicated – for example in terms of their power to create social order, their power over the individual, their efficacy in socialization, their relationship to "identity," and their "negotiability" in interaction.

Interaction is, as we established in Chapter 1, the minimal form of social relationship, because we relate to each other reciprocally when interacting. Now there are many everyday situations that do not require us to take a complementary position towards other participants. We can readily visualize this with the help of Goffman's (1983) interaction format of "ambulatory units" (see Chapter 1): this covers a number of activities that can take place in the presence of others, but are not determined by role complementarity. For example, our participation in road traffic[4] is constituted by our activity as cyclists, pedestrians, car drivers, roller-skaters, etc., and these are activities that are not defined by a social relationship – we do not need another person in order to rollerskate, and even in the presence of other road users there is not necessarily any need for direct contact. But as soon as co-presence turns into interaction, a social relationship comes about. We never know with any certainty in which direction this will "develop," but we can always say with certainty what it is like at present: we can say whether we are strangers or acquaintances, and we can identify different degrees of familiarity, as well as determining what context we know someone from. With regard to face-to-face interaction, we have observed that it is limited by various mechanisms: if there is only one speaker at a time, only one topic can be discussed at a time, and the interaction is also subject to a time limit, then many things that are relevant to the interaction cannot be thematized. These things are present as "background assumptions" which are not (or do not need to be) expressed. Depending on the social event, however, there is always a whole spectrum of aspects of the situation that are not at all relevant for the immediate interaction – be it the color of the chair one is sitting on, the haircut of the person one is talking to or the rain pouring down outside the window. It is possible to mention these aspects, but it is not vital for the interaction and might even be counterproductive. The "normal" range of topics covered in an interaction, however, is linked with the social roles that the participants occupy in relation to one another. These roles bring into play certain reciprocal expectations about how we and the others can and cannot behave.

We have already heard that the consolidation of expectations happens through communication and that it is crucial for the formation of social systems. In Luhmann's[5] conception, expectations "come into being by constraining ranges of possibilities" (Luhmann 1995 [1984], p. 292), by allowing assumptions about what can and cannot happen. In relation to social roles, such assumptions do not emerge spontaneously from the social situation, but precede it. We can see this from the fact that we are able to formulate expectations of people even without any experience of our own – namely in those cases where we can assign these people to a category about which we already have assumptions, without ever having come into contact with this category of people. So even if we have never personally had anything to do with a stockbroker, a psychiatrist or a pool cleaner, we have an indirect knowledge of what we can or cannot expect from people in such roles, and what these people would or would not expect from us if we were to address them in this category. And conversely, we do not draw conclusions about generally expectable role behavior from the concrete role performance of the person we are dealing with (cf. Goffman 2013 [1961]), but compare the specific behavior in the interaction with previous expectations. That is, our assumptions about the many different categories of persons we deal with on a daily basis have, in the first instance, nothing to do with specific individuals, and are thus "anonymized." They also have nothing to do with the specific situation, and are therefore "generalized" (cf. e.g. Luhmann 1995 [1984]; Popitz 1967). In interaction, then, certain requirements for action are pre-structured through roles, requirements that are always repeatable under similar conditions. Thus the role is always more specific, but at the same time more general than the individual performing the role. On the one hand, it comprises only a very precise subset of all conceivable expectations about behavior; on the other hand, however, it is not tied to the individual, but can always be performed by many different individuals (cf. Luhmann 1995 [1984]).

But how do role expectations come about in the first place? According to Talcott Parsons (1962 [1951]), role expectations are based on four value orientations or "pattern variables" (cf. also Parsons's "AGIL" scheme[6]), which are conceived as contrastive pairs of alternative preferences, dispositions and assumptions, as two mutually contradictory and mutually exclusive orientations. Social roles, according to Parsons (ibid., p. 76), are

> the definitions of rights and duties of the members of a collectivity which specify the actions of incumbents of roles, and which often specify that the performer shall exhibit a habit of choosing one side or the other of each of these dilemmas.

This means that the activities and requirements defined in the role go hand in hand with prescriptive value orientations, so that the role incumbents are freed from the burden of decisions about orientation from the start, and tensions between the different possible orientations are already regulated by the given role (cf. Gerhardt 1971). In this scheme the social relationship defined by this means is "intimate" or "anonymous," the role expectations associated with it are "personalized" or "generalized," and the activities included in it are purpose-free or purpose-bound. Here we will explain the four value-orientation alternatives by which role expectations can be defined, based on Parsons's scheme (1962 [1951]).

1. *Affectivity vs. affective neutrality* describes the orientation towards either impulse control or immediate satisfaction of needs; this orientation can be translated into role expectations in terms of the extent to which social roles require us to exclude personal feelings from social relationships or not. For example, the question of whether or not two participants like each other is crucial for the formation of some social relationships (partnerships, friendships), is taken as a given for some relationships (parent-child relationship) and is simply not "role-relevant" for some social relationships (sales assistant-customer, doctor-patient). Affectivity therefore seems to be the preserve of "intimate" or "personal"

relationships, while affective neutrality is one of the role expectations associated with, in the broadest sense, business or contractual relationships, such as those found in connection with work-related roles. Even if we would intuitively say that it *is* important for us whether or not we like our doctors and teachers, as well as our patients and pupils, we are aware of the role expectation that this feeling must not be *treated* as important, to the extent of having consequences for the interaction which undermine the purpose of the social relationship. Taken to extremes, this would mean a doctor refusing to treat a patient she cannot stand, or a school pupil refusing to participate in the lessons of a teacher she does not like. Affective neutrality, however, also includes all the emotions and needs that have nothing to do with the specific person one is dealing with, but nonetheless have no place in the interaction. Showing extreme joy or deep sorrow is as abnormal in "impersonal" social relationships as it is normal in intimate relationships. Various reasons for this may occur to us, but ultimately the key reason is that affectivity, whenever it makes an appearance "counter to expectations," may in some cases modify the nature of the social relationship, potentially making it impossible to retreat behind this line again. In other words, once a relationship has become "personal," it is difficult to find one's way back to an impersonal relationship mode. This can then have counterproductive effects, especially in asymmetrical relationships where the power to make decisions and give instructions is unequally distributed.

2. *Diffuseness vs. specificity* refers to patterns of orientation in which the social relationship is either more or less focused on instrumental or functional aspects. Role expectations are then either linked with the costs, benefits, purposes and results of interactions, or they are more open-ended, without any specific purpose. If the role expectations are "specific," the social relationship is characterized by a clearly defined common goal, which is attainable in the present interaction (and where relevant in the subsequent interaction). Only certain aspects of the other person are relevant to the joint realization of this goal. For example, in the social relationship between the citizen renewing his driver's license and the administrator in the local DMV office, there are clear parameters that determine what both individuals must do, in accordance with their role, in order to achieve the shared objective. The citizen must prove his identity with a suitable document, provide a recent photo or have a photo taken, sign a form and pay a fee; the administrator must enter the details into the appropriate form, attach the photo and send the documents to the relevant department so the driver's license can be printed. "Diffuse" role expectations, on the other hand, are present when the interests and goals pursued in the social relationship are not so clearly definable, and go beyond the current interaction. The role incumbents cannot be reduced to just a small number of predictable behaviors, precisely because the social relationship has no specific objective, and because its "function" is diffuse. If we were aiming for specific, attainable goals in our friendships and family relationships, then the relationships would become obsolete once the goals were attained. Of course the interactions within such relationships can have a specific

joint goal, such as planning a joint holiday. But here again there are no behavioral expectations attached to the roles, which determine who has to contribute what to the planning – who will research the destination, who will make a checklist of what to pack, who will buy the tickets, who will book the hotel, etc. Even in family relationships where such things follow an established routine, where every member of the family has his or her "jobs," these are fundamentally flexible – depending on their age, the children can take on more or different jobs; the father who is usually responsible for the checklist can research the destination this time, etc. In the local DMV office, there is no option for such changes in the division of tasks between the applicant and the administrator. Nor is it expected that they will discuss anything other than what is necessary to achieve their joint objective. A little small talk is acceptable, but not a conversation about their favorite bars, or about custody disputes with their ex-partners. In interaction between friends, or between parents and children, however, any aspect of the other person can become relevant at a particular time: their occupation, their favorite color, their religious convictions, their food allergies. So here too, we can differentiate between a "contractually" predefined interaction, which is only concerned with the intended transaction, and an "open" interaction in which the social relationship is not limited to the intended transaction.

3. *Particularism vs. universalism* concerns role expectations that are expressed in the social relationship as standards for judging the people one is dealing with. This is about evaluation criteria relating to these people as role incumbents in the situation at hand, or in their broader relationships to one another. It is about the distinction between the "rule" (role expectations that are related to the roles relevant in the situation) and the "exception" (role expectations that go beyond the specific situation and cannot be directly deduced from it). The social relationship between supermarket cashier and supermarket customer is determined by "universal" expectations, which can be defined on the basis of the given roles, and which do not go beyond the purpose of the present interaction. It is not relevant whether the cashier and the customer are also long-standing acquaintances or hostile neighbors, whether their children go to the same school, or whether they belong to rival sports clubs – the cashier does not scan the items any faster or slower, and the customer does not pay any more or less for her shopping, depending ("particularly") on which other relationships exist between the two. Of course we are aware of cases in which social relationships become "mixed up" with one another, and, unsurprisingly, irrelevant relationships become critical for decisions. If we talk about "preferential treatment," "discrimination" or "bribery and corruption," what we mean is always an "improper" mixing of social relationships, one that is contrary to role expectations. If, on the other hand, I greet my friend with a hug and merely offer my hand to the woman sitting with him, whom I do not know, this is different treatment, but it is still behavior conforming to role expectations. Particularism vs. universalism is also the typical orientation dilemma in role conflicts, when we are simultaneously addressed in two roles (cf. Gerhardt 1971)[7]: the person facing us is our friend but

also our accountant, our daughter is also our pupil, our fellow party member is also the HR manager of the company we are applying to join, our dentist is also the suspect we have to summon for questioning in a police investigation. Here contradictions arise between the expectations attached to the different roles we simultaneously occupy in the interaction, and we have to rely on the specific situation to decide which role expectations we will base our behavior on (cf. ibid.), and which role has the primary weighting (cf. Goffman 2013 [1961]).

4. *Ascription vs. achievement*, lastly, is a value orientation focusing either on the actual or possible actions of the other person, or on his or her unchanging qualities. The distinction is based on whether a person in this role is expected to perform particular actions or services, and the role is clearly defined by this, or whether such an orientation can probably be excluded, and role expectations are more likely to relate to the subjective assessments of the others. In other words, there are social roles that are defined by the performance of particular services or actions, and social roles that are defined by the ascription of particular qualities. A tiler is not a tiler because we ascribe particular qualities to him, but because certain actions or services can be expected of him within the social relationships he maintains in his role as a tiler. Conversely, a friend is not a friend because she provides friendship services (which could not be clearly defined anyway) when interacting with us, but because we ascribe qualities to her that correspond to the role expectations associated with a friend. Of course this then also means that the tiler – by virtue of the "achievement vs. ascription" difference – does not possess any unchanging qualities: helpfulness, loyalty, discretion, even friendliness or courtesy are not genuinely associated with the role, and do not form part of the specific role expectations linked with a "tiler."

In summary, role relationships and the associated expectations and requirements can be differentiated by means of the underlying value orientations, as follows:

Intimate, personalized, no specific purpose: "community"	Anonymized, generalized, tied to a specific purpose: "society"
Affectivity	Affective neutrality
Diffuseness	Specificity
Particularism	Universalism
Ascription	Achievement

So far we have spoken of clearly differentiable value orientations. Empirically, however, in view of actual social relationships, we can assume that these pairs of opposites actually represent a continuum. Most social relationships fall somewhere between the two extremes, and lean towards either one side or the other. The more intensely we interact with a role counterpart, and the longer our shared history of interaction is, the less the absolute interchangeability of individuals that comes with anonymized and generalized role expectations can – from a subjective perspective – be taken as a given. In functional terms, it is irrelevant who sells shoes to us, and who we sell shoes to, who teaches us mathematics, and who we teach mathematics to, who looks after our children and whose children we look after, as long as all those involved meet the demands of the given roles. And if a person on one side or the other drops out, there will always be someone else to take over the role. And yet over time we "appropriate" many of our "purely functional," purpose-oriented social relationships, in such a way that it is no longer solely the role function, but the person "behind the role" who becomes more important to us: "the doctor" becomes "my doctor," "the professor" becomes "my professor," "the hairdresser" becomes "my hairdresser." And this always leads to a preference for the specific person in his or her generalized role: only in an emergency will I see "a doctor" rather than "my doctor." On the continuum between "intimate, personalized, purpose-free," and "anonymized, generalized, purpose-oriented," then, our social relationships tend to become more personal rather than more impersonal as our interactions become more intense and more frequent. Thus when someone "crosses the line" or "oversteps the boundary," this always refers to role-inappropriate behavior in one and the same direction: what is being crossed is the role-defined boundary in social relationships from the instrumental and functional towards the diffuse and affective – but not in the opposite direction.

Against this background, we will first take a look at the most basic form of social relationship, which is only expressed in a short exchange (such as: "Excuse me, could you tell me what time it is?" – "Quarter to two." – "Thank you!" or "If I'd known the train was going to be so crowded I'd have booked a seat." – "Yes, it really is extremely crowded today." – "Well, I'll keep looking then." – "Good luck!"). The reason why there is no role expression[8] for this minimal form of relationship is probably that fleeting interactions require us to face the other person with completely anonymized, generalized behavioral expectations; we cannot base our expectations on much more than the fact that we are in the same place at the same time. Of course there are also, and we will study this more closely in Chapter 9, typifications that supplement role expectations, and give us (additional) help in categorizing the person we are dealing with. But if we have been wandering around for hours in a strange town, and have finally made up our minds to ask someone the way, we will tend to ask the first person who crosses our path rather than waiting hours longer until a person comes along whom we would really like to ask (whichever typifications we might use to decide this). What we have here, then, is a completely anonymized, generalized behavioral expectation, which can only be explained by the fact that, in our position as someone in need of assistance, we basically assign the role of helper to any person present. Furthermore, the subsequent course of the interaction also follows a particular pattern, which anyone involved in any comparable situation can fall back on. Adhering to interactive moves that conform to expectations not only relieves us of the need to make decisions, and restricts the range of possibilities; this relief from decision-making and restriction of possibilities are also a reason why, in social situations, we are able to turn to complete strangers in the form of "generalized others" (cf. Chapter 12). These are, in the immediate situation, merely representative "members of society," of whom we have generalized behavioral expectations. If we thus assume that there is a fundamental solidarity between strangers in public spaces (see also Chapter 4), we can also say, against this background, that the extent of the behavior based on this solidarity is so clearly limited by the completely generalized behavioral expectation that the social risk we take by asking for and providing help is relatively small. Precisely because the role complementarity in fleeting social relationships is based on a very small number of mutual behavioral expectations, the risk of disappointment is manageable. This also means that when a stranger makes a remark about what they think of something, or how they are feeling, with no purpose other than the need to communicate with another person, this can be treated as completely non-binding, at least by the person addressed in this way – we are not "obliged" to give any more than a suitable response.

The more the pendulum of the social relationship swings towards "anonymized, generalized, purpose-oriented," the more clearly predefined are the associated interactions. There are then pre-existing structures within the interaction determining how impulses can be controlled, goals achieved, purposes focused on and actions or services carried out, and certain interactive moves are automatically assumed to be part of this, while others are excluded. Thus what makes it possible to keep track of and anticipate role behavior is the fact that our role actions are coordinated with those of others (cf. Gerhardt 1971). According to Krappmann (1973 [1969]), however, successful role action requires agreement between the predefined role expectations and the reciprocal role interpretations of the role incumbents. Thus it is quite possible for there to be no full consensus between those interacting about what is included in or excluded from their own and the other person's role. Again, we can use the continuum of Parsons's value orientations to explain this. For example, a lecturer can interpret the expectations made of her in this role as consistently neutral, specific, universalist and achievement-oriented. Inevitably, however, she will find herself in situations in which students evoke affective, diffuse, particular and ascriptive aspects: a student may be unable to submit an assignment on time because he has taken on too much in this semester, because his own wedding has got in the way, because the computer with his data has been lost, because the library book crucial for the assignment was always on loan, etc. Thus the student expects his personal circumstances to be taken into account in the social relationship, while the lecturer expects that these will not be relevant here. Depending on how we look at it, this presents a dilemma or offers scope for value orientation; it is always possible to retreat to the position of "going by the rules," and in this case mark the non-submitted assignment as a "fail." But one can also accept certain reasons for the non-fulfilment of role expectations, and in this case, extend the deadline. According to Luhmann (1995 [1984]), this mainly depends on whether the role expectations are "normative" or "cognitive":[9] true, it is an inherent element of all expectations that they can be disappointed, but within this there are expectations that are resistant to experience, and others that are open to experience. Normative expectations are not impaired by disappointment; regardless of how often the lecturer experiences assignments not being handed in on time, she continues to insist on punctual submission and to give a fail grade in cases of deviation. Likewise, however, regardless of how often the student has the experience that his personal circumstances are not relevant for lecturers, he continues to bring them into the social relationship, because he has the normative expectation of his professors that they will recognize him as a "whole person" (with individual weaknesses, problems and commitments). Cognitive expectations, on the other hand, are subject to a "learning curve": if they are disappointed, we tend to modify or completely abandon them. The lecturer would then, over time, no longer insist on punctual submission of assignments, and might eventually dispense with such deadlines altogether; the student, in turn, would eventually stop bringing his "whole person" into the role relationship, and would accept that only certain aspects of his person are relevant for his role as a student. We can also observe, however, that many role expectations that we might, a priori, regard as normative, binding or obligatory do not have to be any of these things – neither in the present interaction nor, where relevant, in the social relationship in which the interaction is embedded. And we can also see that normative expectations of a role are not discernible from their fulfilment, but from the unchanging, constant nature of the expectation itself.

This, of course, always means potential for manipulation, dissent and conflict, but also for consent and cooperation (cf. Luhmann 1995 [1984]). If all the role expectations in social relationships were *mutually* interpreted as clear and binding, our everyday life would be largely free of conflict and disturbance. The customers at our supermarket checkout would never question the price we scan in, and would never dash back to the aisles to fetch something important they have forgotten. They would never jump the queue and would always have enough money on them to pay for their shopping promptly and with exactly the right change. If, conversely, role expectations were always interpreted as optional and non-binding, we would not have any "everyday life" at all – every social situation would demand that we "negotiate" expectations from scratch, and there would be no schematic sequences of interaction. We could not automatically expect the customers at our supermarket checkout to put their shopping on the conveyor belt, pack it into their bags or boxes after scanning and pay the price we state, etc.; instead we would first have to explicitly formulate these as expectations, and then negotiate with the other person about the extent to which this meets or runs counter to *their* expectations. On the one hand, then, normative role expectations relieve us of the burden of subjective interpretation and allow us to pursue our shared goals and interests with predefined interactive moves. On the other hand, however, the more "complex" the social relationship is, the more complex and thus diffuse the role expectations become. So the further the pendulum swings towards "intimate, personalized, purpose-free," the more strongly, of course, we perceive the other person as a specific individual and not as a "generalized other." And as this happens, generalized role expectations become less able to adequately structure interactions, because the relationship can no longer be exclusively described within a clear, singular "context of purpose." For the supermarket cashier, it is irrelevant whose shopping he is scanning, because the role complementarity between cashier and customer is limited to the singular purpose of shopping and receiving payment. The reciprocal role expectations associated with this are limited, and the moves in the interaction are therefore predictable. In contrast, behavioral expectations that are associated with our roles in parent-child, sibling, friend or partner relationships are directed towards a single, specific, non-interchangeable person. In intimate personal social relationships there is such a far-reaching subjective identification of the person with the role that the two become synonymous: "my pool cleaner" can be any pool cleaner, but "my mother," "my partner," "my child" is a specific person and cannot be just any mother, partner or child.

This brings us to the question of the identificatory potential of the social role. Luhmann (1995 [1984]) observes that the individual takes his orientation from roles, while at the same time identifying as a person; from the "I" perspective, we are not – following the logic of roles – the sum of currently "activatable" fragments or elements of social relationships, but whole, complete individuals, who "more or less" and "somehow" find expression in the roles we take on. The role, according to Kaufmann (2000, p. 70), "is not simply a casing that protects the individual, but the bearer of an order of meanings which define it." We already saw in Chapter 1 that we participate in interactions as "whole persons," at least insofar as we do so with our whole body and our whole physical manifestation. In our corporeality alone, we are already "holistically," personally and individually present, and we perceive ourselves as such. In this sense, we do not regard ourselves as "multiple personalities," which either reveal themselves in the form of roles, or remain hidden, depending on the situation. This is why, according to Popitz (1967), we come to see ourselves within our roles in ways that are determined by the relevant role expectations, but are not limited to a one-to-one equivalence with them; instead they also have something to do with individual attitudes and preferences. In short: every social role has identificatory potential in the sense that we can internalize it as an integrative component of our personality. This can be effectively illustrated with the example of our occupation: if we are invited to "say something about ourselves," our occupation is usually a prominent part of this. For many people, their occupation has a very strong integrative power; in their self-descriptions they "are" the work that they do, even beyond the actually doing of the work ("I am a teacher," not "I work as a teacher"); and often they "are" the occupation which they "have," regardless of the work they are doing ("I'm a trained accountant, but at the moment I'm working in an architectural practice, doing the paperwork"). Of course we can say that occupation is a key indicator of social status,[10] and this is why we tend to circumscribe, elevate, marginalize or even conceal our low-status activities.

With regard to "identification" with the role, however, social status alone is not a sufficient explanation, because then we would have to assume that activities such as stripper, drug dealer, call center agent, shelf stacker or cruise ship entertainer have only a low level of identificatory potential, as opposed to occupations such as dentist, lawyer, factory director, astronaut or film star. Yet this cannot be established as categorical fact. We can, for example, cite Krappmann's argument (1973 [1969]) that *every* social role contains the potential for resistance against total absorption. Even if it may generally be easier for us to "admit" to being an astronaut than a shelf stacker, this does not mean that the astronaut is entirely absorbed by his occupation and that the shelf stacker is not. How much satisfaction and recognition we gain from carrying out an activity depends partly on our attitude towards it, and this is where what Goffman (2013 [1961]) calls "role distance" comes into play: the more the role is designed to entirely absorb those who occupy it, and to "reduce" them to a small number of role qualities, the greater is the probability that, in playing this role, we will distance ourselves from the very aspects that genuinely belong to the role.

Goffman (ibid.) distinguishes here between "commitment" to the role and "embracement" or complete adoption of it. The more regularly we exercise a social role, the stronger our commitment to it – it constitutes a considerable part of our everyday actions, and is thus firmly anchored in our everyday life. This does not yet mean that the role is "a part of us," but in the first instance merely that we perceive the role expectations associated with it as binding, and feel obliged to fulfill them. It is only when we feel committed to a role in this way that we can also distance ourselves from it. We usually do this by signaling to our role counterpart that we are only fulfilling expectations, but do not personally take them seriously or support them: "I personally don't care when you hand in your assignment, but according to the examination regulations you can't register for your bachelor's thesis without this course assessment." Often, however, we express role distance towards third-party observers – we respond with dutiful servility to our manager's absurd request, but behind her back we make faces to show our colleague that our role actions are not congruent with our attitude to them. Embracement of the role, on the other hand, goes beyond commitments and obligations, and thus beyond mere role expectations. We absorb the role, and are no longer able to slip into it and out of it, depending on the situation – our everyday actions are no longer determined by the role, but the role influences our everyday actions even when we are not occupying it, that is, when the social relationship is defined by other roles. Viewed in empirical terms, we are in the realm of clichés here: the teacher who always speaks in schoolmasterly tones, the lecturer who never converses, but always lectures, the general who expects obedience from everyone, the mother who mothers everyone. The role is like a skin we cannot shed, and we are unable to distance ourselves from it. But of course this can also be "imposed" on us, so to speak, by the people we are dealing with – for example when, even among friends and family, the doctor is constantly asked for medical advice, the banker for investment tips, or the father for parenting advice. Here too, those who are "pressured" in this way may feel the need to distance themselves from the role, which threatens to take over their other social relationships.

Here a fundamental problem of role theory arises, one which is still far from being resolved: is the individual defined by his social roles, or by his attitude towards his social roles? Intuitively, we would probably opt for the latter assessment: what constitutes our "identity" is not the expectations that are addressed to us in our different roles, because the expectations are always the same. It is not the fact *that* we fulfill them that makes us distinguishable as individuals from other individuals, but the *way* we fulfill them or, as the case may be, do not fulfill them. According to Kaufmann (2000), however, this is only possible to the extent that attitudes of expectation are restricted to us as specific individuals – i.e. in those social relationships where personal value orientations have priority over anonymized and generalized ones. It is only in our personal relationships that we can adapt our role engagement in the long term to a specific other person, and develop, adjust and modify our definitions of identity, because it is only in our personal relationships that we are perceived and appreciated as specific individuals. However diffuse the general, anonymized role expectations may be, for example in the partner relationship, they nonetheless become specific as standards of behavior which develop in the partners' direct interactions, in their interaction history, and are characteristic of this specific relationship. Behavior conforming to roles makes up only a small part of the actual interactive repertoire, and therefore even role-contravening behavior can only be flagged as such in a small number of situations.

It must be borne in mind, however – as a final point – that the "social corrective" which is necessary to identify and highlight role-contravening behavior remains somewhat obscure outside of interaction. We can illustrate this with the example of professional codes. Professional codes are issued by professional or trade associations, and describe the behavior required for the exercise of the given occupation. Contraventions of such professional codes, however, do not usually occur towards the organization that has issued them (unless the offense is non-payment of one's membership fee), but towards the clients one deals with professionally. In the first instance, then, it is not doctors and their organizations who sanction the behavior of doctors, but patients. And the expectations that I as a patient have of my doctor are not necessarily the same as the professional code, which I am probably not familiar with. For all I know, she might be contravening some aspect of the professional code whenever she treats me, without me noticing a thing. Conversely, of course, my doctor can also disappoint me in expectations that are not covered by the professional code; I can nonetheless sanction her behavior by complaining to her or switching to another doctor. And finally, even if I am aware of a breach of the professional code I am not obliged to report it to the medical council; I can consciously decide not to do so. The generalized behavioral expectations of people occupying certain roles, as formulated, for example, in professional codes, do not necessarily operate either comprehensively or unambiguously in interaction. At the same time, it is only in interaction – and thus in the context of a social relationship – that they can operate at all.[11]

FOOD FOR THOUGHT

Refer to your transcript of the café scene from *As Good As It Gets*. Carol is operating in her workplace in her professional role as a waitress. By now, however, her relationship to Melvin goes beyond the purely professional. Examine Carol's appearances in this scene: does she succeed in separating the "professional" from the "private"? (Pay special attention to the point where she gives Melvin the letter.) Is it possible to speak of a role conflict in Carol's case?

Notes

1 Dahrendorf (1973 [1964]) defines his famous *homo sociologicus* as the bearer of socially preformed roles. In this conception, "role" refers both to the social position of the individual in a particular field of social relations and to the demands society makes of those occupying the roles.

2 For a concise, often-quoted overview of the development and the important proponents of role theory see Biddle (1986).

3 In this context many authors also speak of "norms," and particularly in studies on role theory, there is often no distinction made between behavioral expectations and behavioral norms. This non-differentiation reveals the incompatibility between the functional, static aspect of the role on the one hand (role as constraint) and its dynamic, interaction-dependent aspects on the other hand (role as play) (cf. Furth 1991), a theoretical dispute which we do not want to discuss further here. We will therefore largely omit the term "norm" in this chapter, but will explore it in detail in Chapter 7.

4 In his study on "role distance," in contrast, Goffman (2013 [1961]) treats riding on a merry-go-round – which can also be broadly considered as participation in traffic, and thus as an interaction format involving "ambulatory units" – as a key example of a "situational role." In the case of behaviors described as situational roles (cf. also Gerhardt 1971), however, the starting point for the observation is not interaction, but the performance of an activity and, where relevant, the extent to which we identify with this activity. This is, then, a different approach from that proposed in this chapter.

5 Here it must also be pointed out that Luhmann (1995 [1984], p. 430) assumes that "the ordering performance of roles for actual behavior and behavioral expectations has been considerably overestimated in sociology;" he himself does not explore the concept of roles any further in his work, and instead deals with the significance and efficacy of organizational programs.

6 AGIL = adaptation, goal attainment, integration, latency.

7 This is a narrow and therefore, we believe, easily operationalized definition of "role conflict." Other authors take this to include other kinds of conflict which can appear in connection to the performance of social roles, e.g. "role ambiguity" and "role overload" (cf. Biddle 1986, p. 82).

8 Here we could once again point to the concept of the "situational role," and in the first instance it does seem plausible that certain social relationships are generated

and shaped solely by the event in the context of which they take place. This, however, is not what is meant in the prevalent use of the term; instead it is a "residual category," encompassing any behavior that is mainly determined by situation (and not by position or status). To avoid misunderstandings we will refrain from using this term here.

9 Dahrendorf's (1973 [1964]) often-cited division into "must," "shall" and "can" expectations is not helpful in this conception; from the perspective of the person who has an expectation about another person, it is pure anticipation of what is possible in the context of the specific interaction; from the perspective of the person from whom something is expected, there is always the possibility of fulfilling the expectation or not.

10 According to Linton (1947, p. 50), status is the "position of an individual in the prestige system of his society."

11 Dahrendorf (1973 [1964]), on the contrary, assumes that it is actually the sanctions that make role expectations tangible and verifiable.

References

Goffman, Erving (2013 [1961]). *Encounters. Two Studies in the Sociology of Interaction.* Indianapolis, IN: Bobbs-Merrill. See especially: Role Distance, pp. 85–152.

Luhmann, Niklas (1995 [1984]). *Social Systems.* Stanford, CA: Stanford University Press. See especially: Structure and Time, pp. 278–356; Society and Interaction, pp. 405–436.

Parsons, Talcott (1962 [1951]). *Towards a General Theory of Action.* New York: Harper & Row. See especially: Categories of the Orientation and Organization of Action, pp. 53–109.

Further reading

Berger, Peter L., & Luckmann, Thomas (1967). *The Social Construction of Reality. A Treatise in the Sociology of Knowledge.* New York: Anchor Books. See especially: Primary Socialization, pp. 129–138.

Biddle, B.J. (1986). Recent Developments in Role Theory. *Annual Review of Sociology, 12,* 67–92.

Dahrendorf, Ralf (1973 [1964]). *Homo Sociologicus.* London, UK: Routledge & Kegan Paul.

Furth, Peter (1991). Soziale Rolle, Institution und Freiheit. In Harald Kerber & Arnold Schmieder (Eds.), *Soziologie: Arbeitsfelder, Theorien, Ausbildung. Ein Grundkurs* (pp. 213–251). Reinbek bei Hamburg, Germany: Rowohlt.

Gerhardt, Uta (1971). *Rollenanalyse als kritische Soziologie. Ein konzeptueller Rahmen zur empirischen und methodologischen Begründung einer Theorie der Vergesellschaftung.* Neuwied, Germany: Luchterhand.

Goffman, Erving (1983). The Interaction Order. *American Sociological Review, 48/1,* 1–17.

Kaufmann, Jean-Claude (2000). Rolle und Identität: Begriffliche Klärungen am Beispiel von Paarbeziehungen. *Sozialer Sinn, 2000/1,* 67–91.

Krappmann, Lothar (1973 [1969]). *Soziologische Dimensionen der Identität. Strukturelle Bedingungen für die Teilnahme an Interaktionsprozessen.* Stuttgart, Germany: Klett. See especially: Identität und Rolle, pp. 97–131.

Linton, Ralph (1947). *The Cultural Background of Personality.* London, UK: Routledge & Kegan Paul. See especially: Social Structure and Culture Participation, pp. 36–54.

Luhmann, Niklas (2013 [1997]). *Theory of Society*. 2nd sub-volume. Stanford, CA: Stanford University Press.

Merton, Robert K. (1957). The Role-Set: Problems in Sociological Theory. *The British Journal of Sociology, 8/2*, 106–120.

Parsons, Talcott (1991 [1951]). *The Social System*. New York: The Free Press.

Popitz, Heinrich (1967). *Der Begriff der sozialen Rolle als Element der soziologischen Theorie*. Tübingen, Germany: Mohr.

7

NORMS AND RULES

How we measure social action

In sociology the significance of norms and roles for the social order is a given, but the theoretical exploration of social norms is often subordinated to the sociological interest in deviance and crime. In a classic example of "negative definition," social norms are discerned from the sanctioning of deviation from the norm, usually in the form of punishment. It would be easy to conclude from this that members of society adhere to norms because they otherwise risk punishment, and in the behaviorist tradition the corresponding argument is that sanctions condition members of society to conform to norms. This chapter, however, will not be concerned with conformity and deviation, but with what social norms contribute to interaction, and how they structure interaction. Theoretical concepts dealing with the structuring quality of norms can be found in the work of Talcott Parsons, Claude Lévi-Strauss, Niklas Luhmann and Heinrich Popitz.

In everyday life we encounter the concept of the norm in various places. The first thing that occurs to us may be ISO norms or EU norms. Of course when we speak of norms in sociology, we are not talking about the length of bananas, the size of sheets of paper or the diameter of screw anchors. But technical standards of this kind can also be used to illustrate the significance of social norms. If bananas are needed for a cake recipe, if a sheet of paper has to be folded to the size of an envelope or the right screw has to be found for a screw anchor, then we naturally assume that a certain number of bananas is required for a certain quantity of flour, that a specific envelope fits a specific sheet of writing paper, and that a particular screw fits into a particular screw anchor. Here the existence of norms saves us from having to start from scratch every time, thinking about and testing options – we only have to imagine what the everyday working life of a builder would be if, for every screw she wanted to use, she had to first test every available screw anchor to see if they fit. Social norms perform exactly the same function: they save us from having to develop new courses of action for every new situation if we want to accomplish something (cf. Bahrdt 1984).

Although social norms cannot be expressed in kilograms or centimeters, they can still be clearly named: norms are manifest social rules, which means that they are reflexively available to us. We will come back to this later. The first point we want to make here is that a norm, as a behavioral rule, does not describe what we ought to do, but what we are required to do: it does not express a possible way to behave, but prescribes a behavior (cf. ibid.). As a result, the concept of the norm as a rule of conduct may strike us as obsolete in a modern, plural, individualistic society; of course we obey laws, but beyond that, surely, everyone can do what they want. Or can they?

For example, there is no law stipulating how we have to behave when we want to enter a room with a closed door, in which we presume another person to be present. Nonetheless, we all behave the same way in this situation: we knock and wait to hear "Come in!" Such behavioral norms exist even in regions where rooms or indeed buildings do not usually have any doors – in the Swahili-speaking region of East Africa, for example, one draws attention to oneself by calling out "Hodi!" (roughly translatable as "May I come in?") in front of the open entrance, and waiting for the answer, "Karibu!" ("Welcome!"). If this rule is broken – if we simply go in without knocking – nobody is going to call the police, we will not be taken to court, and there is no "authority" that could be called upon to enforce the rule's validity. At most, the other person will simply respond with "Would you mind knocking before you come in?" That would be bearable, and we might even be able to give a reason for not knocking. So why do we knock? And why do we need to give reasons for not doing so? Why do we not make use of our universal freedom of choice and decide on each occasion whether to knock or not, depending on our mood and needs at the time?

Another example is rules about how to dress on particular occasions, which seem to have largely lost their force in modern, pluralistic, individualized society. It seems that everyone can go around looking however they like – what counts is their own taste, and what they themselves find attractive, practical, comfortable or appealing. And indeed, these days a man does not necessarily have to wear a tie to a formal occasion, or a woman a dress. There are doctors who do not wear white coats, at least in private practices, and students who attend lectures in sports clothes. And yet we are not as "free" in our clothing-related behavior as we might think. For example, the occasions on which we would appear in a bikini or bathing trunks are limited, even on very hot summer days. And it simply feels wrong to attend a funeral dressed in bold, bright colors. Why does this bother us? Why, on a hot day, do we not go to the bank in our swimming trunks to get investment advice, and why – if black does not suit us, and we cannot stand the color – do we not wear a pretty yellow dress to a funeral?

Personal hygiene is another example which shows that we certainly do not always do what we want: of course we might occasionally go out in public with greasy hair, or with dirty, smelly clothes, but we do not feel comfortable doing so. We expect others to look askance at us, or even to demonstratively keep their distance from us. We tend to explain our personal hygiene rationally, in terms of susceptibility to and the transmission of diseases, but if I have not washed my hair for three days or have a large ketchup stain on my trousers, I am sensible enough to know that I am not exposing myself and others to any risk of disease. So why should it matter to me and to others?

And lastly, let us look at the example of waiting in line: if a concert that I desperately want to see is sold out, and I hear that there are still tickets available on the night, I will hurry to the box office. If I find that there are already hundreds of people waiting in line at the box office, then I either join the back of the line in the hope that there will still be a ticket left when I reach the front, or I go home again, because the likelihood of getting a ticket seems too slim. But I do not push in, and I do not use violent or fraudulent means to gain a place near the front of the line. Why do I not ensure that my own interests – urgent and important as they are – are met here? And why do I expect indignant or even angry behavior from others if I do so after all?

The examples show two things: on the one hand, there is no law that would legally sanction our potentially divergent behavior in the situations mentioned. If the laws of a constitutional state are, as it were, codified social norms (like rules and regulations, but potentially with different scope and different consequences when they are contravened), then there is legal security concerning the rules that are in force. I can look them up in law books and invoke them formally at any time, and there are authorities I can appeal to in order to assert my rights. But in areas where human behavior is not regulated by laws, rules and regulations, and rules of conduct are not enforced by any competent bodies, this certainly does not mean that behavior is disordered and random. There are a large number of rules of social conduct that are not normatively binding in a formalized sense, but nonetheless have normative force. On the other hand, the binding nature of the normative rules of social behavior is not something that is only imposed on us from outside; instead, it is something that we ourselves have internalized to such an extent that we *know* when we are contravening these norms. In the case of such rules I am, as it were, my own social corrective: I am conscious of my divergent behavior, and I either feel fundamentally uncomfortable with it, or I must at least be able to legitimize it "to myself." Because this is readily accessible knowledge, I do not have to laboriously recall how normatively appropriate or inappropriate action in a given situation might be constituted. For this reason, a breach of the norm is identifiable, and some form of sanction will be given in response: reprimands, abuse, physical distance, indignant frowns, bewildered questions, etc. All these things are already sanctions, which not only serve to highlight divergence from the norm, but also contain the expectation that the other person will correct himself or herself (cf. Popitz 2006/2017) – whether directly, in the form of an apology or explanation, or indirectly, in a future change of behavior.

Claude Lévi-Strauss (1963 [1958], p. 287) describes norms as "conscious models" of social structure, and in this sense as an expression of the manner in which a society interprets its own social order. On the one hand, we can understand this as meaning that social norms reflect society's consensus about how social order is to be created. The conscious, model-like character of norms thus points to their quality as principles of orientation, which are, as it were, schematically and objectively accessible, and which thereby generate structure. On the other hand, of course, this also indicates that social order is created and stabilized by far more than just the norms we are conscious of; rather, these constitute only that part of the social order which is available to us in the form of interpretations. This means that while society defines itself via norms – in the form of rules, regulations and laws – societal structure can nonetheless not be explained purely through norms. We have already observed in Chapter 3, with reference to Searle (2010), that socially pre-established solutions to problems take the form of "institutions," which relieve the individual members of society from the burden of decision-making. The institutions themselves – marriage, money, private property, the office, etc. – first appear as abstract, mediated figures, which do not yet present any behavioral requirements in the form of "solutions to problems." It is only the regulative rules associated with the institution that directly lift the burden of decision-making. We, therefore, distinguish between constitutive rules, which produce social practice, and regulative rules, which regulate social practice (cf. ibid.; cf. Searle 1969). We can further classify a large proportion of social norms as *manifest* regulative rules, whose main feature is that sanctions can be imposed if they are not obeyed. With the potential for sanctions, the regulative character of the norm is already established, because this implies that a deviation from the norm does not make the social practice itself impossible, but "merely" disrupts its orderly execution. This is restored by means of the sanction, on the basis of a fundamental consensus that the norm applicable in the framework of a social practice always marks what is "right." In our example from Chapter 3, when one team on the all-purpose sports field is playing basketball, and the team designated as the opposition is playing soccer, the one team is not "right" and the other "wrong;" it is not possible to identify a norm from which one team is deviating and the other is not. There is no sanction that could forcibly bring about an orderly execution, because, from the outset, no shared social practice comes about, and it is, therefore, impossible to identify any clear regulations valid for all the players. In this sense, social norms cannot be constitutive of social practice, but can "only" regulate practices that already exist. The capacity for sanctions also means that, in this framework, the rule is acknowledged by all the participants – in fact, one of the main ways we recognize sanctions is that they are understood and accepted as such by all those involved (cf. Bahrdt 1984). We can resist them, defend ourselves or even pretend we have not noticed them, but we cannot interpret them as anything other than what they are – we cannot, for example, treat them as praise or compliments. As Searle (1969) argues, then, social norms are regulative rules (see Chapter 3), which do not constitute a practice themselves, but mark the different behaviors that can occur within the framework of a social practice as expected/normal or unexpected/abnormal. In other words, behavior that conforms to rules is not clearly and exclusively a result of the rule, but could be observed even without this rule – even without an existing norm, people could knock on doors, dress in dark colors at funerals, keep themselves clean or join the back of a line; these are not behaviors that would not exist without the norm. But precisely because norms are regulative rules, they can always, a priori, be either one way or the other, they do not arise "inevitably" from the social practice itself – rules such as whether we eat with knives and forks or with our fingers, whether we generally shake hands when greeting people, or do not do so, or make this dependent on certain criteria,[1] whether we address teachers, superiors or even our parents formally or informally,[2] etc. Thus the social relationship or situation is not created by the rule, but modified by it. Constitutive rules therefore provide room for maneuver, but norms determine what actions are socially desirable within this "room."

For their part, *manifest* regulative rules are social norms because we are conscious of them and because they are reflexively available to us as behavioral requirements. Social norms may be habitualized, self-evident obligations, which we have internalized to the point that we follow them without having to think about them. In cases of deviation, however, we can always identify the exact nature of the deviation (cf. Popitz 2006/2017). In interaction, norms operate as normative expectations – in cases of disappointment, we insist on their importance (cf. Luhmann 1995 [1984]). On the one hand, this means that the expectation is not subjectively corrected and readjusted to fit each situation; on the other hand, though, it also means that if expectations are disappointed this leads to sanctions, as we have already seen (cf. Bahrdt 1984; Popitz 2006/2017). The potential for norm violations to be sanctioned is treated as central by many authors; here we will go so far as to say that it is *only* possible to speak of a deviation from a norm when divergent behavior leads to a sanction. This means, first and foremost, that norms are enforced; this is why the sanction has to make it clear what the wrongdoing was. The sanction refers to the norm that has been violated, because the aim of the sanction is to enforce the norm (cf. Popitz 2006/2017), and the highlighting of the norm by means of the sanction or "punishment" restores the norm. Violations of the law are of course the clearest cases of norm violations. Laws are formalized norms; the idea is that nothing can become a law that has not previously existed as a social norm. In contrast to norms, however, violations of the law can only be sanctioned by certain institutions of criminal justice. And insofar as laws are also norms, norms that do not take the form of laws cannot be enforced by executive and judicial bodies.

Latent regulative rules, on the other hand, cover that area of regular mechanisms of interaction which we are not conscious of, and which can therefore not come into play in the form of normative expectations. Here we can follow

Goffman (1983) in observing that very few rules which help to create the order of interaction have an intrinsic value – i.e. possess an ethic or moral force in and of themselves. This may be the reason why we are not conscious of most of the rules of interaction that we follow. If the rules of ratification, of turn-taking, of self-correction and correction by others, or of reciprocity were not observed in an interaction, we might notice this, but we would not be able to identify the rule that is being broken. These are not social norms like knocking on the door or observing particular dress codes. Nonetheless, the "latent" social rules are part of a normative social order, because they distinguish between conformity and deviation – but because of their "preconscious" nature, they do not imply any clear chances of sanctions.

We have also already established, however, that social norms are in a certain sense arbitrary – they could just as easily take another form. Very few of the norms we encounter are obvious and "logical" in a literal sense, and arise from the situation that they regulate. In fact, social norms instead seem to prevent us from drawing the "logical" consequences from the given situations – opening a closed door when I want to go through it, taking my clothes off if I am hot, leaving my dirty trousers on because I cannot be bothered to change them and pushing to the front of the box office line when I want a concert ticket. Seen in this light, one might think that social norms (including laws, rules and regulations) stop us from proceeding efficiently and economically, and acting in a way that maximizes the benefit to ourselves. But is this the case? We have repeatedly observed that norms relieve us of the burden of making decisions: not only do they save us from constantly having to make choices, but also from having to justify and assert these choices. Furthermore, we assume that applicable social norms are equally valid for all those involved; they do not restrict us as individuals, but regulate our joint actions, and thereby create more and not less coordination and therefore convenience (cf. Goffman 1983). Finally, and for this reason, we should not underestimate the fact that we do not adhere to most norms and rules because we would otherwise be punished. We refrain from the majority of "punishable" actions not because they are punishable, but because of the quality of the action itself, which contravenes values whose rightness we acknowledge and whose validity we approve of (more on this later). That means that our actions cannot be guided solely by our present aims and our desire to avoid certain things, but that there must be some principle applicable beyond this, something that cannot be arbitrarily redefined from one situation to the next.

At this point, it makes sense to return to the connection between social norms and social roles. In the previous chapter, we avoided the concept of the norm, although the relevant literature frequently mentions "role norms" and "behavioral norms." Instead, we worked with the concept of expectation, distinguishing between normative and cognitive expectations (cf. Luhmann 1995 [1984]). The reason we initially gave was that, from a microsociological perspective, role expectations are always expectations about the interaction between the role incumbents, and are expressed in this interaction, but that at the same time social interaction is characterized by a high level of contingency, and always has the potential for dissent and conflict. Even if there are norms of role behavior, their actual normative power to impose order in the interaction is rather opaque, and their effect is weaker the less the person one is interacting with is perceived as a generalized, anonymized other (see Chapter 6). Now, as we turn our attention to social norms, we can explain why this is so. For one thing, norms offer no scope for different possibilities or for personal judgment. We cannot partially submit to a norm, or interpret it as we see fit. Social norms can only be followed or not followed, adhered to or not adhered to. In this, they are similar to regulations and laws, even if they are not set down in writing. So I can either go to the back of the line (observing the social norm) or push in (contravening the norm), but there is no gray area, no middle ground, no room for maneuver.[3] In other words, if it is clear what the underlying norm is, it is also clear what constitutes a norm violation. However, it is not always as easy to decide what the applicable norm is as it is in the case of waiting in line. Civil law disputes often arise when it is not obvious which norm is applicable, or what is covered by the applicable norm in specific cases – for example when it comes to claims for rent reduction or matters of inheritance. We can say, however, that the "gray areas" do not affect the norms themselves (which are always "valid"), but only, where relevant, their specific areas of application and their scope. For another thing, social norms do not compete with each other (at least within a society or its collectives). Norms are always clear and exclusive, and we are always aware of this clarity and exclusiveness. There are not two different norms for knocking or for waiting in line, of which we have to choose which has more weight in a given situation. If roles were "normed" in this sense (as discussed in the previous chapter), then participants could not "legitimately" interpret their reciprocal expectations of their role partner in different ways, because it would always be clear whose interpretation was normatively "correct." Thus when different people reconstruct someone's behavior, their "interpretations" may diverge.

The large field of regulative rules must be differentiated from what we shall refer to here as "habits" (cf. Popitz 2006/2017).[4] Because firstly, not everything that becomes consolidated as "normality" is in actual fact established as the only "right" way to behave. In many societies, for example, it is no longer a violation of the social norm for an unmarried couple to live together, or for children to be born "out of wedlock." That is, in large parts of society this behavior is not subject to derogatory judgments and does not call forth any sanctions; it has become "normal," which is not to say that it is marked as the only right and socially desirable behavior. Secondly, not every regular and rule-governed behavior is actually also socially normed behavior. Most people, for example, will arrange their CDs and books in some sort of order on their shelves (alphabetical order, genres, etc.), and for many of us this kind of order is so important that we always adhere to it – a new book is not simply placed at the end of the row, but is inserted where it belongs, according to our system. But of course we know that behavior that deviates from this is not sanctionable – after all, it is nobody's business whether and how we arrange our books. There are many habits that we turn into rules for ourselves, though we could not claim universal validity for them or demand the same from others – for example, doing ten minutes of exercises every morning, donating €50 to charity every month or separating white clothes from colored clothes when we do the washing. Here too, we accept that what is "applicable" for us does not have to apply to others. Violations of our "own" rules are therefore only sanctionable to the extent that we "punish" ourselves – for example if we skip our morning exercises and then go without a chocolate bar at midday to make up for it. When Bahrdt (1984), in his book "Schlüsselbegriffe der Soziologie" ("Key concepts of sociology"), says that a norm fixes aspects of human behavior that are not yet fixed in other ways, then this can only apply in relation to a social order and thus to the common interest of the members of society. Those things that do not fall into the area of the common interest – as they neither stabilize nor disrupt the social order – are often governed by rules, but are not structured by social norms. Here, however, Luhmann (1995 [1984]) points out that the commitment of members of society to norms can probably not be ascribed to the fact that humans in general value a social order; rather, it is the risky nature of social interaction and the likelihood of disappointment that make it necessary to generalize behavioral expectations by means of norms. We can take this to mean that there is a mutual need to limit reciprocal uncertainties about expectations, so that interaction can proceed successfully. As we have heard in the previous chapters, this is achieved on the one hand through a reduction of complexity in the interaction itself, but on the other hand by means of generalized, normative expectations, which we "bring with us" into the interaction. Here, according to Luhmann (ibid., p. 95), it is the "meaning-specific function" of the generalization to keep meaning "accessible at each specific moment of meaning." In accordance with this, the "meaning" of the norm outlasts situations and events, but also the specific people we are dealing with. It is precisely for this reason that norms operate as "generalizations that must be retained counterfactually" (ibid., p. 326), which we rely on even when we cannot observe them in the given situation. If we see a stampede at the box office, with people jostling and pushing each other aside in order to get one of the last highly-coveted concert tickets, we do not take this as proof that the norm of "joining the back of the line" is invalid; we do not conclude that this norm is not (or no longer) applicable, and has no "meaning." On the contrary, this example at least seems to demonstrate the meaning of the norm, if it stops people from disrespecting and injuring each other in the reckless pursuit of their own needs. We can also see from this example that there is sometimes a very obvious link between norms and "values."

Parsons (1961 [1937]) famously highlighted this connection in his exploration of normative order. The basic assumption, as we have already discussed in the previous chapter, is that the social order is based on norms and values shared by the members of society, and that these norms and values pre-structure collective goals for action. Here values, which precede norms, are comprehensive culturally specific ideas about what should be regarded as useful, desirable and worthwhile for all members of society – for example, health, freedom, equality or prosperity. But these examples also show us that values, in their universality, only describe very general conditions or qualities. As in the case of institutions, they contain no concrete instructions for action – though values are even more general in nature, especially as their implementation or preservation in the diverse institutions can be manifested exclusively or in parallel. We assume that norms – in obvious or in very subtle ways – relate to values. Here too, they differ from what we have called "latent" regulative rules, for which we can neither consciously define violations, nor determine the value that underlies them. What value, for example, underlies the social norm of a clean, tidy appearance? We have already established that "health" cannot be the crucial factor here, if we are talking about dirty clothes or unwashed hair. This only applies, however, in the conditions of a highly technicized, "medicalized" society, where hygiene conditions have been optimized, e.g. through vaccinations against diseases, and regulations on cleanliness designed to stop the spread of pathogens. This means we can assume that "cleanliness" or "tidiness" are not cultural values, but social norms, which have their historical origins in the value placed on health, and which retain their validity even when there is currently, from a "scientific" viewpoint, no danger to health. In this sense, values serve to (latently) maintain structures ("latent pattern maintenance"), and manifest themselves via norms in the framework of situations and functions. Thus it is our commitment to cultural values – an explicitly voluntary commitment, in Parsons's view (cf. ibid.) – that allows us to formulate rules and objectives for action in the form of norms, and to use these for orientation.

In light of this notion of voluntariness (cf. Parsons's "voluntaristic theory of action") we can also explain, finally, why the scope of norms within a society can be defined not just in general, but also in particular terms (cf. Popitz 2006/2017). General norms apply to all members of society, who, on the basis of an assumption of equality, are subject to the same behavioral requirements – as in our opening examples. Particular norms, on the other hand, are based on non-commonalities of groups within society; certain groups allow the enforcement of specific normative expectations which cannot be transferred to all members of society. In secularized societies, this applies, for example, to the many different religious communities, where there are numerous behavioral requirements that are normative in character, and are imposed as binding within the group, but have no importance for the "rest of society." What is important here is that there is a "group public" (Popitz 2017, p. 9) in which the norm is enforced. This is achieved by categorizing subjectively different actions, situations and events as objectively homogeneous: the generally applicable behavioral norm "joining the back of the line" applies to every "waiting" situation in which several people are unable to carry out the same activity at the same time, e.g. buying something at a shop counter, getting into a bus, waiting in a waiting room, etc. The particular behavioral norm of "crossing oneself" when entering a church has the same universal force – it only applies to a particular group, but for this group, it applies in all of its churches, every day, and under any conditions. We can, therefore, say that norms "typify" particular actions, situations and events in such a way that compliant behavior can be presupposed in the form of consensual expectations (cf. ibid.). Here the degree of validity of norms is dependent not least on the willingness of the members of society to protect them, in the future as well as the present (cf. ibid.) – though admittedly such a "willingness" can only be expressed when a norm is actually violated. This becomes particularly clear in the case of media reporting about norm violations as "scandals," a topic addressed by Luhmann (2000 [1996]) in his work "The Reality of the Mass Media." What this generates is a "feeling of common concern and outrage" (ibid., p. 29), which is designed to indirectly strengthen the norm – not in its directly perceptible non-observance, but in the way it is reported. The shared feeling of outrage is, in this sense, not a proper sanction, but the expression of a willingness to protect the norm. The possibility of scandalization also shows that norms must be accessible as general attitudes, even if they are not explicitly applied: "the norm is actually only generated through the violation, whereas before it simply 'existed' in the mass of existing norms" (ibid., p. 29).

FOOD FOR THOUGHT

Refer to your transcript of the café scene from *As Good As It Gets*. Melvin asserts: "I mean, you know, if his parents are alive, I mean, they have to help. It's the rules." But is this true? Is there a social norm that parents have to financially support their adult children? Think about whether parents have to expect any sanctions if they do not support their adult children, and if so what sanctions. Who (what social group or organization) might be expected to impose such sanctions? And could parents who refuse to financially support their adult children perhaps invoke "rules" themselves?

Notes

1 In some cultures, for example, the norm is that men and women who do not know each other do not shake each other's hands. We can also imagine that handshaking is not a customary greeting in youth peer groups, and that it would tend to constitute a violation of the norm if one were to attempt to do so.

2 In the Netherlands it was customary for children to address their parents with the formal word for "you" as late as the 1960s.

3 Which does not mean that we always have to make our pushing in recognizable as such. For example, we can go and stand with someone we know, who has secured a place near the front of the line, start a conversation with him, and move forwards with him. But such behaviors are not evidence of any gray areas, they are simply a strategic attempt to conceal the norm violation.

4 Another possible way to differentiate between rules is the further division into conventions, customs, traditions, etiquette etc. (cf. Bahrdt 1984). However, these demarcations are largely arbitrary, and the terms and definitions sometimes overlap. For example, Tönnies (2001 [1935]) does not distinguish norms from rules etc., but "conventions" (as positive regulations and rules of all kinds for the sake of the general good) from "customs" (*Sitten*) (one does things in the same way they have always been done). Weber (2013 [1922]), on the other hand, understands the "ethical norm" as an abstract standard of behavior, whose binding force is expressed in "conventions."

References

Bahrdt, Hans Paul (1984). *Schlüsselbegriffe der Soziologie. Eine Einführung mit Lehrbeispielen.* 5th edn. Munich, Germany: C.H. Beck. See especially: Soziale Normen (Wertvorstellungen, Verhaltensregelmäßigkeiten, Verhaltenserwartungen, Normenkonflikte, Normenwandel), pp. 48–65.

Popitz, Heinrich (2006). *Soziale Normen.* Friedrich Pohlmann & Wolfgang Eßbach (Eds.). Frankfurt a. M., Germany: Suhrkamp.

Popitz, Heinrich (2017 [2006]). Social Norms. Translation of "Soziale Normen," pp. 61–75. *Genocide Studies and Prevention, 11/2,* 5–12.

Searle, John R. (1969). *Speech Acts. An Essay in the Philosophy of Language.* Cambridge, UK: Cambridge University Press. See especially: Rules, pp. 33–42.

Further reading

Goffman, Erving (1983). The Interaction Order. *American Sociological Review, 48/1,* 1–17.

Lévi-Strauss, Claude (1963 [1958]). *Structural Anthropology.* New York: Basic Books. See especially: Social Structure, pp. 277–323.

Luhmann, Niklas (1995 [1984]). *Social Systems.* Stanford, CA: Stanford University Press. See especially: Structure and Time, pp. 278–356.

Luhmann, Niklas (2000 [1996]). *The Reality of the Mass Media.* Cambridge, UK: Polity Press. See especially: News and In-depth Reporting, pp. 25–41.

Parsons, Talcott (1961 [1937]). *The Structure of Social Action. A Study in Social Theory with Special Reference to a Group of Recent European Writers.* New York: McGraw-Hill.

Searle, John R. (2010). *Making the Social World. The Structure of Human Civilization.* Oxford, UK: Oxford University Press.

Tönnies, Ferdinand (2001 [1935]). *Community and Civil Society.* Cambridge, UK: Cambridge University Press.

Weber, Max (2013 [1922]). *Economy and Society.* Berkeley, CA: University of California Press.

8

FRAMING

How we know what we have to do

Framing is a term coined by Erving Goffman, and his frame analysis is used in many fields of research in sociology. This specific perspective on social situations and social interactions offers an analytical approach to something that usually remains unconscious and obscure in interaction: the culturally shaped background knowledge that we apply to social situations, and on the basis of which we assess, categorize and cope with these situations. So one of our concerns in this chapter is the question of "intercultural communication," or interaction between group members and people outside the group. Here John J. Gumperz's pioneering works on this topic serve to explore the linguistic dimension of framing in particular.

In light of the previous chapters, we might think that the above title makes this chapter seem superfluous. Surely we know "what we have to do" by now – we know the foundations of interaction and the structural features of sequentiality, we know the importance of institutions, we have discussed the mechanisms of reciprocity and of perspective-taking and have examined the function and characteristics of social roles and the efficacy and scope of social norms and rules. All this put together seems to give a fairly good picture of "how we know what we have to do."

We must bear in mind, however, that the majority of the rules and mechanisms discussed previously are not part of our "manifest," accessible knowledge. From a scientific, observing perspective, we can describe, define and categorize these mechanisms and rules, but in social interaction they are not consciously accessible to us – and this is even more true of our assumptions and expectations which precede interaction, and relate to the given social situation in itself.

Our large repertoire of background knowledge about social situations plays an important but obscure role in the immediate interaction.

So far we have only defined the social situation in very basic terms, in line with Goffman, as the physical meeting of at least two individuals who are perceptible to each other. In this chapter, we are guided by the fundamental assumption that the meeting of individuals is "framed" in a particular way and that this framing defines the social situation regardless of the individuals involved. In the following discussion we will look closely at Erving Goffman's (1986 [1974]) *Frame Analysis*[1] and John Gumperz's (1982) *Discourse Strategies*.[2] First, however, we shall try to approach the "framing" of interactions from an "exotic" research perspective.

For many years, the framing of situations was a problematic issue for classical ethnology, sometimes dramatically so, without being acknowledged as such. We can easily imagine that encounters with members of a totally unfamiliar culture on their own terrain constitute a challenge for interaction, in many respects. We do not speak the language, and do not know the prevailing norms; we are unfamiliar with the organization of society; functions and roles are not associated with the same expectations as in our own culture. It becomes especially difficult for us if we are not simply passing through, or wishing to spend a few days in a distant place as tourists, but want to learn something about this society; if we want to study it and find out how social order is created and structured in cultures that are completely foreign to us. It is probably thanks to ethnology that we as social scientists are now aware – and take this into account in our research – that even with the best intentions we do not encounter the new and the unknown as neutral scientists, but as people formed in a particular culture, with particular ideas and experiences of how society "works" (cf. Agar 1980). We are not blank slates, or sponges that absorb new impressions without filtering. Ethnology reached this insight in a roundabout way, by acknowledging the sometimes huge contradictions between the reports of different ethnographers conducting research into the same society. Prominent examples of this are the ethnographies of the Yanomami, and the ethnographic analyses of a village community in Tepoztlán (Mexico). The latter has gone down in ethnological history as the "Redfield-Lewis debate," named after the 2 researchers Oscar Lewis and Robert Redfield, who studied this village community 20 years apart (in the 1920s and 1940s) and arrived at completely different conclusions. Redfield (whose research findings were published in 1930) presented the society of Tepoztlán as a harmonious community characterized by homogeneity and collectivity, while Lewis (whose findings were published in 1951) interpreted the culture in Tepoztlán as conflict-ridden and shaped by struggles for power and territory (cf. Agar 1980). A similar problem arose with research on the society of the Yanomami, who live in the border area between Venezuela and Brazil: the reports of the ethnologists conducting research there, Otto Zerries, Napoleon Chagnon and Jacques Lizot, painted utterly different pictures of the Yanomami – as a "transitional people" between hunter-gatherers and agriculturalists, as a wild, warlike people and as a harmonious, permissive society (cf. Häusler 1997).[3]

Now how is it possible for researchers to reach such different conclusions about the same subject? One problem we can identify is methodology, when different data are gathered and analyzed on the same subject. Otto Zerries, for example, focused on the quantitative analysis of artefacts, which he collected during his stay with the Yanomami; in fact his main interest during his field work seems to have been in their material culture, sometimes with little regard for what the objects he collected meant for the Yanomami in their everyday practices (cf. Häusler 1997).[4] In such collections, of the kind we see in many ethnological museums today, utensils become artifacts, that is, the focus is not on their use, but on the way they are made. We can readily classify a culture in which there are dozens of sorts of spearhead as one where hunting (or war) is especially important. But would we classify a culture in which there are dozens of types of food storage container as one where the storage of leftover food was of particular importance? Would this then be a culture in which food was particularly valued or even one where food was scarce? When it comes to our own culture, in which we have grown up and which has shaped us, we would probably tend to make our understanding of "artefacts" dependent on their use as "utensils." At the same time, we might find it difficult to explain to someone why there are so many sorts of food storage container in an "affluent," "throwaway" society. Thus as adult humans with a specific cultural background, we have strong presuppositions about artifacts, which come from our experiences with them as utensils (by observation or by using them ourselves). We can associate familiar objects with social situations, and identify social situations by means of the objects that appear in them. It is not necessary, however, to be able to consciously assign an overarching "cultural" significance to the objects. In fact, we can see, from the comparison between spearheads and food storage containers, that "cultural categorizations" seem more compelling to us the less familiar the objects are; we resort to them mainly when we have little personal experience of the artifacts in question as utensils.

Chagnon, for his part, investigated the culture of the Yanomami by the method of participant observation, and by way of his personal, subjective experience. In his research reports, he himself is the central actor, toward whom the Yanomami were distrustful or even hostile from the start, making him very aware of his position as an outsider. He also exploited animosities between the villages to persuade his subjects to talk about the inhabitants of enemy villages (cf. ibid.). Thus the hostility and aggressiveness which he himself experienced became one of the leitmotifs of his investigations; not least from his subjective experience, he developed his specific understanding of the Yanomami culture, as one dominated by aggression, ferocity and pugnacity.[5] Now we might intuitively say that our understanding of "social situations" is obviously always shaped by our subjective experiences. But we also realize that, in our own culture, we are quite capable of separating our subjective experience from the "objective meaning" of the situation. We "know," for example, what a job interview, a trip in an elevator, or a game of ice hockey "is," and are not solely reliant on our subjective, immediate experience in order to "understand" social situations. What is more, we would not generalize our subjective experience in the form of a "cultural interpretation," because the relevant schemata of interpretation are already available to us. If we are not familiar with these schemata, however, it is at the very least difficult to avoid including our personal experience as an immanent part of the social reality that presents itself to us.

Lizot, lastly, also conducted his research as a participant observer, but expressly rejected the aim of explaining the Yanomami culture in sociological terms, and instead undertook to describe them "from the inside out." He did not want to focus his investigation on how he experienced things, but on how the people he encountered experienced things. At least in his research reports, he completely minimizes his role as a participant, and gives the impression that he is documenting the Yanomami culture in a kind of "self-description," by projecting himself into the individuals and even describing their feelings and thoughts. Evidently, he became so close to the people during his stay that he was even able to depict sexual acts from his own perspective (cf. ibid.). Does this mean that his impression – that the Yanomami are a harmonious, permissive society – is the "most authentic"? Häusler (ibid.) instead concludes that Lizot is deliberately selective in his reports in order to give this impression. Even if this is not necessarily the result of Lizot's subjective experience (as in the case of Chagnon), it is probably due to his obvious enthusiasm for a society in which sexuality was apparently not taboo – or at least not in the same way as it was in his own culture at the time he was staying with the Yanomami. This shows the impact of our culture on the way we, as fully socialized members of society, look at other societies: it can (and usually does, unconsciously) make us relate the new things we experience to what we know already, and judge them accordingly, be it positively or negatively.

What is interesting for us here is that, taken together, these various approaches to a foreign culture – via objective materiality, subjective experience and (potentially unconscious) comparisons to one's own culture – provide a good description of what becomes relevant for us in social situations. Each situation "consists" of its physical, material reality, of the subjective interpretations of the individual and of generally applicable schemata of interpretation, which are available to all the members of the society in question. When we find ourselves in a foreign society, we can, of course, perceive it in its materiality, and experience it subjectively, but what we lack, at first, is access to the schemata of interpretation that are generalized here.

And this is what is crucial. We interpret the situation according to generalizable categories, which we do not define ourselves, and which are not part of the immediate interaction. That is, we do not produce the situation by our arrival, but we come upon something which we categorize in a particular, predefined way, from which we then draw conscious conclusions and also generate unconscious behaviors (cf. Goffman 1986 [1974]). When we say that "different peoples have different customs," we are referring to the problem that the categories we use to interpret social situations are culturally prefabricated, and may be different in other cultures. The dilemma is that we cannot simply adjust to new situations, but are reliant on the frames that are familiar to us. These are so firmly embedded that even if we explicitly undertake to be "unprejudiced," this is not possible. As stated previously, this presents a challenge for ethnology: research findings must always be tested to see how much the analysis is influenced by the culturally predefined "frames" of the interaction with the people being studied.

Like Goffman (1986 [1974]), we will take frames to mean principles for the organization of interaction, which allow us to categorize and comprehend situations. Even in social contexts that are completely unfamiliar to us, framing enables us to give meaning to aspects of a situation that would otherwise be meaningless. Goffman uses the expression "primary frameworks" (ibid., p. 21) to refer to classes of schemata which are related to each other in a particular way, and serve as a basis for the members of society to develop an understanding of their social world. It is only with the help of such schemata of interpretation – Gumperz (1982, p. 131) speaks of a "channelling of information" – that social events can be located, perceived, identified and categorized: they are not based on interpretations that we have already undertaken as individuals, but make these interpretations available a priori to all members of the given society. We see this especially from the fact that, when first assessing a situation, we do not reflect on the meaning of most aspects of the situation; no cognitive loop takes place, in which we first distinguish the meaning of the chair from that of the table, or contemplate the significance of another person's presence. Thus we are guided by a "background understanding" of the social situation, which allows us to accept the conditions and consequences of our own and others' behavior as given, more or less without reflection, in the form of categorical standards (cf. Goffman 1986 [1974]). Framings also fix the direction of our attention in a particular way, making us unconsciously separate the main events of the social situation from the secondary events. This focusing is only possible because a certain weighting is present from the start; for example, we pay attention to the events on the stage and not to the parallel events in row seven of the auditorium, without having to think about what might be "more important" or "more relevant."[6]

We can get a clearer idea of the extent to which framing affects our understanding of situations and events by looking at one of Goffman's examples (ibid.). Imagine a woodcutter who is sawing up a tree, and a magician who is performing the trick of sawing a person in half on stage. The act of sawing is, from a technical point of view, the same, but the framing within which it takes place gives us clear indications of why we understand the one as "real" and the other as "fabricated." In the latter case, this includes the fact that the action takes place in front of an audience, and that the person carrying out the action is a magician, and dressed for the part. We, therefore, know from the outset that this is not "really" a person being sawn in half, but a trick designed to make us believe this. Even if we consider that the trick could go wrong, we await the outcome of the action – we do not run out of the room screaming and call the police. Here the nature of the performance is a component of the social framing, which we do not have to interpret in this specific situation in order to know what is happening. Here too, of course, we can once again note that other cultural schemata of interpretation in other societies could permit a completely different interpretation of the situation – for example as a public execution. The possibility of distinguishing between "real" and "fabricated" sawing also shows, however, that frames can be modulated if the "original" meaning of an action is transformed in the context of games, experiments, parodies, ceremonies, etc. The important thing here is that the transformation of the frame is also a framing, which provides us with prefabricated schemata of interpretation. But these do not have to be fixed and static, as we discussed in Chapter 5 with reference to the Nixon example; Goffman (1981) uses this example in his reflections on "footing" to point out the possibility that even unambiguously framed situations can be transformed in the immediate interaction itself by a change in the attitude of the participants. We must understand this, however, as a conscious, active change in the framing of the situation by the participants, which we can assume to be a fairly rare occurrence. Because the prerequisite for this does seem to be that the participant who changes the "footing" – in such a drastic way that previous definitions of the situation no longer apply – not only has a particular power over the other participants, but also misuses this power.

Different frames, then, restrict the range of possible behaviors a priori, because they prescribe certain patterns of interpretation which guide our behavior. According to Goffman (ibid.), however, the available schemata of interpretation are not relevant in the same way for all those present. To borrow another of Goffman's example, a game of chess is relevant as "chess" for those playing it, while some of the other people present may be content to identify it as a "game," and others may see it as a "cultivated pastime." One observation that particularly applies to collective social events, however, is that the social framing "brackets" the event in a distinct way:

> Activity framed in a particular way – especially collectively organized activity – is often marked off from the ongoing flow of surrounding events by a special set of boundary markers or brackets of a conventionalized kind.
> *(Goffman 1986 [1974], p. 251)*

This "bracketing" of collective undertakings is temporal and spatial in nature, and is thus not crucial for the content of the event, but for the fact that it takes place and is separate from "outside": what is happening at this place at this point in time is the event (e.g. the lesson, the work meeting, the wedding), everything else is not. At such events, we often observe ritualized introductions and terminations (cf. ibid.) – the ringing of the school bell, the team leader's greeting and farewell, the arrival and departure of the bride and groom. Such clues not only give information about the beginning and end of an event, but also signify a predefined understanding about what will happen in the meantime.[7] Thus if there is a shared understanding, preceding the concrete situation, that the ringing of the school bell signals the beginning of the lesson, then what follows will be a school lesson, and neither a work meeting nor a wedding. This is not only equally understandable for all those present, they also *rely* on it (cf. ibid.). It is possible that the framework we apply to a concrete situation does not fit – that there is something different going on from what we initially assume. In these situations, however, those directly involved must in each case signal to each other what frame the situation actually has, by means of "keying" – by indicating, for example, that it is not a real fight, but a simulated one (cf. ibid.). The difficulty many spectators have in deciding whether wrestling is a real fight or just a show is probably due to the contradictory "keys" given by the participants: there are playful exaggerations and aspects of theatrical performance, but also real blows and real injuries.

With J.J. Gumperz, we turn to the interactional dimension of framing or contextualization, and within this, the linguistic dimension. The basic assumption is as follows:

> channelling of interpretation is effected by conversational implicatures based on conventionalized co-occurrence expectations between content and surface style. That is, constellations of surface features of message form are the means by which speakers signal and listeners interpret what the activity is, how semantic content is to be understood and *how* each sentence relates to what precedes or follows. These features are referred to as *contextualization cues*. [...] Roughly speaking, a contextualization cue is any feature of linguistic form that contributes to the signalling of contextual presuppositions.
>
> *(Gumperz 1982, p. 131; emphasis in original)*

Contextual presuppositions can be realized linguistically in many different forms within the horizon of our linguistic repertoire: as linguistic registers or codes, as dialects or changes in style, in lexical or syntactic modes of expression and in the use of sayings and of strategies for opening and closing conversations. On the one hand, we use such realizations in interaction to give indications of how we understand the situation. On the other hand, the way we speak depends in equal measure on the event in question and on our interlocutors and the other participants. Every social framing of a situation, then, prescribes to a greater or lesser extent how we are to behave, linguistically, and we fulfil such conventional expectations even if we remain unaware of them. We speak differently to children than to adults, and differently to peers than to superiors; we select a different linguistic register at a conference than at a family breakfast; our linguistic behavior when we are being observed by unfamiliar third parties is different than it would be in a private conversation. Linguistic realizations are therefore a crucial aspect of social situations, to which we schematically give predefined meaning, even beyond their content. An obvious example is the speaking of dialects (here we do not mean what is commonly known as a "regional accent," but a linguistic variety). Regardless of the possibility of reduced comprehensibility

– even dialects of a standard language are not necessarily comprehensible for all speakers of the standard language – dialect speaking is, in Germany at least, limited to interactions in certain groups, that is, the speakers of the dialect in question. Thus dialect marks, from the outset, members and non-members of the group, i.e. insiders and outsiders; but while the insiders usually have the standard language in their repertoire as well, most outsiders are not proficient in the dialect. A social situation in which dialect is spoken is therefore framed in a particular way by means of this aspect – namely as an "insider interaction," for which outsiders do not have the required linguistic skills. Whatever is then treated as relevant on the level of content, the dialect is a keying signal: for both outsiders and insiders, it marks who "belongs" and who does not.

While this is a simple example of framing through language, we can also imagine events in which it is the frame of the social situation that gives us insight into how certain utterances are to be understood in certain situations. We have already addressed this question in Chapter 2 on sequentiality, where we were concerned with how "common ground" is created through interaction. With regard to the framing of situations, we can now expand this question to consider what common ground is already predefined by the social situation, and how linguistic realizations take their orientation from this. Here Gumperz (ibid.) offers the example of the utterance "Tickets, please," which can only make sense, in literal terms, in very specific contexts, i.e. in places where the possession of a ticket is mandatory (especially when using public transport). Outside such a context, the utterance appears to make little sense; nonetheless, we would not be completely helpless if it were addressed to us, as we could automatically interpret it as reflecting the transformation of a frame – and probably as a joke, game or metaphor. But this also applies to situations in which we identify the person making this utterance as someone who does not have the authority to demand a ticket from us – for example, a little girl playfully imitating a conductor in a busy train. Because we can identify this as a game, we are prepared to play along – we might show the girl our ticket or even claim we do not have one, but we will not seriously explain to the child that (and why) she is not in a position to demand to see our tickets. At first glance, according to Gumperz (ibid.), such evaluations of situations seem to be individual interpretations of inherently contradictory linguistic realizations. On closer inspection, however, we must notice that these are interpretative strategies which are potentially available to all speakers with a particular cultural background:

> We can thus talk of human communication as channelled and constrained by a multilevel system of learned, automatically produced and closely coordinated verbal and nonverbal signs.
>
> *(Gumperz 1982, p. 141)*

Thus linguistic contextualization cues, pointing to how an utterance is to be understood (taken seriously, or as a joke, game, metaphor, etc.), can only work if there are shared schemata for the interpretation of emphasis – for example in the distribution of prosodic accents, as in the example, "Who do I have to thank for *that*?" as opposed to "Who do I have to *thank* for that?" Adept speakers of the language can tell from the emphasis in the first utterance that this is meant ironically – the speaker is signaling that, because of an unknown third person, something has happened to him for which he is not in the least grateful. This is contrasted with the second emphasis, which signals that the speaker wishes to identify the person who had done something good for him. The speaker relies, as it were, on the addressees using the contextualization cue to understand the intended meaning in the intended sense.

An interesting contextualization cue examined by Peter Auer (1999) is the distinction between "du" and "Sie," the informal and formal words for "you" in German. While the transition from the formal "Sie" to the informal "du" can generally be regarded as marking an increase in solidarity, the problem is that there is no provision for a transition in the opposite direction – we could not offer the formal "Sie" to a person we call "du," even if we had every reason to do so, or if we felt that a "re-formalization" of the social relationship was appropriate – for example in the case of a divorce. This means that we may not be able to draw any clear conclusions about a social relationship from the fact that the people involved call each other "du." From the perspective of this chapter, however, it can also be observed that the non-retractability of the informal form of address is not due to the individual interpretation of the interaction or of the social relationship; instead, right from the outset, the assumption of solidarity implied by situations in which people call each other "du" means these situations are framed in such a way that one can no longer retreat from the "du."

Linguistic realizations, then, can be an aspect of the framing of the social situation, they can be determined by the framing of the social situation, and of course they can be both at the same time: in Germany, the use of dialect might be a significant aspect of the framing of the event "village festival," while at the same time the event "village festival" frames the occasion in a manner that encourages the use of dialect. Herbert Willems (1997, p. 59) argues along similar lines when he describes Goffman's frame analysis as "two-dimensional:" as a system for analyzing the conditions of social interaction, and as the analytical practices of the interactants.

If we conclude by returning once more to the problem of "contradictory ethnographies," we can note that the culturally shaped schemata of interpretation that are genuinely available to us may be what prevents us from understanding the strange and the unfamiliar. But they can also prevent us, as researchers, from understanding what is personal and familiar, simply because these are preconscious, non-reflexive assessments of situations, in which we do not really know what categories we are creating. And this is also true of the informants we work with in most social science studies: while they are acting, the actors involved usually have no awareness or only a very limited awareness of the objective structures of meaning of their interactions and life practices, and hence they can only reconstruct them in a laborious and rudimentary manner. There will always be some discrepancies between what people do and what they can say about it (cf. Gumperz 1982). The latent, taken-for-granted background assumptions and culturally determined schemata of interpretation can therefore only be revealed in a systematic scholarly analysis.

FOOD FOR THOUGHT

Refer to your transcript of the café scene from *As Good As It Gets*, watch the film scene and try to work out how you actually "know" what is going on here. Consider why, for example, you do not classify the scene as a panel discussion, a marital counselling session, or a sports contest. Analyze which features of the situation you ascribe which categorical meanings to.

Notes

1 Here it should be noted that this work, like others by Goffman, engages intensively with questions of dishonesty, dissimulation and deception. We will not focus on these reflections in this chapter.
2 In the chapter "Contextualization Conventions," Gumperz is partly concerned with the problem of how situations are influenced by language; here, however, we mainly consider his reflections on the opposite case. Auer (1999) notes, importantly, that Gumperz's understanding of context is essentially linguistic and not social.
3 A major scandal among the experts was caused by Patrick Tierney's book "Darkness in Eldorado: How Scientists and Journalists Devastated the Amazon" (W.W. Norton & Co. Ltd. 2000). The book contains serious allegations against several Amazon researchers: they are accused of bringing disease and war to the Yanomami, and exploiting them economically and sexually.
4 He went so far as to persuade the Yanomami to repeat the dances that took place in the evening and at night during the daytime, so as to have better lighting for camera shots. Häusler (ibid., p. 82) compares this with the idea of repeating the final of the soccer world cup the following day, when the result is already established: "How enthusiastic and committed would the two teams involved be?" (tr. by N.B.)
5 This view has been continually contested by other researchers, see, for example, Ferguson (1995).
6 In scholarly research on social events, this sometimes means that the social framing of the interaction also guides the scholarly focus of the study, so that "secondary events" are assumed to be irrelevant for the analysis (cf. Suerig 2011).
7 We can therefore say that greetings and farewells begin and end interactions, but do not bracket the event, because the mere act of greeting someone/ saying good-bye does not determine what will happen after the greeting and what has happened before the farewell.

References

Goffman, Erving (1986 [1974]). *Frame Analysis. An Essay on the Organization of Experience.* Lebanon, NH: Northeastern University Press. See especially: Primary Frameworks, pp. 21–39; The Anchoring of Activity, pp. 247–300.

Gumperz, John J. (1982). *Discourse Strategies.* Cambridge: Cambridge University Press. See especially: Contextualization Conventions, pp. 130–152.

Further reading

Agar, Michael (1980). *The Professional Stranger. An Informal Introduction to Ethnography.* New York: Academic Press.

Auer, Peter (1999). *Sprachliche Interaktion.* Tübingen, Germany: Niemeyer. See especially: Kontextualisierung, pp. 148–174.

Ferguson, R. Brian (1995). *Yanomami Warfare: A Political History.* Santa Fe, NM: School of American Research.

Goffman, Erving (1981). *Forms of Talk.* Philadelphia, PA: University of Pennsylvania Press. See especially: Footing, pp. 124–159.

Häusler, Christian (1997). *Kopfgeburten. Die Ethnographie der Yanomami als literarisches Genre.* Marburg, Germany: Förderverein Völkerkunde.

Suerig, Inken (2011). *Students as Actors in Supporting Roles. Video Analysis of Classroom Interaction Systems as Multi-Participant Events.* Osnabrück, Germany: Hochschulschriften der Universität Osnabrück.

Willems, Herbert (1997). *Rahmen und Habitus. Zum theoretischen und methodischen Ansatz Erving Goffmans.* Frankfurt a. M., Germany: Suhrkamp.

9

TYPIFICATION

How we know who we are dealing with

This chapter deals with the categorizations we use to interpret not social situations, but social relations. We regard "typification" as an important structuring aspect of interaction, yet it is scarcely dealt with in-depth in social theory. The exception is the sociology of knowledge, a field which we do not otherwise refer to in this book, since it is linked to the theory of action rather than interaction theory. Accordingly, we acknowledge and discuss Alfred Schütz and Thomas Luckmann's classic approach as "the only one out there," developing a revised concept of "typification" which can help to explain structure in interaction. We show that typifications ("pre-judgments") in interactions enable us to deal with information and action requirements that are not pre-structured by roles, frames or norms, but by subsumptions which always take place when we associate people's observed or reported behaviors with a pattern.

When we interact, we are not guided solely by role expectations, we do not behave purely in conformity or non-conformity with normative requirements, and we do not only follow rules. These aspects, which lay claim to universal validity, do have a major impact on our actions, but this is not the whole story. "Structure" goes beyond these things. As we have already seen, we also insert individuality into interactions, in various respects. This is not meant as an empty phrase, like those everyday words of wisdom which we modern people are always quick to agree on: e.g. that we are all special, that we all have our idiosyncrasies, our particular styles, opinions and tastes, etc. In the present context, our concern is to determine the proportions of individuality and subjectivity that are relevant for the development of structure. This will be a central theme in Chapter 12, which is about the element of decision-making in interactions. But individuality plays a part even prior to decision-making, in the way we perceive situations and the people we interact with.

On the one hand, this is because universally valid rules, norms and role expectations do not have a direct effect, as it were. We must first relate them to the specifics of the given situation and the person we are interacting with. We must make classifications, and this does not happen arbitrarily. On the other hand, these general patterns only allow an inadequate grasp of social relationships. This does not apply solely to close, long-term social relationships, such as couple or family relationships, in which the specific individuals are crucial. The fact is that in concrete situations we always register more than what is "governed" by universally valid patterns. A specific café, for example, is not just a café, but is also part of a particular milieu or a particular social class, and the waiter does not confront us only as a role incumbent, but also as a specific person, whom we always "categorize" partly in terms of gender, age or origins. In order to be able to operate "skillfully," i.e. in an appropriate and knowledgeable way, we are therefore reliant on action-structuring patterns of a different kind, patterns that are more closely tied to our individual experiences. In sociology, these patterns are referred to as "typifications."

"Type" and "typical" are terms that are familiar to us from everyday language. In everyday life, when commenting on the way people act, we sometimes talk about typical behavior or typical actions. For example, we say something is typical of men, women, Germans, senior citizens, New Yorkers, teachers, janitors, etc. It becomes apparent from these "typifications" that they describe a sort of subsumption which always takes place when we associate people's observed or reported behaviors with a pattern. We then regard the people in question as representatives of this pattern. We perceive their gender, origin, age, occupation, etc. as sources of expectable behaviors, which we prepare for and classify accordingly. Patterns of this kind already play a part in our initial deductions about behaviors and characteristics: in other words, typical attributes help us to identify a man, someone from New York, a senior citizen, a teacher. When we talk about other people in this way, admittedly, these are often negative typifications. That is, we attribute negative behaviors of an individual to a particular group of people, and we assume that these negative behaviors have their origins in negative characteristics which are representative of all members of this group. Here we see two important differences between "type" and "social role." First, typification, whether or not it contains a value judgment, concerns groups that can be far broader than social roles (e.g. "New Yorkers," "women"), or far narrower (e.g. "class 10a," in which all the pupils are "overachievers"). Second, the typification itself is not about the behavioral expectations we have of a particular group (even if we derive the expectations from the typification), but about the ascription of behaviors to particular characteristics.

In all the aforementioned cases we have not invented the pattern we refer to; instead, we find confirmation of something that we think already exists. To begin with, then, these patterns are not especially "individual," but are understood by us to be common and widely shared. This is also something we refer to when we say this kind of thing; it is only the assumption of intersubjectively *shared* interpretations that makes utterances such as "Typical man!" comprehensible. "Typical," then, always implies that something is stereotypical as well. In some cases, these are interpretations that are extremely common and simplistic. We are familiar with them, even if we do not wish to appropriate them (perhaps because we are men, New Yorkers, or teachers ourselves). In some cases, however, more specialized, less common knowledge is referred to; special expertise is required in order to be able to classify and apply a pattern of typical behavior in a certain situation. Not everyone knows (or thinks they know) that a given behavior can be ascribed to the fact that the person in question is a teacher, a sociologist or a waiter. Here particular knowledge or experience is needed – on the part of both speaker and listener.

This applies all the more to those typifications that concern specific people in their individuality, when we use "typical" to characterize relatives, friends or colleagues in their specificity, in phrases such as "Typical Harry, he always flies off the handle straight away," or "Typical Helen: all talk and no action." Here too, these "typifying" assessments have a structuring effect on our actions: we will be wary of criticizing Harry, and will not automatically expect Helen to behave in accordance with her own assessment of the situation.

From a sociological viewpoint, there is nothing extraordinary about the examples that occur to us when we consider everyday phrases that include the word "typical." Typifications are not only present in situations where we talk about them explicitly. They are not the exception, but are omnipresent. Whatever we may think of this – and it is generally not seen in a positive light, because it involves a subsumption[1] – we cannot generally get by without this kind of pre-judgment.

There is a sociological theory explaining why this is so. It was developed mainly by Alfred Schütz and Thomas Luckmann (Schütz 1981 [1932], 1962; Schütz & Luckmann 1973). These theoretical reflections will be the starting point for the subsequent argument, but we want to make it clear from the out-set that Schütz and Luckmann make no distinction between social roles and "types." Much of what the authors refer to as "typification" is what we, along with Talcott Parsons (see Chapter 6), would assign to the formal category of the role. As noted at the start, "types" and "roles" are, in an "interactionist" (but also in a structuralist) argument, not only not the same thing, they can also be clearly distinguished from one another. We will return to this point.

Schütz and Luckmann understand typification as an elementary process in the everyday world. Types are schemata of interpretation which help us to order our world. This is not (only) about our ruminations on life, the universe and everything in moments of leisure. Instead "interpretation" has a very practical side here, with direct relevance for action. This is about schemata that we bring to interactions, schemata that determine our understanding of the actions of our interaction partners, and guide our own actions. They generate the expectations we have in the different situations, expectations by which we measure the actions of others, and which we use as the basis for our own actions. We can state that basically everything we have discussed in the previous chapters and will discuss subsequently is dealt with in Schütz and Luckmann's work under the concept of typification.

The texts of Schütz and Luckmann contain various versions of a theoretical explanation for this. Some of these are quite fundamental, and are tied to philosophical assumptions about the workings of human consciousness. In a preliminary theoretical derivation, the argument is put forward that our perception of reality generally involves typification (cf. also Chapter 5). This concerns not only social objects in a narrower sense, but all the objects we perceive. If an object is to become present in our consciousness, we must have access to a schema corresponding to the given object, "a schema of striking thematic elements that belong together, a schema that has been formed in prior experience and solidified in the subjective stock of knowledge" (Luckmann 2003, p. 15, tr. by N.B.). If things are registered by us, if they enter into our consciousness, then this is because a corresponding schema is "automatically appresented" (ibid., tr. by N.B.). In other words, objects in the world become "real" for us because, and to the extent that, they correspond to the patterns with which we perceive the world.

We have to imagine that we wear what might be called "mental spectacles," with which we give meaning to the world. The schemata or types that order the world for us are obviously very diverse, but have a common basic shape. This should not be imagined, however, as a pattern or template, filtering our perception according to whether things fit or do not fit. Instead, Luckmann (cf. ibid.) speaks of a thematic core, embedded in a field, which is in turn surrounded by an "open horizon." On this level of abstraction, these are inevitably rather vague characterizations. The talk of the schemata having an "open horizon," or somewhat blurred edges, is plausible, however, if we bear in mind that they have to have a certain experiential openness, because otherwise we would not learn. Even if the schemata have been transmitted to us by other people (parents, teachers, etc.), our own experiences always lead to modifications. It is possible to imagine, for example, that a small child, based on her previous experience, might see all furry, four-legged animals (these would be the "striking thematic elements that belong together") as "dogs," until new experiences make her apply further differentiating features to the type (e.g. barking, tail-wagging), and simultaneously form another type, "cat" (a furry four-legged animal that does not bark, but miaows).

For typifications of *social* objects, there is another very general theoretical explanation, one that we do not share, but nonetheless wish to outline here for the sake of completeness.[2] Back in the first chapter, we pointed out the central assumption in the argument of Schütz, or Schütz and Luckmann, that understanding of others (*Fremdverstehen*) – that is, understanding the meaning of others' behavior – is fundamentally precarious. According to Schütz and Luckmann in their various writings on the subject, it is impossible for us to adequately comprehend this meaning. This is plausible if – and only if – meaning is attributed to the subjective experience of individuals, as in the tradition of phenomenology and the sociology of knowledge, which the authors follow. Here meaning is tied to the content of each person's own consciousness, and only what appears to be directly given in our own individual consciousness is meaningful. Under this premise, the meaning of others' behavior is fundamentally closed to us, as we have no direct access to their consciousness. If the subjective meaning we associate with our actions is largely based on our own experience, then it is only the individual who really has access to this meaning. An understanding of others, i.e. an understanding of the subjective meaning of the other person, is, strictly speaking, impossible. We must make do, using the other person's behavior and utterances to cast light on the meaning of his or her actions. Such "objective" attributions of meaning, however, can never be more than an approximation. In this context, typifications are introduced as a kind of necessary makeshift: in order to at least roughly grasp the meaning of the observable behaviors of others, we use interpretive schemata of typical actions.[3]

In the present context, however, typification interests us neither as a fundamental way of perceiving the world, nor as a means of bridging the supposed chasm between self-understanding and understanding of others. Instead, our concern is to describe it as a necessary element in interactions. In the following discussion, we will, therefore, foreground a third theoretical derivation, which is a better match for this focus on interaction theory, and is largely independent of the derivations mentioned above. Here typifications are considered in the context of the distinction between closeness and distance in social relationships (cf. Schütz & Luckmann 1973). The basic idea is simple: the more relationships are characterized by social distance and anonymity, the more important types become.[4]

In this respect, Schütz and Luckmann roughly divide social relationships into fellow humans (*Mitmenschen*) and contemporaries (*Zeitgenossen* or *Nebenmenschen*)[5] (Schütz 1974, p. 245ff.; Schütz & Luckmann 1973, p. 103ff.). Even if this distinction does not seem altogether clear in everyday language,[6] these terms nonetheless serve to describe two contrasting types of social relationship. Relationships with "fellow humans" are characterized by a high density of interaction, i.e. frequent face-to-face interactions ("encounters," in Schütz and Luckmann's terminology), in which the other person is "directly experienced." Typical "fellow humans" are therefore family members, friends, but also colleagues or neighbors. Contemporaries, on the other hand, are only experienced indirectly. Face-to-face interactions are isolated incidents, if they occur at all,[7] we know little to nothing about the other people as individuals, and the relationship is therefore largely anonymous. Typical encounters with "contemporaries" are thus what we would call role relationships – in shops, on buses, in administrative offices, and in general, interactions within the public sphere.

What this differentiation between proximity and distance means for interaction is described by the authors using the simple example of increasing spatial distance and the associated transformation of a fellow human into a mere contemporary:

> I find myself face to face with an acquaintance. He excuses himself, shakes my hand, and departs. He turns around and calls something out to me. He is still farther, waves to me once more, and disappears around the corner.
> *(Schütz & Luckmann 1973, p. 69; see also Schütz 1974, p. 246)*

This is associated with a qualitative change in our mutual experience of each other. True, my knowledge of this acquaintance is still "first-hand" knowledge, even if spatial co-presence is no longer given, but the immediacy of the "thou-orientation" is missing. Direct experiences are replaced by memories, ideas and images – until the history of the interaction is resumed in face-to-face inter-action. The distinction between physical proximity and distance can also be understood as a gradation of forms of communication: face-to-face interactions, then phone conversations, then written correspondence and lastly messages passed on by third parties. This is associated with a "decrease in the abundance of symptoms" and an increase in social distance (ibid., p. 69): in a sense, we lack the material to adequately understand our interaction partner as a concrete per-son, as discussed in Chapter 1.

In theory the previous example of the gradual transformation of a "fellow human" into a "contemporary" is accurate: to the extent that I have no infor-mation acquired in direct experience about the attributes of the specific other person, I am reliant on mediated information, on imputations and suppositions about the other person's actions, in order to adjust my own actions accordingly. With increasing social distance, these assumptions must necessarily become more abstract and schematic. They can no longer relate to specific individuals, but to "someone;" they can no longer relate to perceptible, but only to general attributes. My expectations of how others will act are no longer based on my own experiences of a specific person, but on generalized knowledge about the likelihood of actions and sequences of actions. Typifications are thus the inter-pretive schemata produced by relationships in conditions of social distance and anonymity.

We have already established in Chapter 6 that the crucial aspect of role rela-tionships is not the direct experience of them, but the indirect knowledge of abstract, reciprocal behavioral expectations, which we connect to the social roles and not to the role incumbents. True, Schütz and Luckmann also note that *Ihr-Beziehungen* or relationships with contemporaries (referred to in the English translation as "they-relations") are oriented toward indirect knowledge:

> The reference point of the they-orientation is inferred from my knowledge and from the social world in general [...] . My knowledge of the social world is typical knowledge concerning typical processes.
> *(Schütz & Luckmann 1973, p. 75)*

But as they do not work with the concept of the social role, the attitudes of expectation linked with these relationships – as typifications – are always developed from the subjective point of view of the individual and are comparatively vague; as if I were adapting my actions to people (not roles!) that I do not know, but whom I suppose to exist, and whom I expect. Schütz's favorite example (Schütz 1962, 1974; Schütz & Luckmann 1973) is postal workers, whose "typical" actions I count on when I put a stamped, addressed letter in the mailbox. In the words of Schultz and Luckmann (ibid., p. 76), in doing this I have signaled a "wish," and have acted "in the expectation" that "certain contemporaries" (postal employees) will "interpret my wish" and "conduct themselves accordingly." We believe that the corresponding attitudes of expectation can be understood more concretely in terms of role theory. But the question of how and to what extent role expectations can be understood as typifications is not our concern here. What is interesting in the present context is when typifications go beyond the stocks of knowledge that provide orientation for relations with "contemporaries." If my partners in relations with "contemporaries" are types, then they are not people. They are absent; I only presume their existence, or presuppose it in my actions. But what if "contemporaries" become "fellow humans;" what if types become real partners? What if I interact face-to-face with others whom I have previously only perceived as types?

Interaction in relationships with "contemporaries" is overlooked, or at least not given any particular prominence, in the writings of Schütz and Luckmann (and also in those of Parsons). This is probably because the theoretical model is constructed in such a way that "fellow human" and "contemporary" are a pair of opposites, and the "direction of development" of the typification goes from proximity to distance, as described previously. In line with this, there are subdivisions of the two types within this direction, i.e. both "fellow humans" and "contemporaries" are divided into smaller groups, under conditions of increasing anonymity and abstraction; there is, however, virtually no reflection on the opposite direction of development. And yet this is relevant in terms of interaction theory. How, for example, do I deal with an increasing "abundance of symptoms" in the interaction if I cannot relate it to previously experienced knowledge about the uniqueness of my interaction partner?[8] Again, the answer is typifications.

We thus assume that typification is not restricted to contemporaries; it is too fundamental for this. If we assume that our perception of the world is generally shaped by typification, then we cannot *not* typify. Typification is ubiquitous. Our knowledge of the social world, therefore, consists of typifications.[9] If – as Schütz and Luckmann (1973) argue – we inevitably inject our "stock of knowledge" into relationships with "fellow humans" as well as relationships with "contemporaries," then we typify in every interaction, and we typify everyone, including the people who are close to us. We even typify ourselves. We do this, for example, whenever we say "you know me," "I'm not usually like this" or "that's not like me." Our overall self-concept, the identity we have gained in biographical reflection, also takes the form of a typification (cf. Hahn 1987, 1988). But what form does a typification have?

Types are structures of meaning, and like all structures of meaning, types cannot be seen, felt or tasted. They can therefore not be "measured." Moreover – as mentioned at the outset – our explicit knowledge about them is limited. The development and "application" of types in everyday practice are primarily pre-reflective processes. Unlike social norms, we do not have an especially clear idea of them. We cannot unambiguously identify them. It is possible, though, to analyze them, and to gain a better understanding by reflecting on them. In order to define a typification that is relevant for our actions, then, we must become aware of what is subliminally influencing them. We must identify what we see as "belonging" to the concepts of – for example – man, waitress or New Yorker, that is, what attributes and behavioral expectations we associate with them. Even the attempt to carry out such an analysis is very instructive, if we put aside the question of how successful it is likely to be.[10]

If, for example, we set ourselves the task of determining how we typify men and women in social terms (gender), we soon realize that this will be a fairly complex undertaking. As Schütz and Luckmann (see previous) have already noted, such general types are composed of a plethora of sub-typifications: men and women in terms of their physical behavior, their clothing, their communicative style, their preferences, their attitude towards a number of inherently "typical" areas of life (work, children, love, sport, art, technology, academia, etc.), in a number of inherently "typical" situations. We also realize very quickly that types – as already noted – are not classifications or definitions which can be used to make one-to-one correlations. They are not a set of characteristics from 1 to n, determining whether or not a specific social object is a man, a waitress or a New Yorker. Instead, there are more or less relevant characteristics, there are clear cases and borderline cases, there is variance. Even if certain expectations are not fulfilled, this does not mean we will say, in every case, "That isn't a man."

Against this background, Luckmann's aforementioned obscure and abstract reflections on the "thematic core" in its "field" with an "open horizon" become more clearly defined. There can hardly be a more apt description for the form of a type than these concepts of a relevant core and somewhat blurred boundaries or edges. In everyday language, we give expression to this when we talk, for example, of a "real man," a "proper waitress" or a "true New Yorker." Other people are also men, waitresses or New Yorkers within the terms of the relevant typifications, but the specific examples we refer to with these phrases somehow match these typifications in a special way.

But how do we arrive at the types with which we organize our actions? A further effect of the attempt to analyze our own typification of men and women is the realization that the ensemble of attributes and behavioral expectations contains both social (in the sense of "generally valid") and individual, idiosyncratic elements. In part, our expectations will be linked with elements of a "gender role." Or at least we will believe that this is so, in various respects, when we think that men *are supposed to* take care of the family income, protect their female companions in certain situations or take the lead when dancing. Another part of our expectations, however, will be the result of our individual experiences, which we have built into the typification. Often we will directly combine our individual experience with general social expectations, automatically seeing them as confirmation of "what men and women are like." Sometimes, however, we will become aware of the element of specificity of our experiences – particularly if the corresponding expectations are disappointed in later experiences. For example, I could have held the view that the medical profession was "typically female" because my mother was a doctor, but then (in the 1950s) I would have had to observe that there were actually hardly any women working in this profession. Or I might imagine that "psychologists" are men, and then have to realize (at the beginning of the 21st century) that more than three-quarters of psychology students are women.

In general, types are made up of two elements: elements of society's stock of knowledge, which we share with other members of society, and elements which are part of our particular experiences. The latter is especially important for the present context; after all, this is the reason why we are devoting a separate chapter to typification. Apart from the pathological case of prejudices that are impervious to experience, types are open to experience. While social norms are upheld even in concrete cases of norm violation (which we understand as "deviations"), types are different: when reality does not meet our typical expectations this has a lasting, disconcerting effect on us. In line with this, the above-mentioned experiences will lead to a restructuring of our complex of types relating to "male and female occupations."[11] Types, then, are always in part a reflection of our individual life history, and our typifications thus add an individual element to interactions.

The question of how types evolve must engage with a dialectic of the new and the familiar. In theory, it is possible to treat type-formation as the development of something new, or as an engagement with something familiar, a restructuring. Both strategies can be found in the sociology of knowledge. However, the arguments about type-formation as the development of something new, arising "in the original situation of the acquisition of knowledge" (Schütz & Luckmann 1973, p. 165), are scattered, and are as vague as the reflections on types as a way of perceiving the world. Empirically, the greatest "initial openness" is found where interactions have comparatively little role-based pre-structuring, as in relationships between married couples, parents and children or friends – that is, in the original relationships with "fellow humans."

The crucial thing is always that a type produces a context of meaning. This is associated with an abstraction, i.e. the typical is separated from the concrete, unique, specific aspects of the situation and the people we are dealing with. Here similarity (between situations and people) and repeatability (of attributes) play a part. I assume that there is something unchangeable in the behavior of the others (cf. Schütz 1974), but this does not mean that we conduct measurement series and form average values in everyday life. Instead, we have to think of it like this: in certain situations, and with regard to particular topics, schemata of the previously described form develop out of existing predispositions and individual experiences; these schemata stand the test of time and are thus consolidated.

It is easier, on the other hand, to describe the development of types not as "original," but as a restructuring of pre-existing patterns. We do not form types "out of thin air," but come to situations with predispositions, based on social typifications that have been transmitted to us by significant others (the important people in our lives). As part of our individual stock of knowledge, these patterns have proven their worth in practice, i.e. we have been able to act and interpret "successfully" with them. However, this is only ever provisional – we are, after all, open to experience! In certain respects, the patterns can also be proven wrong by reality; they are then restructured, and the schema is modified:

> In other words, a type arises from a situationally adequate solution to a problematic situation through the new determination of an experience which could not be mastered with the aid of the stock of knowledge already on hand. Here that means: with the aid of an "old" determination relation.
> *(Schütz & Luckmann 1973, p. 231)*

At this point it makes sense to consider some empirical examples, in order to take a closer look at how types are formed and how they "work" in interactions.

It should have become clear from what has been said so far that any sociological study of a research field (family, classroom, business, administrative organization, soccer game, etc.) should expect the actors and groups of actors to typify each other. This is one key to defining the particular kind of interaction that predominates in a specific family, classroom, etc. Thus the nature of the interaction in the Smith family will depend partly on how the husband and wife typify each other as man or woman, and what general typification of "male" or "female" is at work here (cf. Gildemeister & Robert 2008; cf. Maiwald 2010). And the relationships within a classroom will be partly shaped by how the pupils and the teacher typify each other, and what typifications are prevalent among the pupils ("overachiever," "cool," "nerd," etc.). Moreover, we know from the previous sections that such typifications are not identical to the conscious opinions or theories that the interaction partners can express about each other. Typifications are, to a large extent, pre-reflective.

A vivid example of how typifications can "function" is found in an analysis by Ilja Srubar (2009). This is about typification strategies when dealing with a particular kind of social distance. The background is a research project which takes the example of the merger between two automotive groups, VW and Skoda, to examine intercultural communication in multicultural companies. The German and Czech managers interviewed in the project not only encountered each other – as role incumbents – in conditions of social anonymity, but also – as members of different cultural groups – in conditions of mutual foreignness, strangeness or unfamiliarity (*Fremdheit*). In respect of the latter, the participants did not have access to either existing typifications or typifications with claims to universal validity. At the beginning, there was only the mutual expectation of cultural difference, which immediately found expression in various translation problems. Even after general linguistic differences and specific differences in technical terminology had been overcome, differences still remained; these were mutually perceived as an expression of foreignness.

The two cultural groups responded to this with heterotypifications,[12] though these were restricted by the overall need for cooperation. The participants were aware of the divisive potential of typification based on national oppositions:

> On the part of the Germans, the foreignness was therefore translated into the terms of a semantics of system difference, which had happened to the Czechs for historical reasons, by no fault of their own. On the Czech side, the preferred strategy was the personalization of disconcerting experiences: this relativized the cultural foreignness and foregrounded an 'anthropological' distinction between 'good' and 'bad' people, irrespective of socio-cultural background.
>
> *(Srubar 2009, p. 171, tr. by N.B.)*

This did not, however, alter the fact that there were substantial differences on the level of everyday collaboration in the style of work of the German and Czech managers, which were perceived as problematic by those involved. While the characteristics of the German style, according to Srubar, included a focus on flat hierarchies, discursive, consensual decision-making, thinking in projects and visions and flexible decision-making autonomy, the Czech style involved a focus on technical competence, hierarchical organizational structures and fast, authoritarian, but at the same time flexible and situation-oriented decision-making. Ironically, these styles of work led to exactly opposite modes of behavior in everyday collaboration. While the German managers, seeing the negotiations as open-ended, acted formally and emphasized their power and competence, the Czech managers – in the light of their perceived clear hierarchical position and the technical competence attributable to them – took an informal, egalitarian stance.

We can see the potential for conflict. And the groups of actors involved also perceived the differences in their perspectives, and tried to understand the unfamiliar practices of the other group in the pragmatic contexts of action. In order to facilitate a practical approach to the foreigners in the everyday collaboration, however, types and interpretive schemata were also developed. These strongly reflected each group's own ideas of normality, and contained corresponding elements of judgment: in the Czechs' view, the German semantics of management was translated as "ideology" (ibid., p. 173), and their decision-making style was seen as long-winded and inflexible; in the Germans' view the Czech emphasis on technical competence and flexible decision-making was interpreted as the absence of a systematic approach, and as pettiness. For all the prejudices at work here, these typifications were always incorporated into an overall focus on collaboration. It could be said that it was only the new backdrop of normality (the notion that "that's what they're like") that allowed intercultural communication. In the case in question, this cooperative process of communication was boosted by the fact that the groups inserted their heterotypifications into the communication process itself as proposals for describing and explaining the situation. It became apparent "that there was a consensus about the acknowledgment of the mutual foreignness, and that the heterotypifications were accepted as types of description of this foreignness, and used as communicative shorthand" (ibid., p. 175, tr. by N.B.). In the interactions, "that's what they're like" became "that's what you're like."

The example once again shows clearly, as we have already heard in Chapter 6, that role expectations are not enough to structure interactions. This is not only true under conditions of mutual unfamiliarity, but also under conditions of relative familiarity. In conclusion, we will illustrate this once more with reference to our film example, considering the role of waiter/waitress. What are the role expectations of a waiter or waitress? We can order food and drinks, and they will be brought to us; we will be served in the same way as everyone else; the essence of our relationship to the waiting staff is that this service is provided to us, and we pay for it; the waiter or waitress has a certain expertise, that is, he or she knows what food and drinks cost, knows roughly how long it will take until they are served, can make recommendations; we can expect a certain degree of friendliness when they address us, etc. Such expectations belong to the role, or to the complementary role pair "waiter-customer." All of this is also important for the interaction, because it gives it structure, independent of the specific situation. But it is not enough to enable us to interact "skillfully."

Let us assume we are in an establishment that we have been able to successfully identify as a café or restaurant. The problem then begins with the fact that the role itself does not give us any direct information about how we can tell who, among those present, is a waiter or waitress. Certainly, there may be obvious clues that are connected to the performance of the role: we see people serving other people, or we see people wearing a money belt with a notepad and pen. And if we do not see that, then there is work clothing that makes identification easier. But this is where the typifications begin (if they have not already done so), as there are several "typical" versions of this (black suit, suit pants with a white shirt and black vest, black pants with a white jacket; sometimes a long or short apron, sometimes a T-shirt with the name of the café, etc.). And it may also be that there is no workwear or uniform. The extent to which we perceive each of these possibilities as typical (or find it disconcerting) depends on the knowledge we have acquired second-hand and on our personal experience.

But we do not simply notice the nature of the work clothing; it is also associated – often involuntarily – with further typifications. These may concern the type of café or restaurant we are in ("exclusive," "trendy," "bistro," etc.), but also our expectations about typical behavior from the waiting staff. For example, we would be baffled if a young waitress in jeans and a T-shirt were to assume a rather stiff pose, leaning forward slightly, and ask "Good evening sir, have you made your selection?", and conversely, we would not expect a waiter aged around fifty in a black suit to say, "Hey guys, have you decided what you want yet?" But the subsequent behavior in the course of the interaction is also subject to typifications. We can perceive waiters as "well-trained," "bumbling" or "stressed," and can adjust our behavior accordingly, by enjoying the service, giving our order as clearly as possible, or being willing to make allowances. And how do we respond if we are served in a grumpy or even unfriendly manner? We can assume that there is a negative typification of our own person at work, typical of this kind of restaurant (for example in a Michelin-starred restaurant, if we are unsuitably dressed, or uncertain of how to "behave" in such an establishment), or we can see it as typical of the city we are in (for example, New Yorkers are typified as unfriendly, and Berliners as flippant. Does a waiter's ironic joviality reflect the type of restaurant he is serving in (a beer garden), or his origin (Bavaria)?

Sometimes we are cautious with typifications, sometimes we are particularly quick to make them (especially on holiday, in a strange place); this may depend on what type of person we are. But we can never dispense with typification altogether, because the general parameters of interaction (which can themselves be understood as type constructs, in terms of their form), are never enough to enable us to deal adequately with the abundance of information we are confronted with in social situations. To put it generally: the special contribution of typifications in interactions is that they enable us to deal with information and action requirements that are not pre-structured by roles, frames or norms. We cannot help but notice the particular features in the interaction, assign these to types and adjust our actions accordingly. And if we ourselves do not do this, the waiter or waitress definitely will (cf. Girtler 2008).

FOOD FOR THOUGHT

Refer to your transcript of the café scene from *As Good As It Gets*. What typifications exist, in general, for cafés and restaurants? How would you characterize the café in the film example? What sort of menu and prices can be expected here? What are the clues that point to these things? What makes the waitress a waitress? What typifications do the actors carry out? What sub-typifications are they made up of?

The art agent Frank Simon justifies not being able to drive to Baltimore himself with the fact that he has "a high-maintenance selling painter coming through." Why is this a sufficient explanation? Consider what the brief typifications "high maintenance" and "selling painter" imply. How do you imagine this type? Describe him in as much detail as possible.

Notes

1 Perhaps this is also the reason why the attributes mentioned in this type of phrase are usually not especially positive ones.

2 In anticipation of the objections likely to be raised here: we are aware that this representation contains some oversimplifications.

3 At this point we will give an indication of why we do not share this position: objective structures of meaning, institutions, general or universal validity – all these things are more than bridges between consciousnesses that are closed to each other. Moreover, such a fundamental distinction between self-understanding and understanding of others is empirically not the rule but the exception within interaction, as already established in Chapter 1.

4 Talcott Parsons also emphasized the difference between "intimate" and "anonymous" in his "pattern variables" (see Chapter 6).

5 The German prefixes *mit* (with) and *neben* (beside, alongside) suggest that these are people who live either with us or alongside us. This meaning is not conveyed in the English translation. This also concerns the translations of some of the other terms coined by Schütz and Luckmann, which is why we abstain from using them here.

6 In modern German both these words are more common in in written language than in everyday language; *Mitmenschen* (fellow humans) does have connotations of a certain social proximity, but *Mitmenschen* are also contemporaries (*Zeitgenossen*), and to a certain extent the converse is also true – when, for example, we say that someone is an *unfreundlicher Zeitgenosse* (a disagreeable person, literally: an "unfriendly contemporary").

7 In fact, the concept, in its narrower sense, does not envisage any interaction between contemporaries, or at least none that is face-to-face. We will return to this later.

8 At one point the authors imply that, in "institutionalized patterns of action" such as that of buyer and seller, there is the possibility "that, even when one meets his fellowman, one may 'hold back' from the living we-relation and replace it, so to speak, with a they-relation" (Schütz & Luckmann 1973, p. 77). This is quite obscure, and the subsequent explanatory example suffers from the fact that it once again contains "real" fellow humans – friends – towards whom the narrative ego takes an observing and correspondingly distancing attitude. Elsewhere, although only in the German original, Schütz (1974, p. 245) concedes that we also approach strangers, in the public sphere, in a "face-to-face thou-orientation" ("umweltliche Dueinstellung"). But again, the contemporaries in the public sphere are subsequently treated as mere types. We believe these passages point to the need (as we have argued) to make clearer analytical distinctions between relationship type and interaction type: face-to-face interaction is one thing, close social relationships are another.

9 Here, however, knowledge of rules is more than typification.

10 An operation like this is really not straightforward, since this is not (just) about what we think, that is, our explicit ideas about something, but mainly about our implicit attitudes, which we apply in concrete interactions. And this requires a certain analytical distance from ourselves and our actions. Some deep-seated attitudes may only be revealed by experience – or analysis by third parties.

11 How this restructuring occurs depends on individual circumstances: I can now regard the medical profession as "male," or psychology as "female," or I can, in response to such experiences, shift the occupational complex from the thematic core of typifications of men and women to the periphery.

12 Typifications of the behavior and the attributes of the members of the other group.

References

Endreß, Martin (2006). *Alfred Schütz*. Konstanz, Germany: UVK. See especially: Grundlegung der verstehenden Soziologie: Der sinnhafte Aufbau der sozialen Welt, pp. 65–79; Das wissenssoziologische Profil der Lebensweltanalyse, pp. 99–118.

Luckmann, Thomas (2003). Von der alltäglichen Erfahrung zum sozialwissenschaftlichen Datum. In Ilja Srubar & Steven Vaitkus (Eds.), *Phänomenologie und soziale Wirklichkeit* (pp. 13–26). Opladen, Germany: Leske + Budrich.

Schütz, Alfred (1962). *The Problem of Social Reality. Collected Papers 1*. Maurice Natanson (Ed.). The Hague, the Netherlands: Martinus Nijhoff Publishers. See especially: Common-sense and Scientific Interpretation of Human Action, pp. 3–47.

Schütz, Alfred (1967 [1932]). *The Phenomenology of the Social World*. Evanston, IL: Northwestern University Press. See especially: The World of Contemporaries as a Structure of Ideal Types, pp. 176–214.

Schütz, Alfred, & Luckmann, Thomas (1973). *The Structures of the Life-World*. Vol. 1. Evanston, IL: Northwestern University Press. See especially: The Mediate Experience of the Social World, pp. 68–92; The Structure of the Social Stock of Knowledge, pp. 304–318.

Further reading

Berger, Peter L., & Luckmann, Thomas (1967). *The Social Construction of Reality. A Treatise in the Sociology of Knowledge*. New York: Anchor Books.

Gildemeister, Regine, & Robert, Günther (2008). *Geschlechterdifferenzierungen in lebenszeitlicher Perspektive*. Wiesbaden, Germany: Springer VS.

Girtler, Roland (2008). '*Herrschaften wünschen zahlen': Die bunte Welt der Kellnerinnen und Kellner*. Vienna: Böhlau.

Hahn, Alois (1987). Identität und Selbstthematisierung. In Alois Hahn & Volker Kapp (Eds.), *Selbstthematisierung und Selbstzeugnis: Bekenntnis und Geständnis* (pp. 9–24). Frankfurt a. M., Germany: Suhrkamp.

Hahn, Alois (1988). Biographie und Lebenslauf. In Hanns-Georg Brose & Bruno Hildenbrand (Eds.), *Vom Ende des Individuums zur Individualität ohne Ende* (pp. 91–106). Opladen, Germany: Leske + Budrich.

Maiwald, Kai-Olaf (2010). Vom Schwinden der Väterlichkeit und ihrer bleibenden Bedeutung. Familiensoziologische Überlegungen. In Dieter Thomä (Ed.), *Vaterlosigkeit. Geschichte einer fixen Idee* (pp. 251–268). Berlin, Germany: Suhrkamp.

Srubar, Ilja (2009). *Kultur und Semantik*. Wiesbaden, Germany: Springer VS. See especially: Strukturen des Übersetzens und interkultureller Vergleich, pp. 155–178.

10

STRUCTURAL PROBLEMS OF ACTION

How we adjust to the circumstances

The concrete material world in which every social interaction necessarily takes place is seldom accorded a central position in sociology. No real theory on the importance of the material world for interaction exists; there are, however, a limited number of studies focusing on the effects which spatial conditions have on interaction. Here we give a detailed presentation of two of these studies: Stefan Hirschauer's analysis of elevator travel, and Tilman Allert's reflections on traveling by plane. Both examples make it clear that "objects themselves" possess a structuring force – after all, they are "brute facts" which must be dealt with, regardless of the quality of the social relationship and the social situation in other respects.

So far we have dealt with a number of *social* mechanisms that play a role in interactions. But we do not only interact sequentially, we do not only have recourse to institutions such as norms and definitions of situations, we do not only enter interactions with experience-based predispositions, and we do not only try to adapt our emotions to contexts of interaction – rather, we are always dealing with an actual *matter* as well. We are not simply talking about something, we are also working on something, engaging with something. The "common ground" of interactions always includes a connection to things. This not only makes a difference externally, but is also relevant for structure.

If, for example, we want to spend a convivial evening with friends, undertake a difficult mountaineering expedition, serve an elaborate dish to a paying guest, or resolve conflicts in divorce proceedings, then the manner in which we interact will – in part – have to do with the fact that a convivial evening, a mountaineering trip, a five-course menu and a major marital crisis are very different things. "Conviviality," for example, obviously involves an emphatically symmetrical style of interaction, only disrupted by the asymmetry of host and guest. In contrast, the mixture of hierarchy and solidarity in the relationship between a mountain guide and her rope team can undoubtedly be ascribed to the knowledge disparity between those involved on the one hand, and the risky nature of the undertaking on the other. It can be assumed that the hierarchically rigid structure in top restaurants has something to do with the need for a division of labor that will lead to high-quality production under severe time restrictions, in processes that can only be formalized to a limited extent. And it seems obvious that consensus-oriented conflict mediation in divorce proceedings should include both the asymmetry of expert advice and interaction "on an equal footing."

So once again, it all seems to be quite mundane: we have to take into account the material circumstances of the interaction. And therefore we do. But here are the problems: the matter at hand is never expressed "nakedly," so to speak, i.e. totally undisguised and free of social mediation. The "givens" are not simply given. On the contrary, they are always culturally mediated, as is already clear from our examples: while the preparation of elaborate dishes is probably an undertaking that is similar in most cultures, the same can certainly not be said for "convivial evenings," "mountaineering" and "dealing with divorce-related conflict." Ideas about acceptable forms of conviviality, and about who is admitted to them, vary considerably from one culture to the next; in some areas there are neither mountains nor leisure time (and the ideas of "recreation" and "natural beauty" are unknown), and even in some EU countries divorce-related conflicts are a relatively recent development.[1]

Nonetheless, material circumstances and requirements have a structuring force, which is not limited to cultural precepts and interpretations. Whether we like it or not, things constitute a touchstone for interaction, which must adapt to them, and in this respect, they actually are "given." Yet their influence has a different quality to that of norms and rules. Here, too, there is a kind of conformity and deviation – except that we cannot really talk about conformity and deviation here. Instead what is at work here is a "material logic," which we must adapt to in – and insert into – interactions. If we do not do so, then we are not punished by the law, but – as a Soviet president once said – by life. We are not sanctioned by confusion, disapproving looks or the police, but our actions fail and cause frustration. And yet in everyday practice, it is often not easy to say what the problem is, and in this respect the distinction between manifest and latent becomes relevant. Sometimes we know (or think we know) what element of our actions was not appropriate to the matter at hand. But sometimes we do not even realize there is a problem. This is especially true when we are not acting in accordance with our own patterns, but are following culturally and organizationally prescribed patterns. There are, for example, a number of occupations where at least certain aspects of work organization do not directly address the matter at hand, for example when people get "buried in paperwork," or decisions are delayed indefinitely because they have to pass through a number of committees and subcommittees. This can make people bitter, fed-up, and frustrated, leading to conditions that are vaguely referred to as "stress" or "burn-out."

Seen in this light, the question of how to determine the significance of the matter at hand for the structure of the interaction no longer seems so trivial. But to what extent is this even possible, if we have to simultaneously refer to the relevant cultural, situational and subjective understanding of the material conditions of the interaction, *and* distance ourselves from them, in order to assess relatively invariant aspects? This is probably *one* reason why there is not really any discursive tradition in sociology concerned with analyzing the material dimension of interaction.

True, there are approaches to material connections in social theory, such as Niklas Luhmann's distinction between the material, temporal and social dimension (Luhmann 1996 [1984]), or Jürgen Habermas's discussion of how action is related to the world (Habermas 1986 [1981]). There are anthropological approaches that aim to theorize the relationship between the body and the world of things (e.g. Leroi-Gourhan 1993 [1965]; Kaufmann 1997; Latour 1993), and there are studies that explore the significance of objects in processes of knowledge acquisition and transmission (e.g. Knorr Cetina 1999). For the questions we are seeking to answer, however, these discursive strands are in some cases too general, in others too specific, and overall, not "interactionist" enough. Of course empirical analyses – such as those examining workflows – often consider how material circumstances or "givens" influence the structure of interaction and relationships. But this generally tends to be ad hoc and related to the specific object under examination.

What all of this means for this chapter is that we are dependent on discussions of specific examples. In the following two sections we will consider and to some extent expand on two such examples, each of which offers a careful analysis of the material dimension in interactions. A further advantage of these analyses is that the matter at hand is, in each case, relatively uncomplicated and widely known: taking an elevator and traveling by plane. We will first demonstrate how this can be analyzed, then use these insights in the final section to formulate a basic idea of how, in general terms, the structuring power of objects can be imagined.

In his 2005 essay "On Doing Being a Stranger: The Practical Constitution of Civil Inattention," Stefan Hirschauer examines the distinctive features of traveling by elevator. Here he is not concerned with which people travel by elevator, and how much they do so on average, nor is he concerned with their subjective associations with elevator travel, or with the feelings of discomfort, frustration or perhaps even joy they experience when doing so. He does observe *how* people travel by elevator, and *what* they do while doing so, but these behaviors are not considered on their own, as it were – there are no calculations of how common certain characteristics are, for example, or definitions of types of elevator passenger. Instead, behavior while waiting for the elevator and in the elevator is systematically analyzed to determine what elevator travel *is*, in contrast to other modes of locomotion. What consequences does it have to venture into "an optically closed cage for 6 to 10 inmates, with automatic doors and aluminum walls, going through a vertical tunnel in a public building, i.e. a place where *strangers* come together?" (ibid., p. 43). The specific behaviors are attributed to this – and are thus defined as typical reactions to the structural parameters set by the artifact and the conditions of its use.

Let us begin with a few behavioral patterns. Most of these are likely to be familiar to anyone who has a certain amount of experience of this means of transport. In actual fact, we act in a fairly uniform manner in the following respects – for example when we get into an elevator, look for a space and adapt our position to the number of passengers entering and exiting. If we are the first to enter the elevator, we will choose a spot that seems particularly advantageous in view of the forthcoming journey, for example a position at the front next to a side wall if we want to get out again straight away, or a place at the rear wall if we want to go further and anticipate that people will get out before us. If other passengers are already present, we will stand as far away from them as possible. We "automatically" form geometric shapes, triangles or quadrilaterals, depending on the number of passengers. If the elevator becomes more crowded, this is no longer possible, but we still take care to position ourselves neither too close nor too far from the people standing around us – with the exception of colleagues or acquaintances traveling with us, to whom we may stand closer. We can concur with Hirschauer (cf. ibid.) that positioning follows the rules of maximization of distance (as additional passengers enter the elevator they stand as far away from each other as possible) and equidistance (they try to make the distances between them as equal as possible).

There is a considerable degree of uniformity not only in *where* we position ourselves, but in the manner in which we do so. We stand in such a way that we neither turn our face nor our back towards the others. No one stands with their face to the wall, or face-to-face with another passenger. Nor do we stand immediately behind each other, facing the door. Instead, we position ourselves at an angle to each other that could be characterized as a "half-turn" towards each other. If the elevator becomes emptier, we move away from each other again, but with a certain time delay, and not returning to the same positions as before.

Why is this so? It is partly to do with the material circumstances of the elevator as a mode of transport, circumstances to which we must submit. The architecture, for example, is cell-shaped, defining what is "the front" and what is "the back," and how much space we can lay claim to. Here the design principle is to fit as many people as possible into the space, i.e. we should expect that that it will be a tight squeeze. One of our sources of information here is the notice that is usually displayed in the cabin, stating the maximum number of occupants or the maximum weight. Furthermore, unlike buses and trains with their rows of seats, there are no fixed places to get our bearings from; instead, we are required to "populate" a relatively open space. In addition, the elevator is an automatic or externally controlled means of transport; this not only means that we have to know our destination in advance (and we take this into account when choosing a place to stand), it also shapes the nature of the journey: there is no possibility of hesitating, lingering or having a short conversation as one might in the stair-well. Furthermore, there is a chance of stopping unexpectedly or traveling in an unanticipated direction (if the elevator is summoned to other floors). The fact that we usually cannot see into or out of the elevator car has a similar effect. It makes our perception of the change in location abstract, only communicated by the electronic floor indicator, which – as will become apparent – plays a special part in the perceptions and interactions of the spatially and temporally disori-ented passengers.

But positioning, or behavior in general in an elevator is not solely deter-mined by the material circumstances; rather, the requirements imposed by the material circumstances confront the requirements of the interaction system. It is only the interplay between them that explains the patterns mentioned praviously. The rules of maximization of distance and of equidistance are an answer to the problem that spatial proximity and distance in interactions can be interpreted by the participants as signs of a personal relationship, indicating either affec-tion (relatively close proximity towards each other) or dislike (relatively great distance from one another). This is precisely what is avoided in an elevator, as a public space, a place of encounters between strangers.[2] The way we stand in a full elevator – turning neither our back nor our face to the other passengers – also follows this requirement: our bodies are kept in a state of tension between turn-ing towards and turning away from the others, between paying attention to them and ignoring them. And if, after some of the passengers have left the elevator, we hesitate before moving slowly into the more distant positions that are now pos-sible, then this is to avoid giving the impression that we are distancing ourselves from the other passengers. Thus a particular kind of social relationship charac-teristic of public spaces is produced interactively: a relationship beyond friend-ship and enmity, one in which a minimal level of cooperation and potential for cooperation is maintained,[3] without any personalized interaction occurring.

In an elevator, however, the production of this strangeness or unfamiliarity (*Fremdheit*) takes place under exceptionally difficult conditions, due to the par-ticular spatial proximity associated with it. This is especially obvious from the fact that eye contact becomes a problem in an elevator. Why? Because staring at the other people present is seen as an attack, and because mutual eye contact, as we know, means interaction, and interaction is avoided. Because of the lack of stimuli offered by its décor – compared to a rail compartment, for example – an elevator car offers little to fix our gaze on. We look at the floor indicator, the ground, our own feet, a bag; we stare at an advertising poster, or look past the others towards the exit. In this way, we establish "sightlines" that allow us to avoid eye contact. We also use techniques for shifting focus which allow us to glance briefly at the others without being looked at, and conversely, lowering our gaze intermittently offers brief opportunities to be looked at (again, this serves to avoid meeting anyone else's gaze). If the elevator is very crowded, however, the floor display ends up being the preferred object for passengers to look at.

Such a "minimization of presence" (see previous) by largely avoiding eye contact is not only characteristic of elevator travel, but of interaction in public spaces in general. The aim is to interactively create something like "relationlessness" or "unconnectedness" – Goffman (1971, p. 219) speaks of "civil inattention." This paradoxical structure of strangeness is primarily achieved through rules of eye contact and avoidance of eye contact, such as the rule that pedestrians who are about to walk past each other first look at each other openly from a "suitable distance," then lower their gaze and thus avoid interaction.[4] Here mutual presence is only partially given. In an elevator, this is different, as we are actually present for a certain period of time. Furthermore, the relatively confined space, as described previously, calls for a more complex "regime of the gaze." But at the same time – a point that should be added to Hirschauer's analysis – avoiding eye contact is even more important here than in the more fleeting encounters in the street.

This has to do with the close physical proximity – and even physical contact – that can prevail in elevators. Proximity is not just a potential "relationship sign" which has to be avoided, it also means – when it can no longer be avoided – a situational curtailment of the "territory of the self" that we have marked out (Goffman 1971, p. 28f.), or of our "personal space." What is meant by this is the cultural equivalent of flight distance in the animal world: an imaginary protective space that surrounds us wherever we go. If strangers enter this space, this causes displeasure and a tendency to retreat. Unlike the flight distance specified in the behavioral program of animals, personal space is flexible, since there are socially defined situations in which strangers can legitimately come closer to us than this, and traveling in a fully-occupied elevator (like waiting in line) is one of them. But even if people do not really "invade our personal space" in these situations, interactive precautions must nonetheless be taken so that the appearance of intimacy does not seem "intentional." The point is to combat an impression that might be given, and to compensate for the spatial proximity with demonstrative indifference.

These, then, are the requirements of elevator travel to which we have to adapt. Before we continue to explore the idea of a structuring of interaction through material circumstances with another example, we would like to visualize the particular structuring power of circumstances with a theoretical example of "non-adaptation." Because of course, the "material constraint" of the elevator (combined with the interaction system) is not an absolute constraint. Regardless of the relative uniformity of the behaviors described previously, it is possible to act differently. This sometimes leads to sanctions, in cases where rules of the interaction system are violated: if someone comes too close to us we demonstratively move away; if someone looks at us for too long we may ask, in annoyance, "Is there a problem?". But not always. Imagine someone who wants to get to the office of Department XY very quickly, storms onto the lift, and then realizes that he does not know what floor Department XY is on. To be on the safe side, he presses the buttons for three floors at once, thus earning the disapproval of the other passengers. He gets upset that the elevator is moving so slowly, is surprised and annoyed that it stops when none of those present want to get out, becomes angry at having to change his position when new passengers get in, and holds the door open at each of the floors he has chosen, so he can get his bearings, etc. The result of this sort of behavior, which is not modified to meet the material requirements, is that courses of action quite simply fail, leading to conflicts and frustrations.

Our second example is about planes. The plane is a mode of transport that shares a number of characteristics with the elevator. Here too, strangers come together to travel, and here too, passengers are spatially and temporally disoriented, and largely restricted in the perception of their movement. There is, however, a substantial difference in the distances covered. With an elevator, we move in a single dimension in a space dictated by a building; with a plane, we travel through space towards a distant destination: we make a journey. This is why Tilman Allert, whose analysis we will be referring to in the following section, examines flying in relation to the general question of "settledness" and spatial mobility, in his 2008 essay "Das Flugzeug als Kommunikationsraum" ("The plane as a space of communication"). This offers an analytical frame of reference which makes it possible to define the specificity of flying as one form of locomotion among others, and to get some distance from everyday interpretations. According to Allert (ibid., p. 62, tr. by N.B.), flying is characterized not only by a "transitory break in settledness," like any journey, but also by a "transitory crisis of location," and by the fact that this is a "risky overcoming of space."

What is meant by the former is that we, as air travelers, are not easily able to relate to our movement. This is not a problem when we travel on foot, by bicycle, by car or by train. There we are able to relate the time and the distance covered to each other; we know where we have come from and where we currently are. This is different in a plane. If we have a window seat, we may possibly, in favorable conditions (daylight, no clouds), be able to gain some clues about where we might be from the topography of the landscape below. As a rule, however, and for the duration of a flight, we do not know this from first-hand experience. It is easy to imagine a flight ending at the point of departure, and the passengers only noticing this after landing, when they are on the ground again. As in an elevator, then, we are largely disoriented. We can tell that there is a "crisis" here, or at least a definite need for orientation, from the fact that, thanks to modern technology, passengers on every flight are given constant updates on the location, altitude and speed of the plane. But this is mediated information – it is not directly experienced.

So what about the "risky overcoming of space?" Objectively speaking, flying is not especially risky, or at least the statistics tell us it is less risky than driving one's own car. Has flying not become just as routine as train travel for "modern humans?"[5] Is it not the case that it is now rare for passengers to applaud after a "successful" landing? (an unmistakable sign that flying is or was felt to be non-routine and risky). To what extent, then, can we actually talk – in this respect – about material circumstances that influence interaction on board? Does this not apply solely to a small group of people with a "fear of flying?" The first observation to be made is that we cannot simply stop while flying. For the duration of the flight, the passengers are tied to a location, the cabin, and to a group, their fellow travelers. They form a community bound together by necessity. It is neither possible to withdraw from the situation, nor to remove other actors. If a plane has to turn around, for example, to eject drunk and disorderly passengers, this is always worthy of mention in the newspaper. Nor is it possible to simply open a window. Of course, this is also the case in modern high-speed trains, but in a plane, we know that we are extremely high up, in an environment that is essentially hostile to life (the altitude itself, the temperature, the air pressure). Lastly and most importantly: however safe flying is, and however routine it has become for many people, risk is still an astonishingly prominent topic during a flight. Not only in the instructions for emergencies which are announced to passengers on every flight, and in the guidance given during the flight if turbulence is to be expected. Sometimes the same captain who invites her passengers to "enjoy the flight" before take-off will wish those transferring to another flight a "safe onward journey" on landing.

What else can be said about the behavioral requirements imposed on flight passengers by the material circumstances? There is a stark contrast between the bridging of distance allowed by a flight and the forced immobility of the participants. Restricted space is the key characteristic of the situation in the cabin. As in the elevator, the idea is to fill the passenger area with as many travelers as possible, though in this case the economic motives of the airlines (but also those of the passengers themselves – hence the name "economy class") are obviously the crucial factor. Legroom is an expensive luxury.[6] But space restrictions define not only the seats, but also the "public" space. In view of the large number of passengers, the narrow aisles, the small number of toilets, and the comings and goings of the food and drink trolleys, every movement is a logistical challenge. In short, flying is linked with a major reduction in our autonomy of action; the time spent on a plane "resembles a stay in a total institution" (Allert 2008, p. 66, tr. by N.B.).

While Allert also considers the "reactions" of the passengers to these circumstances, we shall concentrate on another group of actors in the following section: the flight attendants. A critical difference between flying and taking the elevator is that here we are dealing not only with passengers, but also with people who are present for professional reasons: pilots and flight attendants. This fact itself is also connected to the material requirements. A plane does not fly (fully) automatically and is not remotely controlled, but has to be flown by a person. And it is obvious that such a large group of passengers, on a long journey in the conditions described previously, needs a certain amount of supervision and care. In terms of interaction on board, the first thing to be noted is that the presence of professional actors results in a different inside–outside relationship than that associated with the elevator. It is a little like a restaurant: as a passenger, one enters a clearly demarcated space with a group of people (flight attendants, pilots) who clearly hold responsibility for or "sovereignty" over this space. The pilots and flight attendants play the role of hosts, and as such they greet and welcome the passengers.

What is striking is how explicitly this is done. The pilot greets the passengers as a collective, over the public address system, once they have taken their seats. Although the pilot is not seen at any stage, she introduces herself by name – as if her personal identity were important, rather than the skills that can be expected by virtue of her role. This unobtrusive highlighting of the non-routine is in contrast to the emphatically casual, almost mumbled tone in which she delivers her speech, making it clear to all the passengers (and presumably this is the intent) how unperturbed she is by the upcoming event of the flight. As we have already discussed, Goffman (2013 [1961]) uses the term "role distance" to refer to those behaviors which express that the tasks at hand fall well below one's abilities: all this is routine, almost boring. The flight attendants, on the other hand, greet every passenger individually as they board the plane. This is not simply an emphatically friendly demonstration of approachability. Rather, it simultaneously shows each passenger who is responsible for this space, leaving no room for doubt.

This ambiguity gives an indication of why the flight attendants are a particularly interesting part of the role complex of air travel. For them, the material circumstances described previously give rise to different and quite contradictory requirements: they serve and control simultaneously. This is probably one of the reasons why airlines insist on uniform-like clothing, which symbolizes authority. In this particular place, hospitality not only means taking care of the passengers' well-being, compensating for the narrow, confined setting with attentiveness, little comforts and a touch of luxury, and minimizing expectations of risk with a demonstrative show of nonchalance. It also includes controlling activities, to ensure that the flight proceeds safely and smoothly. The flight attendants not only inform passengers about the safety features of the aircraft; they also check and if necessary insist that luggage is properly stowed, seatbelts are fastened and smartphones switched off. They must also deal with passengers who cannot adapt to the material (and interactive) requirements, intercepting any potential for situation-dependent "deviance." Here Allert (2008, p. 66f.) cites two main types of reaction: "passage compensation" (argumentative behaviors seeking to compensate for the passenger's forced immobility) and "passage protest" (rudeness and vulgarity, expressing a feeling of "permitted regression" in the non-routine situation of flying).

These forms of reaction can be regarded as examples of what happens in the case of flying if we do not conform to the material requirements. What is interesting is that there are also examples like this on the part of the professional actors, in the form of "overconformity" among the flight attendants. This overconformity is not instigated by the flight attendants themselves, but is due to a particular understanding of their role, which is encouraged by the airlines: we are talking about the question of the appropriate level of "emotional labor." The fact that conscious management of their own feelings plays a greater part in the actions of flight attendants than in most other service occupations has to do with the material requirements. If the location itself offers next to no comfort, then it is obvious that the burden of producing comfort falls mainly on interaction. This can be seen as one material reason for the emphatic friendliness of flight attend-ants in interaction – not only in the way they speak to passengers, but especially in their facial expressions, i.e. their demonstrative smiles. At the same time it seems reasonable to assume that this is also – as part of the previously described control function – the best means of producing conformity (as stated, it is not possible here to use the threat of exclusion as a sanction; conflicts must be resolved within the situation). This is the second reason for this emphatic friendliness. However, Arlie Hochschild has shown in her analysis "The Managed Heart" (1983) how far the smiles of flight attendants have gone beyond these requirements and have been integrated into the marketing strategies of the airlines: flight attendants are required to "really" smile, to continuously inject "real," i.e. personal feelings into what are actually impersonal, role-based relationships. "Emotion work" becomes "emotional labor." And this produces a particular kind of frustration, a feeling of emotional alienation.

We have not presented these analyses of interaction under the conditions of elevator travel and flying because we assume these are particularly important objects of microsociological study. Instead, our concern – for want of a general model – was to give an idea of how much the material requirements in interac-tions influence their structure. The analyses seemed particularly suitable for this because they take a comparatively "direct" approach to the problem. Their start-ing point is not the subjective interpretations of those involved, nor is it their practices. Instead, it is attributes of the things, spaces, and technologies, which are in each case initially "translated" into the qualities of a particular form of locomotion, into conditions for action and interaction in these contexts.

We suggest that this can be generalized in interaction theory terms: the mate-rial circumstances of a context of interaction generate *structural problems for action*, which affect those involved whether they like it or not, and therefore become rel-evant for the interaction between them. The problems are always specific ones.[7] The task for analysis is to examine each of these problems and identify their consequences for the context of interaction. Here it is necessary to determine the different positionality of the participants with regard to the overall problems, because specific requirements are connected with these different positions.

Unlike normative, institutional requirements, etc., these material require-ments do not constitute an obligation. They should be understood, rather, as a continuous confrontation with "brute facts" (see Chapter 3),[8] which must inevi-tably be dealt with in action. Of course, I can underestimate certain requirements, deny them, or simply not see them, because I lack the experience or training.

But then this has consequences, as in the case of our examples of "deviance." This allows us to visualize the structuring power of things. But this structuring power affects not only the negative or positive consequences of action. First and foremost – as the analyses were intended to show – it affects the structure of interaction. Structural problems must be overcome interactively; they are something that automatically becomes part of the common ground of the interaction as a shared point of reference. In more precise terms, interaction is faced with the problem of turning the shared material point of reference into common ground.

Even if the examples of the elevator and the plane may suggest that this is the case, "material requirements" does not refer only to dealings with the technicized world. It can also mean natural circumstances of any kind. The sociological perspective of translating material requirements into structural problems is always the same, whether we are carrying out research into mountaineering or cooking. We can even analyze a given landscape, and its spatial (geographical, geological, meteorological, biological) features as a starting point for problems affecting action: what requirements would arise if people were to settle there?[9] Or we can consider the human maturation process as a problem which every individual and every society has to contend with. What challenges must be overcome? What social institutions and patterns of interpretation are developed in response to this?[10]

Lastly, we wish to point out a further aspect which influences the material dimension in interaction: their organizational setting. In our air travel example, we can already see that interaction on board is partly shaped by the division of labor between the professional roles involved and other parameters of work organization. This is generally the case, at least in work-related interactions. A concrete exploration of material requirements is always embedded in an organizational context: it is dependent on the organization of work, the collaboration between different roles and entities and the legal parameters. Here it is entirely possible for the requirements of the "original problem" to be in conflict with the established organizational procedures for processing the problem.

The material requirements may also be primarily social, however, and the matter at hand may be a social problem: the sale of products, the transfer of knowledge, the resolution of social conflicts, the treatment of diseases, care, the acquisition of new insights, the solving of technical problems, etc. As simple as our proposal is, its analytical implementation can be highly complex, faced as it is with the challenge of determining what the general requirements of scholarly knowledge acquisition, jurisprudence or political action *are*. It is obvious that they exist, and that these fields of action and interaction are characterized by particular problems. But claiming to be able to define them, and to decide on particular formulations, seems difficult, not only in view of the complexity of the respective problem areas, but also in view of the abundance of (competing) theories. Such theories have always existed, and in some cases they themselves form part of the fields of action and interaction – for example as professional orientational knowledge. At this point we cannot explore the related methodological problems in any more depth; instead, we will point, on the one hand, to famous examples of such an undertaking (cf. Weber 2004 [1919]). On the other hand, we can also point out that the microsociological perspective, because of its focus on the interactions in laboratories, courtrooms, medical practices, etc., does not require abstract theories, but heuristics – for the concrete requirements in concrete situations.

FOOD FOR THOUGHT

Refer to your transcript of the café scene from *As Good As It Gets*. Consider the café situation from Carol's point of view. What material requirements is she faced with? Try to identify as many as possible.

What particular requirements are added when there are large numbers of customers in the café? As a customer in a café, one sometimes has the impression that the waiting staff "purposely" do not notice when customers at other tables want to give an order. What could be the material background of such an "avoidance of perceptibility"?

Notes

1 In Ireland, for example, divorce was only made possible by a change to the constitution in 1995.
2 Unless one is really friends with or acquainted with a fellow passenger. Social proximity is then also expressed by physical proximity. Such a dyad, however, positions itself in the same way as the individual passengers towards all the other passengers.
3 In the case of the elevator, Hirschauer (2005, p. 52) ascribes this to the fact that it leaves open the possibility to "actualize the virtual community" in the event of a crisis. The possibility of responsiveness, however, points not only to the risks of elevator travel (getting stuck), but also to more harmless opportunities for cooperation such as asking for the time or for the location of a particular office.
4 In this context the everyday phrase "taking a second look" can be understood as an offer of a relationship.
5 Indeed, one often encounters people in trains who obviously have more experience of traveling by plane than by train (and who assume, for example, that seats will be numbered in a single sequence throughout the train rather than car by car).
6 Which in turn allows considerable "distinction gains."
7 In any case we see few opportunities for useful generalizations. At best these might be made about the nature of the relationship between inside and outside, about approaches to natural objects (inanimate/ animate) or social objects, or about the inclusion of role incumbents or "whole persons" etc. (wherever that may lead).
8 Literally so: the "brute facts" discussed in the philosophy of science are not "brute" because they are understood as "natural," or "not socially mediated," but because they are able to upset our ideas about the way the world is made. This power plays a part not only in the process of cognition, but also in everyday practice: in the structuring of our actions.
9 Such analyses have been carried out by Fernand Braudel (1995 [1949]) (the mountain ranges, plateaus and plains of the Mediterranean).

10 Talcott Parsons (1962), for example, described the American idea of "youth" as a particular kind of reaction to the requirements of the developmental phase of "adolescence." And in view of the previous reflections, the model of human developmental phases devised by the psychologist Erik H. Erikson (1963 [1951]) can be seen to be appealing because he conceives these phases from the perspective of certain crisis-like problems, which every individual must cope with in the course of growing up.

References

Allert, Tilman (2008). Das Flugzeug als Kommunikationsraum. Handlungsformen, Vergemeinschaftungstypen und Berufsprofile an Bord. *Sozialer Sinn, 2008/1,* 57–72.

Hirschauer, Stefan (2005). On Doing Being a Stranger: The Practical Constitution of Civil Inattention. *Journal for the Theory of Social Behaviour 35/1,* 41–67.

Hochschild, Arlie (1983). *The Managed Heart. Commercialization of Human Feeling.* Berkeley, CA: University of California Press.

Further reading

Braudel, Fernand (1995 [1949]). *The Mediterranean and the Mediterranean World in the Age of Philip II.* Vol. 1. Berkeley, CA: University of California Press.

Erikson, Erik H. (1963 [1951]). *Childhood and Society.* London, UK: Vintage Books.

Goffman, Erving (1971). *Relations in Public.* New York: Harper.

Goffman, Erving (2013 [1961]). *Encounters. Two Studies in the Sociology of Interaction.* Indianapolis, IN: Bobbs-Merrill.

Habermas, Jürgen (1986 [1981]). *The Theory of Communicative Action. Volume 1: Reason and the Rationalization of Society.* Cambridge, UK: Polity Press. See especially: Relations to the World and Aspects of Rationality in Four Sociological Concepts of Action, pp. 75–101.

Kaufmann, Jean-Claude (1997). *Le cœur à l'ouvrage. Théorie de l'action ménagère.* Paris, France: Armand Colin.

Knorr Cetina, Karin (1999). *Epistemic Cultures: How the Sciences Make Knowledge.* Cambridge, MA: Harvard University Press.

Latour, Bruno (1993 [1991]). *We Have Never Been Modern.* Cambridge, MA: Harvard University Press.

Leroi-Gourhan, André (1993 [1965]). *Gesture and Speech.* Cambridge, MA: The MIT Press.

Luhmann, Niklas (1996 [1984]). *Social Systems.* Stanford, CA: Stanford University Press. See especially: Meaning, pp. 59–102.

Parsons, Talcott (1962). Youth in the Context of American Society. *Daedalus, 91/1,* 97–123.

Röhl, Tobias (2015). Die Objektivierung der Dinge. Wissenspraktiken im mathematisch-naturwissenschaftlichen Unterricht. *Zeitschrift für Soziologie, 44/3,* 162–179.

Weber, Max (2004 [1919]). *The Vocation Lectures. "Science as a Vocation," "Politics as a Vocation."* David Owen and Tracy B. Strong (Eds.). Indianapolis, IN: Hackett Publishing Company.

11

EMOTIONS

How feelings become part of social action

The social dimension of feelings is the subject of the sociology of emotions, and here too there are various approaches. A common feature of all these approaches is that they are not concerned with the affective quality of feelings per se, but with the 'controlled' or 'learned' quality of feelings in social interaction. An important difference between the various approaches is whether they interpret expressions of emotion as 'means to an end' in the social relationship, e.g. in connection to status and power, or – as we argue here – as a form of socially regulated management of social situations. Here we refer to the sociological works of Erving Goffman, Sighard Neckel and Arlie Hochschild, which enable us to understand that expressions of feeling in social interaction are always in part an expression of how we understand and cope with the 'emotional demands' of social situations.

At first glance, "feelings" do not seem to be an object of sociology; instead we see them as the core terrain of psychology. It is psychology that deals with emotional states, states of mind and the emotional experiences of individuals, researching, analyzing and where relevant treating these. In the first instance, this has little to do with "society" – especially as we are accustomed to seeing our feelings as our inalienable "property," as a crucial constitutive element of our subjectivity. Our feelings are an expression of how *we* experience a situation, and this is ultimately incommunicable, because it is tied to "having" these feelings: their particular expression, their timbre and their intensity cannot be measured by others. How would we know how "strongly" someone feels something? Gestures and facial expressions are ultimately only external forms of expression. In everyday life, when theorizing about what might be going on in another person's mind, we, therefore, tend to assume that this is unknowable. Thus if there is a "subjective meaning," a meaning that is fundamentally closed to other people, to intersubjective understanding, then it is the meaning of our feelings. We can all only experience things for ourselves, and experience involves the emotions.

This chapter will be concerned with the social side of feelings, and we will be arguing that feelings – regardless of their highly subjective experiential quality – are quintessentially social, (not by virtue of their existence, but by virtue of their effects). And this becomes really interesting when it comes to determining *in what way* feelings play a part in interactions. In Chapter 5 we saw that feelings are learnt very early in the process of socialization: by means of "affect attunement," which occurs interactively when we take the perspective of others. We are therefore able, even later on in interactions, to adopt the other person's perspective and to adapt our actions accordingly. This perspective is conveyed via linguistic structures of meaning, but also by those based on facial expression. As socialized subjects, we are very good at developing, in interactions, an ad hoc understanding of what the other person's emotional forms of expression mean. This not only applies to basic emotional states such as joy, fear, pain or anger; we can also detect more complex emotional states from people's facial expressions.

Here we must take note of two important aspects: on the one hand, spontaneous, affective expressions of feeling (such as jumping in fright, bursting out laughing, grimacing in disgust, or blushing) are not strictly speaking "communicative," because they are not a controlled selection, consciously made by those "expressing" themselves in this way. There are many such "spontaneous outbursts" that we would prefer to avoid if we could – blushing is a good example of this (we will come back to this later). But of course such expressions of emotion have a very specific and important informational value for observers, even if nothing is being intentionally communicated.

We can test this by finding a reproduction of the painting *The Forge of Vulcan* by Diego Velasquez (easily found with an online search engine) and immediately covering up the left-hand side of the picture. Now let us consider the second blacksmith from the right, abstract this figure from the context of the painting and ask ourselves in what situations this man could have such an expression on his face. We might think of situations such as this: the man could be a soccer player who has just been given a red card by the umpire, out of the blue. What would he say now? "That's ridiculous! I didn't do anything!" So what feeling does his face express? Incredulous astonishment. If we now uncover the left-hand side of the painting, we see that the facial expression is well suited to the scene depicted in the painting: after all, it is no everyday event for a god to visit a forge.[1]

On the other hand, however, in the course of our socialization we have also cultivated a number of our facial and bodily expressions of emotion in such a way that they do not always occur as affective reflexes, but form part of certain complexes of behavior. We *display* a friendly attitude by smiling; we *signal* an expectation by raising our eyebrows; we *indicate* that we are discontented or disconcerted by frowning. In these examples, we want to use our facial expressions to communicate something specific to the other person. In this case, of course, they are not merely "reflexive," but "communicative."

The following section, however, will not be concerned purely with the interpretation of expressions of feeling, but also with the feelings themselves. In what way are the feelings we have dependent on interactions? What role do they play in interactions? The example of Vulcan's blacksmiths offers a preliminary clue: we can see here that certain feelings fit certain situations. "Embarrassment" and "envy" are good examples to help us visualize this. Can the relation between a situation and the "fitting" emotions possibly also help to explain why we "have" these feelings in the first place?

People can mainly tell that we are embarrassed when we blush, but other common signs of embarrassment are looking down, avoiding eye contact with others, covering our face with our hands, putting our hand over our mouth or raising our shoulders and ducking our head. In all these behaviors, we see the desire to escape from the shameful, embarrassing situation by "shrinking" and hiding – and thereby also shrinking and hiding the embarrassing episode itself. While we may feel vicarious embarrassment at events in the media, or relive the feeling when remembering our own previous experiences, embarrassment is primarily something that arises situationally in face-to-face interactions. Something has gone wrong; we present ourselves to the other people present (or are confronted) with a behavior that does not match our own self-image. It is situations where we behave inappropriately or make a bad impression; where we make a faux pas or blunder; where we trip over or act clumsily when we should have been poised and confident. All these things can make us feel awkward, ashamed and embarrassed. Hardly anyone is likely to be completely free of these unpleasant feelings. Some will have them more often, and this is not necessarily because of character traits (shyness, lack of confidence), but may, for example, have to do with the fact that the milieu we are currently in is not the same as the one we come from. We may be new starters in a career or a company, and not yet familiar with the special customs and language found there, or we may have risen above our social origins, but sometimes have trouble behaving "as befits our status."

On this basis, it seems obvious to see embarrassment – or the stronger feeling, shame – as the "social feeling" par excellence (Scheff 2000). We are constantly monitoring whether our actions correspond to our self-image – a self-image that not has only idiosyncratic traits, but is largely identical to the ideas of the group. The feeling of shame or embarrassment that arises when we do not match this self-image can be seen as evidence that at least the person experiencing this feeling assumes there is agreement about what constitutes generally acceptable behavior. If we were deliberately engaging in divergent behaviors as an explicit alternative, then we would not be embarrassed – we would be intentionally provocative, challenging or "unabashed." Embarrassment, then, is about those modes of conduct that are assumed to be seen as normal, matter-of-course and appropriate by all those involved. Being embarrassed or ashamed means admitting that we do not meet these standards, and at the same time it is an expression of the fact that we perceive this as an inadequacy. Basically, what we are saying is: "Yes, it's true, I've behaved wrongly, I should have behaved differently." At the same time we are demonstrating – to others, but also to ourselves – that we are capable of learning, working on the well-known principle that self-aware-ness is the first step towards self-improvement. We can then view embarrass-ment or shame as an independent element that helps to produce conformity to notions of social normality (Scheff 1988), an element that derives its strength from the fact that it is located within ourselves: embarrassment is an expression of "self-socialization."

There is a wide range of sociological literature on the topic of "shame" or "embarrassment," for example on the historical changes in the boundaries of shame (Elias 1994 [1939]), on shame and social inequality (Sennett & Cobb 1973), or on the relationship between shame and social control (Scheff 2000). In these studies, the feeling is primarily analyzed as a link between the more general social structure and the individual. But how is this connection between individual and society produced *interactively*? To explore this question, we will take a closer look, with Goffman (1956), at how the feeling arises in interactions, and what consequences it has for the interaction itself. One of the things that will become evident here is that this is not just a problem which the embarrassed or ashamed individual has to deal with on their own.

For Goffman, embarrassment and embarrassing situations, in general, are phenomena of crisis, which draw our attention to certain general structural fea-tures that are characteristic of interaction in conditions of normality. Another cornerstone of his analysis is the observation that embarrassment follows actions which destroy one's claim to a generally acceptable self. But this requires expla-nation. Why is this about a "self" at all? And what is actually meant by this? The first observation to be made is that embarrassment is not simply a matter of mistakes we make. If we are learning an instrument and constantly play the wrong notes, we are not embarrassed. And even if we have done something wrong in the context of our work, we do not necessarily have to be embarrassed. So this is not about our technical or professional skills as such. Instead, embar-rassment has a moral component; it implies that we have violated moral expec-tations by acting in a certain way. But as Goffman rightly remarks, these are moral expectations of a particular kind. Not every breach of moral expectations leads to embarrassment. If we have done something morally wrong, we do not feel embarrassed, but guilty. Embarrassment is not guilt. If we are embarrassed, this is not just about what we have *done*, but rather we always see it, in part, as a reflection of what we *are* (cf. Scheff 2000). It, therefore, seems reasonable to assume that moral expectations are at stake which concern us in a particular way *as individuals*.

But to what extent is it actually possible, in this context, to speak of "self" or "identity," as Goffman (1956) does? This is unlikely to mean identity in a com-plex sense – a reflexively attained idea of who we are and how we have become this.[2] If this was not already clear, it becomes so when he talks of the "multiple selves" (ibid., p. 270) we possess. Instead, he has something else in mind, a kind of unity of the person, which is related to the specific context of interaction, and takes into account "as what" we wish to act and to appear in each case. At the bank counter, I am unlikely to aspire to look like an insider of the banking industry, but I will want to appear to be a generally capable person and a competent market participant. It is different in my profession or in what I see as my milieu: here my actions are always partly intended to demonstrate membership and belonging.

There is a German saying which is instructive here: "Ist der Ruf erst ruiniert, lebt sich's gänzlich ungeniert" – "Once your reputation is ruined, you can live completely without embarrassment." The possibility of embarrassment always depends in part on whether or to what extent we have a "reputation to lose," or to what extent we have to "keep face."[3] "Face" is the expression Goffman uses for this in later work (cf. especially Goffman 1967). So this is not about role attributes, even in cases where we act in conformity with roles (e.g. within the framework of our professional role), but about us as individuals who are perceived by others. Thematically, there is a reciprocal relationship here between the aspirations and expectations of those involved in the interaction. This is also revealed in the embarrassing situations themselves. What happens in situations where someone involved in an interaction has acted in a way that has not fulfilled the expectations of a generally acceptable self, and where he shows, with signs of embarrassment,[4] that he has noticed this? For a start, he will not be alone with this feeling. Embarrassment is infectious. If he has been exposed by another participant, she will also be embarrassed – in view of his embarrassment – at having exposed him. But this is also an unpleasant situation for the other participants, indeed for the whole interaction system. If the other people involved in the interaction are tactful, they will try to make it seem as if they have not noticed the embarrassment. If this is not possible, all those involved are faced with a problem. This is because – after the discredited action and the signs of embarrassment about it – the assumptions under which the interaction operated are no longer applicable. The context of interaction is disrupted; an important element of the "common ground" has been lost. The interaction can no longer continue unproblematically. There are only two alternatives: the exclusion of the embarrassed party – which the others can achieve by turning away from him or persuading him to leave the scene – or a "repair": if the embarrassed person is not to be excluded, the assumptions about the acceptability of his self must be put into effect again, for example by normalizing the embarrassing behavior ("it could happen to anyone"). This is then a task for the interaction system as a whole.

Interaction is thus characterized by an interplay between successfully projected claims to an acceptable identity, and the confirmation of these claims by the other participants in the interaction (cf. Goffman 1956). If all goes well, we reassure each other, in interactions, that we are full members of the interaction system – and furthermore: of the milieu and the society we are in. In other words, we reassure each other of our psychosocial integrity. We do not have to do this explicitly by patting each other on the back or paying each other compliments. It simply happens in the smooth execution of the interaction itself, in which no one "loses face." Embarrassing situations, however, draw our attention to the fact that this does not happen "on its own:" if psychosocial integrity is produced interactively, then it is always on trial, always in danger. This is a task that must be continually performed in the interaction system. Here emotions play a key role.

If embarrassment or shame is, in a sense, *the* social feeling, can envy then be seen as its counterpart, *the* "unsocial feeling?" The two emotional states have one thing in common, in any case: they are based on a comparison. But whereas in the case of embarrassment we compare our actions with our expectations of ourselves (and others do the same), envy seems, at least superficially, to be less self-referential. This is about a comparison with one or more specific persons, in which we notice, firstly, that they have more than us – a higher income, a bigger house, a nicer body, a faster car, greater talents, greater public recognition, etc. This comparison does not always inspire admiration, however ("I'd like to be like that too"), or ungrudging recognition ("lucky her!", "good for her!"). Often what happens is a negative judgment, and not simply in the sense of a cognitive judgment ("I don't think it's good," "it's undeserved," etc.), but in the sense of a complicated emotional state: envy.

Sighard Neckel's (2000a/b) and Rainer Paris's (2010) analyses are to some extent concerned with explaining the "unsocial" nature of envy. This becomes clear simply from the fact that this feeling – unlike embarrassment – is regarded as illegitimate by society. "You're making me jealous" is an expression that can be only be used if it is not meant altogether seriously. And if we are discrediting a third person in a conversation, we can be silenced with the comment: "You're just jealous."[5] But references to "sinfulness" – in the Catholic tradition, envy is one of the seven deadly sins – do not fully explain this rather complex emotional state, particularly the social genesis of its unsocial aspects.

To do this we need to look more closely at the nature of the comparison from which envy arises. First, it is always related to the *concrete possessions* of the other person: his or her car, house, beauty, talent, or higher income. Another aspect of the feeling of envy, according to Neckel (2000a), is the idea of the world as a zero-sum game: I lack what the other person has, and I lack it *because* he or she has it. From here we could deduce proximity to the feeling of relational, romantic or sexual jealousy. The latter, however, is always about "wanting to have" a specific person in a specific relationship triad. Envy, in contrast, is about the possessions of the other person; it is also more abstract on the relationship level. True, feelings of envy arise mainly in our immediate social environment; they usually relate to neighbors, friends, colleagues or relatives – after all, we need a certain degree of knowledge about the circumstances of the person we envy in order to compare ourselves with him or her in the first place. And yet the connection that the envier creates between himself and the person he envies is an imaginary one. The logic of the zero-sum game makes this clear: with my envy, I *make* someone my rival, even if this is far removed from any reality. I *act as though* her property were something exclusive, to which I am actually entitled. This applies even to those cases in which there really is a direct competitive relationship (the award of a contract; the prize or promotion that went to someone else rather than me). The feeling of envy suppresses the mediated nature of every competitive relationship; it focuses on the rival, not on the conditions in which the competition was decided. (And from here it is but a small step to resentment, because the imaginary nature of envy encourages emotionally charged prejudice.)

Another thing that is clear is that possessions, for the envious person, are not merely something external. The feeling of envy involves not only a comparison between what I possess and what another person possesses, it also includes an identification between person and possessions.[6] For the envier, "having" is "being," and having more, therefore, means being more. Or to be more precise, having less means being less. Because, according to Paris (2010), there is a destructive motive inherent in envy, and this is what ultimately makes it "unsocial." It is not just about wanting to have the other person's possessions, but about destroying them. The basic attitude is not "If I had what the other person has, I'd be happy," but "If the other person didn't have that (either), then I'd be happy."

Unlike embarrassment, then, envy is not a risk that is always present in interaction, because unlike embarrassment it does not arise directly in interactions. The person who is envied has not denied anything to the envier – this is something that the envier merely imagines. But like embarrassment, envy makes it clear that there is something wrong in the relationship structure. What is it in this case? At first, the starting point seems to be something individual, a damaged self (cf. Neckel 2000a): without the feeling of having lost out, there is no envy. In modern societies, however, there is a safeguard against envy: the principle of merit (cf. Neckel 2000b). This principle – to put it in abstract terms – links participation in social opportunities in life (such as income or status) with (mainly work-related) achievements, and therefore also connects the person with his or her possessions. However, this occurs in a "decentralized" way, as it were; as the source of possessions, the person only appears via the intermediary of his or her achievements. It is assumed that possessions are – in principle – well-earned. The idea of merit is something that unites the members of a society in which it prevails. This is not only "worthwhile" for the person who is successful, but also for those who are working towards this, and whose actions show that they have adopted this standard of value. Under these circumstances, it is not only those whose performance meets with particular success in comparison to others who can be certain of social recognition, but also those who have simply done "good work."

Thus the idea of merit can be understood as a way of disciplining the feeling of envy. Conversely, as Neckel (ibid.) points out, envy can be seen as expressing a loss of social order. As the principle of merit as a social value is eroded, and only the logic of actual success counts (regardless of how it has been achieved), so too does the disciplining function of the principle dwindle, and the likelihood of feelings of envy grow. Even in a society which is theoretically a meritocracy – one in which positions are assigned on the basis of achievement or performance – there are many areas in which this principle is not obvious or even seems questionable. A typical example is the frequently criticized "manager salaries" and "manager bonuses:" again and again, people ask what performance could possibly justify an income of several million dollars per annum, and whether the work done by a nurse is not just as "valuable" as that of a CEO. Such considerations certainly call into question a social order in which managers' salaries exceed those of nurses many times over. And in this respect, envy is not merely an idiosyncratic emotional state, indicating a personal sense of inferiority (however this may have arisen); instead, it reflects a pathology of the social order, which is unable to adequately legitimize people's different levels of participation in opportunities in life.

A key assumption of the sociology of emotions is that emotions are important – in the sense of "structure-forming" – because, in combining affect and emotion, they constitute an instinctive and therefore very strong impetus for our actions. The mere existence of feelings is not "social," but feelings are a powerful motor of social action. This notion of a "deep-seated" basis for action is supported by the fact that we find it hard to criticize our emotions. They are there, in the form of a directly and physically experienced evaluation of social situations. They thus provide substantial motivation for actions. However, the analysis of the feelings of embarrassment and envy suggests that emotions should not simply be assigned to the subjectivity of the actors. On the contrary, they seem to show, from the start, a close connection to social situations. Feelings are not only brought into interactions by us; they also reflect certain structural aspects of the situation. We shall risk a generalization here, and view *feelings* in general *as representations of structures of interaction.*[7] They are always *positionally bound*, i.e. they reflect the interaction or situation from the position which we occupy in it. In this respect, they function as a "sensorium" for structures of interaction, which becomes relevant for action because it supplies us with strong motivations. Social structures that penetrate to the level of emotions might, therefore, be considered to be especially "momentous" or to have a particularly lasting impact. In light of this, emotions should perhaps be understood not so much as a separate force or factor in forming the structure of interactions, but rather as a separate dimension of this structure itself. This seems to be what Arlie Hochschild (2013, p. 4) has in mind, in any case, when she says that "it is through emotion that we know the world," and that the critical factor for our actions is whether something (a situation) "feels right" or not.[8]

But how do we deal with feelings? As discussed previously, feelings constitute strong motives and triggers for action, due to their special "presence:"

> It is not we that have feelings, but the feelings that have us. [...] Feelings [...] are psychological events that happen to us, something that cannot be

intentionally brought about and wished for, but which instead has a fundamental and lasting effect on our wishes.

(Paris 2010, p. 11, tr. by N.B.)

At the same time, feelings are a sort of sensorium for interaction and relationship
structures. What happens to us as a psychological event is always also a response
to the situations in which we find ourselves. But that is not the whole story. The
way we feel is not only related to the immediate situation; rather our emotional
life is subject to general social parameters that go beyond specific situations.
One of these parameters is the standards of emotional control. Social convention demands that we do not immediately follow every impulse – be it emotions
connected to our drives, or to social situations. Norbert Elias (1994 [1939]) in
particular pointed out that the process of social modernization is always in part
a process of "civilization" in this respect: the standards of self-control rise, and
we internalize these standards in such a way that they usually govern our actions
"as a matter of course."

We are not helplessly at the mercy of our feelings, then. The normative expectation is that we will control how and how much we allow emotions to determine our actions. The social parameters also concern the nature of the feelings
themselves, however. Not only are we urged to "pull ourselves together," to "not
let ourselves go," or generally speaking, to *show* feelings in a particular way; we
are also encouraged to *have* certain feelings in certain situations. There are norms
for this too, "emotional rules," which determine in which situations we are supposed to feel love, grief, anger, etc. A prominent example of such norms has to
do with modern couple relationships. Talcott Parsons (1954 [1949]) pointed out
that married couples do not simply love each other (or not) as a matter of fact.
Rather, we are normatively obliged to love our partner, given that the feeling of
love is the only legitimate basis for entering into a couple relationship in modern
times. And as Giddens (1992) stresses, in recent decades this has also applied to
the preservation of the relationship: we must not only have loved our partner
once, we must continue to love him or her. Other motives (such as upward social
mobility, financial support, social recognition, fear of being alone) are no longer
admissible or at least require justification.

But what if we do not fulfill these requirements? What if we do not love
(enough), if we do not, in the situations where it is expected of us, feel the appropriate pride, grief, sympathy, joy or anger? What if we harbor inappropriate feelings such as envy or jealousy? The answer is that unless we want to persist in our
feelings contrary to these requirements, we will carry out "emotion work." We
will try to feel "properly;" we will make an effort to influence the feelings we
have so that they correspond to the way we think we ought to feel (cf. Gerhards
1988). With this work, we not only influence action itself, we also try to influence the motivational basis for action. Thus the self-socializing effect that can
be attributed to embarrassment as an interactive event (cf. Goffman, previous) is
generalized and shifted "to the inside."

The concept of "emotion work" goes back to an essay by Arlie Hochschild (1979). Discussing Goffman and Freud, she is mainly concerned to find an approach that will allow what might be referred to as a case-specific examination of how people deal with emotions:

> The very topic, sociology of emotion, presupposes a human capacity for, if not the actual habit of, reflecting on and shaping inner feelings, a habit itself distributed variously across time, age, class, and locale.
>
> *(Hochschild 1979, p. 557)*

This is not just about the "general," then – about feelings as a response to structures of interaction, about general normative parameters – but about the manner in which, in particular situations, specific individuals in a given era or a particular social milieu perceive the general requirements regarding their own emotional life, and how they deal with these. This approach is offered by "emotion work," which is "the act of trying to change in degree or quality an emotion or feeling" (Hochschild 1979, p. 561).

Once again, the starting point for this is a comparison. We compare the feelings we actually have in concrete situations with what is expected of us by virtue of general emotional rules. In everyday language, these rules are expressed in utterances such as "You shouldn't feel so guilty. It wasn't your fault," "You have no reason to be jealous. Nothing happened!" or "So, how are you feeling? Today's your big day!" We cannot help making such comparisons. This happens automatically, as the emotional rules are a part of our subliminal knowledge of rules. Sometimes, in the case of a discrepancy, we become aware of our "emotional inadequacy." If we then carry out "emotion work," this is a conscious activity – but only "if." Because the way we deal with the discrepancy, whether we persist in our feelings, whether we carry out emotion work, what "techniques" we use to do so, all this depends on us and on the particular circumstances – and this is exactly what sociologists should be investigating.

A vivid – if not exactly everyday – example of such an analysis is offered by Steven M. Ortiz (2011). He examines the situation of the wives of professional athletes (baseball and football players). These women are confronted with a number of special requirements in their marital life, and therefore their emotional life, including special emotional rules that they must begin by learning. For a start, the media attention focused on them demands a considerable amount of "face work" (see previous), in terms of both public and private life. The women soon learn, for example, that their presence at games is under observation. The "rules of game etiquette" demand a certain interest in the game, which includes suppressing feelings of disappointment with the men's performance, or annoyance about things that happen before or during the game, and putting on a "happy face" that signals support. But even in the domestic context, it is expected that their emotional life will be subordinated to the special requirements of their husbands' careers. This calls for a considerable degree of emotion work – from the point of view of those involved, in any case. Thus worries and upsets in connection to family life are suppressed in favor of interested and supportive feelings. Anger and frustration, which would actually be justified in view of certain behaviors of the husbands, are curbed out of consideration for the men's particular emotional tension, and so as not to endanger the peace in the short periods of shared domesticity. In addition, the constant presence of female fans demands a particular approach to jealousy, and sexual desire is also something that – in these particular living conditions – must sometimes be suppressed, and sometimes cultivated, as it were, in order to fulfil one's "marital duties." We may question how "special" or "particular" these conditions of life and/or marriage are. What is striking, in any case, is the extreme asymmetry in the performance of emotion work, and the fact that this work is not only invested in the relationship itself, but also in the husband's professional success – here emotion work is at the expense of these women's emotional well-being.

FOOD FOR THOUGHT

Refer to your transcript of the café scene from *As Good As It Gets*. Consider Carol's speech act: "I want your life for one minute, where my big problem is somebody offers me a free convertible so I can get out of this city." Is this an expression of envy, as we have defined it here? Is there also a reference here to an idea of "merit"? Give reasons for your answer.

How might Frank be feeling as he leaves the café? What advice would you give him in terms of "emotion work"?

Notes

1 Another good opportunity to practice this is the portraits of emotions by the American cognitive researchers Aleix M. Martinez and Shichuan Du (Martinez & Du 2012). Here too, it is helpful to imagine social situations in which one might have the facial expression in question. Things are more complicated when we look at the busts of the Austrian Baroque sculptor Franz Xaver Messerschmidt. This is probably because these are exaggerated representations.

2 See also the remarks on the question of identity in Chapter 5.

3 This is dependent on both the context of interaction and the individual. In order to be embarrassed, the individual must identify with the milieu in which he or she has a "mishap." But there must also be normative standards present in the interaction, allowing modes of conduct to be attributed to the individual as a person in terms of appropriateness or inappropriateness.

4 As if it were not bad enough already, signs of embarrassment can be embarrassing themselves. Why? Not only because they make obvious the discrepancy between our self-image and our current self-representation. But also because our own aspiration to self-confidence has been destroyed by the signs of embarrassment – a further reason to be embarrassed.

5 Political strategists use this to brand criticism of social inequality as "class envy."
6 And thus a kind of personification of possessions. This is due to the assumption of exclusivity, such as would be expressed in real competition for an exclusive commodity (the first prize, the only painting). From this perspective envy actually is close to (relational) jealousy; it is an imagined jealousy, so to speak.
7 This hypothesis remains to be tested, of course, i.e. other emotional states would also have to be examined to see to what extent they can be understood as a reflection of interactive structures.
8 Hochschild (2013, p. 32ff.) tries to pursue this idea further with the concept of "empathy maps." We do not have space here to explore the questions that arise from this: to what extent we can actually be sure of our feelings, or to what extent we always have adequate access to our feelings.

References

Goffman, Erving (1956). Embarrassment and Social Organization. *American Journal of Sociology, 62/3*, 264–271.
Hochschild, Arlie R. (1979). Emotion Work, Feeling Rules, and Social Structure. *American Journal of Sociology, 85/3*, 551–575.
Neckel, Sighard (2000a). *Die Macht der Unterscheidung. Essays zur Kultursoziologie der modernen Gesellschaft*. Frankfurt a. M., Germany: Campus. See especially: Neid – Ein Gefangenendilemma, pp. 73–81.
Neckel, Sighard (2000b). *Die Macht der Unterscheidung. Essays zur Kultursoziologie der modernen Gesellschaft*. Frankfurt a. M., Germany: Campus. See especially: Blanker Neid, blinde Wut? Sozialstruktur und kollektive Gefühle, pp. 110–130.
Paris, Rainer (2010). *Neid. Von der Macht eines versteckten Gefühls*. Waltrop, Germany: Manuscriptum.

Further reading

Elias, Norbert (1994 [1939]). *The Civilizing Process. Sociogenetic and Psychogenetic Investigations*. Oxford, UK: Blackwell Publishers.
Gerhards, Jürgen (1988). Die sozialen Bedingungen der Entstehung von Emotionen. Eine Modellskizze. *Zeitschrift für Soziologie, 17/3*, 187–202.
Giddens, Anthony (1992). *The Transformation of Intimacy. Sexuality, Love & Eroticism in Modern Societies*. Stanford, CA: Stanford University Press.
Goffman, Erving (1967). *Interaction Ritual. Essays on Face-to-Face Behavior*. New York: Pantheon Books. See especially: On Face-Work, pp. 4–45.
Hochschild, Arlie R. (1997). *The Time Bind. When Work Becomes Home and Home Becomes Work*. New York: Henry Holt & Company.
Hochschild, Arlie R. (2013). *So How's the Family? and Other Essays*. Berkeley, CA: University of California Press.
Martinez, Aleix, & Du, Shichuan (2012). A Model of the Perception of Facial Expressions of Emotion by Humans: Research Overview and Perspectives. *Journal of Machine Learning Research, 13*, 1589–1608.
Ortiz, Steven M. (2011). Wives Who Play by the Rules: Working on Emotions in the Sport Marriage. In Anita Ilta Garey & Karen V. Hansen (Eds.), *At the Heart of Work and Family. Engaging the Ideas of Arlie Hochschild* (pp. 124–135). New Brunswick, Canada: Rutgers University Press.

Parsons, Talcott (1954 [1949]). *Essays in Sociological Theory.* New York: The Free Press. See especially: The Kinship System of the Contemporary United States, pp. 177–196.

Scheff, Thomas J. (1988). Shame and Conformity: The Deference-Emotion System. *American Sociological Review, 53,* 395–406.

Scheff, Thomas J. (2000). Shame and the Social Bond: A Sociological Theory. *Sociological Theory, 18/1,* 84–99.

Sennett, Richard, & Cobb, Jonathan (1973). *The Hidden Injuries of Class.* New York: Vintage Books.

12

PRACTICE *OR* THE PRESSURE TO ACT

This chapter, lastly, offers a specific perspective on the contribution of "actors" to the development of structure in interactions. Based on the works of George H. Mead and Ulrich Oevermann, we elaborate a model of "decision-making" not as a primarily rational procedure, but as a mostly unconscious, yet "creative" process, i.e. a process that always has at least the potential to transform structure. This potential is inherent in the sequential organization of interaction.

If we review the previous chapters of this book, there is no overlooking the fact that "the general" predominates. The focus is on formal and material structural parameters for interaction. Either structure is already there before interaction takes place, or a structure that is independent of the specific interaction partners develops within the interaction. The "particular" has played a subordinate role so far. Representatives of symbolic interactionism could object that this is a strange sort of interaction analysis we are advocating here. After all, they might argue, this analysis lacks the crucial element, those who are "inter-acting:" the actors. Now it should have become clear that we have in fact presented a special version of interaction analysis – one in which the theoretical emphasis is not only on the dyadic relation between two interactants, but which stresses that aspects of a mediating third element have always played a constitutive role here.[1] In the terminology of systems theory, this is "society:" institutions, frames, norms, roles. There are also structural parameters of human sociality, which are even more general then this macro level of specific societies: sequentiality and reciprocity. But it is true that there must be more to it than that. The contribution of actors to the development of structure in interactions still has to be defined.

At the same time, it is important to note that the question of the particular contribution of the actors only presents itself as a question of theoretical

importance once the general structures that precede or overarch concrete interactions have been analyzed. Because then it cannot simply be answered with the
statement that it is actors who are interacting. Instead, it is necessary to define the
point at which they do not act as representatives of society/ sociality. What could
this point be? The codes that are usually used are "creativity," "innovation" or
"self-will." It seems reasonable to acknowledge such an element of creativity in
interaction – partly because it matches our self-image as members of modernized
Western societies. And yet, when we consider this as sociologists, we are equally
quick to back-pedal, and to regard what seemed at first glance to be especially
creative or individual as "socially influenced" or even "socially determined."
Must "actor" not ultimately be understood as a more or less complex embodi-
ment of social structure, mediated by socialization and life history?

This brings us back to one of the fundamental questions of sociology: the
question of the relationship between individual and society, this time in the form
of the relationship between autonomy and heteronomy (actions influenced or
determined by others). We will begin with two assumptions. On the one hand,
we assume that there *is* such a thing as autonomy. We make decisions, and do
not simply follow society's rules. This makes intuitive sense, since decisions are
part of social life. When the waiter asks us which of the two dishes of the day
we would like, then we have to answer, however strongly we believe in social or
neurophysiological determinism. And sometimes these decisions lead to innovations; whether on a large or a small scale, our actions can change structures. On
the other hand, we assume that this element of decision-making or innovation
can hardly be understood as an exotic exception in social life, which is added to
the normality of structural reproduction, continuity and routine as a result of
external influences. Instead, we need a model that always considers the actors'
"creativity" as a possibility. Once again, the classical sociologist who has made a
major contribution in this respect is George Herbert Mead.

In fact, Mead (1992 [1934]) also begins his analysis with the socially bound
nature of all action, and of the individual personality. He is already able to show in
his theory of human communication that human verbal communication always
contains an element of perspective-taking (see Chapter 5). If I say to somebody:
"Could you close the window?", then even if I am not an especially sensitive
person (or in other words, whether I like it or not), I am considering the position
of the other person. But even if I am not paying any particular attention to the
position of the person I am addressing, this position is present in my speech. This
is already apparent from the phrasing I have chosen. If I said "Hey, could you
close the window already? I can't concentrate with all that noise," this would be
a different position. But with my choice of phrasing, I have addressed the other
person as (for example) someone who has said quarter of an hour ago that she was
going to close the window because of the noise, but has not yet done so.

Every speech act contains this element of being "tailored" to the position of
the addressee. Language forces me to choose my utterance depending on the
position of the addressee. I can try, in anticipation, to "strike the right note,"
but the other person can still criticize the tone of my utterance, even if it is only

with a reaction such as "Relax, I'm onto it." Or in the terminology of behavioral theory, to which Mead felt indebted: my linguistic utterance is not only a stimulus for the person it is addressed to, but also for myself, through the fact that I am speaking. In order for this to be possible, both interaction participants must have access to intersubjectively shared structures of meaning (see Chapter 5).

If communication is always "social," in the sense of this kind of perspectivity and the utilization of universal structures of meaning, then the personality of the individual must also be social, according to Mead. As he sees it, the elementary units that make up the personality are mutually interlocking expectations, or in other words complementary roles. The central question is then how the complementary roles are organized. Mead (1992 [1934]) explores this question with reference to the maturation process of the individual, and distinguishes two states or stages, as it were. The first stage consists of the development and differentiation of individual role complements, which do not yet have much connection to each other. The paradigmatic example, for him, is childish role play. Children play mother and child, cowboys and Indians (or they did in the past, in any case), shop assistant and customer. One element of play is that children can – as a matter of course – take either role position, and can, therefore, switch roles. But they largely operate within these role dyads, without being able to establish a connection between them and without having any sense of play as play.

One decisive step in the personality development of adolescents is then connected with a change in the organization of expectations, a sort of synthesis, which is associated with a fundamentally different understanding of social actions. Mead (ibid.) illustrates this by comparing the rule-governed game with (role-)play. To play a game of soccer, for example, it is necessary to be able to adopt the perspective of a whole nexus of roles. So I am not just the center forward awaiting the crucial pass from other members of the team. I also know the roles of the other parts of the team, how they relate to each other, and what this means for me; I know you have to play differently when leading three nil and when trailing three nil; I obviously know the constitutive rules of the game; I know when it might make sense to break them, and I know how to react to a rule violation by the opposing team.

The other person I relate to in my actions is no longer a "particular other," nor is it a number of particular others, each of whom I relate to in a specific role relationship – though this continues to be important, as shown by talk of a "well-oiled" or "well-coordinated" team. Instead, the entity I am interacting with here is – as Mead calls it – a "generalized other." This refers to the combination of all the expectations or attitudes towards the individual that can exist in a collective:

> The attitude of the generalized other is the attitude of the whole community.
> *(Mead 1992 [1934], p. 154)*

Internalizing this generalized other is, as it were, the integrative task that all young people have to perform. The idea is that once they have achieved this, they are able to apply the different expectations of society to themselves in interactions:

> only in so far as he takes the attitudes of the organized social group to which he belongs toward the organized, co-operative social activity or set of such activities in which that group as such is engaged, does he develop a complete self or possess the sort of complete self he has developed.
>
> *(Mead 1992 [1934], p. 155)*

Thinking and acting is only possible if we adopt the attitudes of the generalized other towards ourselves.

Now Mead could have left it at this analysis. The insight gained would be that if all goes well, "society" always operates within us, whatever situation we find ourselves in. This does not always work equally well, and sometimes we deviate from the expectations of the "generalized other," but ultimately this only confirms the validity of these expectations. Theories of this kind do exist. Emile Durkheim's (1961 [1905]) and Talcott Parsons's (1956) theories of socialization are essentially constructed in this way. For Mead, however, such an analysis of the social constitution of personality is insufficient. It can explain neither the actual impact of personality on interaction, nor how an identity, a reflexive self-relationship, is able to develop.

Mead's (ibid.) crucial idea is that the personality (the "self") should no longer be understood as a monolithic object which takes effect in interactions. This means a break with the everyday view, in which we see (and indeed have to see) people as entities who can be held responsible for their actions. In this respect, he does something similar to what Sigmund Freud did before him with regard to the human soul: he divides the personality into different elements, which are in a dynamic relationship to each other. Unlike Freud, however, with his distinction between ego, superego and id, Mead has only two elements, which he calls "I" and "me." His model also has a more obvious dynamism than Freud's, as these elements can only be understood in the context of a certain dialectic within action.

The intended meaning of this distinction can be deduced at least in part from the terms chosen. "Me" is the pronoun used situationally to point to oneself as an object. For example: "Who's there?" – "It's me"; "Better you than me." "I," on the other hand, is used to refer to the self as a linguistic subject. If we bear in mind that in Mead's view any self-observation or self-addressing is only conceivable as an adoption of the perspective of the social group, then it makes sense to understand the "me" as a placeholder for "society within me," so to speak; it is the entity that helps me to understand situations of interaction, and, most importantly, reminds me of what is expected of me in these situations. The "I," on the contrary, is the entity that reacts to this, the entity that acts:

> The 'I' is the response of the organism to the attitudes of the others; the 'me' is the organized set of attitudes of others which one himself assumes.

> The attitudes of the others constitute the organized 'me,' and then one reacts toward that as an 'I.'
>
> *(Mead 1992 [1934], p. 175)*

In terms of interaction theory, the first thing to be noted here is this: I do not merely react to external stimuli (actions of others, material requirements), but my perception of the situation (in a broad sense) has always interpreted these stimuli already, in the light of the structural and normative parameters of society. So ultimately I always turn external stimuli into "internal stimuli" (if we want to retain the terminology of behavioral theory). But this does not overcome my problem, the question of how I should act; on the contrary, this is just the start of the problem. To resolve it, according to Mead (ibid.), we must envisage another entity, since a structured exhortation to act is one thing, but the action itself is another. I must respond to the action of the other person, I must take action myself, take up a position. And an entity that is exhortative in nature cannot do this. This is the task of the "I."

In actual interactions, the whole process is multilayered and correspondingly complicated. As soon as I have acted, this action is again subjected to scrutiny by the "me," and the result may be, for example, that I am ashamed of or embarrassed about what I have done (as we saw in Chapter 11). But my embarrassment, and the way I manifest it, can, in turn, be understood as an action. Because a critical appraisal of my performance in the specific situation does not necessarily have to lead to a feeling of shame or embarrassment, at least perhaps not with such intensity and in a way that is visible to others. My embarrassment as an action can then, in turn, be criticized in the light of my "me" – leading to a "shame loop," i.e., I am ashamed of my own shame, or embarrassed about my own embarrassment. And what is more, even the "me" does not remain untouched in this dynamic of action. Our inner understanding of the social world does not stay completely the same from youth onwards. Even if we assume that many fundamental attitudes remain comparatively stable, we will still modify our "me" in the light of our experiences in interactions (How did we act? How did we rate these actions? How did others rate these actions?). On closer examination, then, "I" always becomes "me."

Such reflections tend towards a theory of personality development or identity formation, and indeed the "I/me" dialectic can be seen as the motor of this development. But this is not our concern in the present context. Instead, we are trying to determine what it is that actors really contribute to the formation of structure in interactions. We can now say, based on Mead's model, that the "I" is crucial in this respect, as an element of spontaneity. We can gain a better understanding of what this is about by investigating when the "I" becomes especially tangible. This is the case in situations of crisis: the pressure of having to act is felt with particular clarity when we are in a crisis, i.e. when we no longer know what to do next. What we refer to as a personal or existential crisis is a prime example of this. But we can talk about a crisis in a broader sense whenever the stream of action is interrupted, whenever we can no longer "carry on" unreflect-ingly, either because a previous course of action has failed, or because we face a task that we cannot cope with easily, i.e. by applying a tried and tested pattern of action. Mead (1964) studied this situation in an essay entitled "The Definition of the Psychical." Here he stresses, among other things, that it is precisely in these situations that we become aware of ourselves as actors, in our subjectivity. At this point, however, we shall stop following Mead and turn to a more recent the-ory in which this model is developed further – Ulrich Oevermann's reflections on *Handlungszwang* ("being forced to act") and *Begründungsverpflichtung* ("being under obligation to provide a justification/ rationale").

In the framework of his theory of "life practice," Ulrich Oevermann takes up Mead's reflections on the dialectic of "I" and "me." For Oevermann, the concepts of "crisis" and "routine" are central. His model can best be explained in the context of an analysis of how something new comes into being (cf. Garz & Raven 2015; Oevermann 1991). Here the idea of the crisis is of major theoretical importance, although crises – fortunately – are generally the exception in every-day practice. Fortunately, because although we seek a little variety now and then, we find crises, by their very nature, exhausting, and therefore tend to build up routines. Something new, however, can only emerge in those situations where proven patterns of action are no longer effective. As soon as this idea has been expressed, it seems obvious – how could it be any other way? After all, the new would otherwise be the product of something old, familiar, tried and tested – but not new. In sociological terms, however, this idea is very important, because it means we do not have to simply offload the question of the emergence of the new onto psychology, or classify it as inexplicable ("a flash of inspiration"), but can instead make it accessible to sociological study. This is done by defining the new as an element within action, and within interaction.

What characterizes all situations of crisis, then, is precisely what Mead took as his starting point for defining subjectivity/ the psychic: routine, self-evident action is no longer possible. At the same time, we cannot evade these crisis situations. We have to act. This is an aspect that did not yet emerge so clearly in Mead's work. Oevermann (1991) speaks here of *Entscheidungszwang* ("being forced to make decisions"): even if we are indecisive or try to avoid the crisis situation, we have made a decision – in favor of hesitation or evasion. This is an idea that is not fundamentally new in sociology. It means another break with everyday experience, a break that is important for the understanding of social reality. When we talk about "decision-makers," for example, or when we say that "something has to be done now," this reflects a different view, and one that dominates our approach to everyday life. It is characterized by the notion that decision-making and action involve a sort of "positive" attitude, an attitude of "taking things in hand" and "making a difference:" "Just do something!"

But a different concept of action has been proposed for sociology, dating back to Max Weber (2013 [1922]) at the beginning of the 20th century: for sociol-ogy, he argued, acquiescence or omission should also count as action. Even the various forms of "rational choice theory" (subsequently referred to as "RC theory"),[2] while positing that the actions of individuals are based on calculations, do not assume that these calculations are consciously deployed in the way they might be for the choice of a holiday or a home loan. In other words, decisions can, as it were, take place behind the actors' backs, even if they themselves make the decisions. We *have* acted, even if we only think that we really ought to have done so. And we make decisions even in situations where we do not think we are doing so, because it all feels so natural and normal. In short, regardless of *how* we behave in relation to a decision-making situation, we always take up some position; we always assume an attitude towards the world with regard to the question at hand. And sociology must take this into account. It cannot restrict itself to those decisions that seem normatively appropriate, that embody activity – and thus, in turn, imply the attribution of responsibility to individuals. To do so would be to overlook a relevant section of reality.

This is an idea that Oevermann (see previous) not only makes particularly clear with the concept of "being forced to decide;" he also, following Mead, identifies its position in microsociological terms: as an inevitable reaction to crisis situations. As in Mead's "I/me" dialectic (see previous), "being forced to decide" does not stand alone. Its counterpart is "being obligated to justify" (*Begründungsverpflichtung*). For Oevermann (1991), it is these two elements together, as a "contradictory unit," that characterize *practice*: having to make decisions in interactions, and then being required to defend these decisions to oneself and to others. But why do we need to justify our decisions? And why are we in this case not "forced," but "obligated" to justify ourselves? The need for justification arises, in a sense, from the nature of a decision. We will discuss this in the following section, where it will become easier to understand why "being forced to decide" and "being obligated to justify" are two parts of a *contradictory* unit. At this point, it will suffice to point out that Oevermann (ibid.) is revisiting an idea from Hegel (2008 [1821]), according to which every action, in principle, lays claim to rationality, and must, therefore, be justifiable. But while justifiability is inherent to a decision, we are not "forced" to make our justifications available: we cannot escape the decision-making situation, but we can refuse to justify our decisions ("No idea," "Just because," "Why not?"). This lends something of an ethical aspect to this part of practice, which is why it is an "obligation" rather than a "compulsion."

But let us first turn to the question of what actually constitutes a decision. As already mentioned, the concept of the decision is exceptionally important not only in the context of the theory of life practice, but also in that of other influential theories, especially in the different versions of RC theory. Here too, action is essentially understood as a matter of making decisions or choices. As RC theory is generally also seen as "microsociology" (see introduction), and as it has, at first glance, some similarities with the models of Mead and Oevermann presented above, it makes sense to examine the differences between them. This works best if we consider the question of what a decision is.

One example: we are standing in front of a supermarket shelf and choosing a tube of toothpaste from among those on offer. This is obviously a decision. It does not involve any particular crisis, though, especially if we always buy a certain brand. Still, it can rightly be said that at some point we must have made a decision, that is, a real choice between different options. And furthermore, we are constantly confronted by new products, so the decision-making situation is continually refreshed, as it were. While there is usually little sign of any decision-making pressure or difficulty here, given the very small sums of money involved, we can easily imagine other choices (a car, a rental apartment or a house) that do involve pressure and difficulty, due to their greater financial impact.

How do we approach this problem of choice? One thing all theories of rational choice have in common is the idea that there are essentially two components to this approach. The first is that, when choosing between two objects (these can also be actions), we fundamentally base our decision on the assumption that the preferred object will offer us the greater benefit. The criteria for evaluating the available objects are then determined with regard to this benefit. The second component is that this evaluation takes the form of a calculation. I compare the objects in question systematically, with regard to their relevant qualities, and choose the object that offers the greatest overall benefit in this respect. The calculation is important, because it would otherwise not be a "rational" decision.

Of course, this is a completely normal procedure in everyday practice. In the examples mentioned, we would even expect something of the kind: "impulse buys" would be unusual, at least in the case of cars and houses. And it may therefore be intuitively plausible to apply this model of calculated maximization of benefit (as RC theory has done) to decision-making situations that do not at first glance seem to match the model, e.g. the choice of a partner, the decision about whether to have a child, the decision about whether to end a marriage. Indeed some would say that the model has been successfully tested on situations of this kind. In such cases, however, it could seem questionable whether it makes sense to speak of maximizing benefits, and whether the assumption of a calculation is realistic.

In fact, there has been a broad discourse in which both components have been subjected to critical scrutiny. And one of the main differences between the varieties of RC theory lies in the way they each understand the benefit and the calculation. We will not explore these questions at this point, partly because they are especially hard to answer if "benefit" is defined so broadly that it can be linked with the assumptions of evolutionary biology, and if calculations are seen as working unconsciously as well as consciously. The main reason not to explore this approach further, though, is that it strikes us as categorically underdetermined for a methodological investigation of decision-making processes – because the concept of rational choice obliterates something that is essential for decision-making. So once again, what is a decision?

First, it is a process that involves a crisis. This does not fit into – and has not found its way into – RC theory. As we have seen, in the paradigmatic cases of decision-making, the starting point for "being forced to decide" is a crisis, in the form of a manifest failure of convictions and patterns of action. For example, the dissolution of a marital relationship constitutes a profound personal crisis. This element of crisis, however, cannot be connected with the element of choice. Nonetheless, an attempt is made to do precisely this in the form of so-called "frame selection:" the assessment that "this is a bad marriage" is declared to be an act of choice (cf. Esser 2002).[3] A crisis, however, cannot be chosen; we can be struck by a crisis or plunged into a crisis, and if the crisis is within a social relationship, then we ourselves are part of the crisis.

Second, there is still something crisis-like about the resolution of the crisis, even in those cases where a decision is in line with social expectations, and does have its origins in a manifest failure of convictions. Noteworthy examples of such weak points or fractures in social routine are the choice of a career and a partner. Here too, "being forced to decide" implies a "gap" or "gulf" in action (cf. Searle 2001), which must be overcome. This applies even to the choice between dishes of the day or toothpaste brands, although it is less striking here. We become aware of it, however, in practical decisions of a different kind: when we are faced with deciding between one career or another; when we wonder whether to give something to this beggar, and not the next; when we wonder, as our child lies screaming with rage on the supermarket floor, whether it might be better to buy him that candy after all. But whatever decision-making situations we bring to mind, there is always an element of uncertainty about the rationality of a decision that has to be made, and this uncertainty cannot be completely eliminated.

This second element of crisis, like the first, is overlooked in RC theory, and is incompatible with it. This is because the theory works on the opposite assumption: the decision is absorbed into the calculation; it is nothing but the execution of its anticipated result. If the calculation determines the decision, however, then it is no longer a decision. In Oevermann's terminology, one characteristic of decisions is that they are open-ended, not a foregone conclusion. However much we try to protect ourselves with calculations when we have to make a decision, we nonetheless never have a complete rationale for our decision. In fact, we ourselves do not exactly know how we will decide until we have decided and acted. As we know, it makes a difference whether voters are surveyed when entering or when leaving the polling station. We must not forget that the "I" is the entity of spontaneity.

In light of the above, we can also formulate a further, microsociological explanation for "being obligated to justify" (*Begründungsverpflichtung*). If I do not have, in advance, a complete rationale for my anticipated decision, then it is obvious that I will endeavor to construct one after the fact. And this is simply in order to gain clarity about my own actions. Here *Begründung* comes to have not just the Hegelian meaning of justification, but also an element of reconstruction, of explanation of one's action.[4] We can now also see the extent to which "being forced to decide" and "being obligated to justify" constitute a contradictory unit. This is because the decision itself occurs under conditions of openness, while the obligation to provide a rationale aims to understand the decision that has been made as (pre)determined.[5]

If, then, we must assume an irreducible leeway in decision-making, then we must be able to name an entity that fills this space. In Oevermann's (2005) model, this is "life practice" (*Lebenspraxis*). This is also referred to as the "source of transformation," the "decision-making center" and the "center of the autonomy of social life" (ibid., tr. by N.B.). These rather flowery, metaphorical labels are due to the fact that it is not easy to conceptualize what this is about, since it is not a matter of simply attributing decision-making to individuals, as we do in everyday practice. In everyday practice it is accepted that the actors decide, must decide, have decided. We as individuals are held responsible for our actions. But in sociological terms, little is gained from this attribution. Because the individual, the "person," not only embodies the element of decision-making, but also the generality of society (the "me," in Mead's terms), which requires the decision and prescribes the framework of possible decisions. A different terminological marker is therefore required; in Mead's work this is the "I," in Oevermann's it is "life practice." What is crucial for the present context is that the framework of Oevermann's theory allows us to identify this element of autonomy and of potential structural transformation more clearly as something inherent *in the structure of the interaction itself.*

How are we to define the new element that can arise in the overcoming of a crisis? For whom is it new? Is this a matter of general innovations, in the sense that, for example, scientific, artistic, economic or political innovations can claim to be valid throughout society, or even universally valid? Is it more a matter of "local" achievements? Or is the new limited, in the end, to my own life, or to those close relationships that I am part of? In actual fact, of course, it is about all of these things. It is only possible to determine what can be regarded as new by considering the structure that has been transformed. The spectrum is broad: from innovations that might be in the running for a Nobel Prize (abstract knowledge), and political revolutions with significance for world history (political practice), to things that will be done differently, from now on, in a company, organization or community (organizational structures), right down to the changes that can take place in our relationships with our partner, our child or ourselves, e.g. in the context of a therapy (family relationships, self-relationship).

An innovation, then, means the transformation of a structure; it means that at one point in a sequence something will be done differently than before and that this change will be substantive and have a lasting effect – whether it be in our personal relationships, or as part of a larger collective. This applies even to the major "revolutionary" transformations, which must of course also happen on the micro level of interaction in order to become a reality.[6] Transformation means that we choose a different option than before, and establish new options, as a result of our substantive criticism of certain situational conditions (role requirements, frames, norms) in interactions.

But not every crisis leads to an innovation. That might be desirable, but the decisive factor is ultimately the manner in which the crisis is resolved. We may simply be unable to cope with a crisis; we may apply old and inappropriate patterns to new situations; we may try to avoid the crisis by not seeing it (i.e. refusing to see it), or by defining it, contrary to reality, as a non-crisis. In short, there are many varieties of failure. But in each case, of course, a decision has been made. And how we deal with the obligation to provide a rationale is then a further crisis-like problem, where the issue is whether or not we succeed in facing up to failure and integrating it into the "me."

Thus the contribution of actors to the formation of structure in interactions is at its most pronounced in situations of crisis; this is where it is most clearly discernible. But this contribution also takes place in routine situations. In other words, it takes place in every part of a sequence of interaction. Life practice is always involved: in principle, a decision is made at every point in a sequence as to whether a transformation or a reproduction of the structure will occur. Thus life practice always decides what form the structure will assume. Here it operates either as the representative of established structures, or as the representative of the actor's own subjectivity. Only after the fact does it become apparent in what manner subjectivity has made use of established structures (be it structures of society or those of the self), even when making a transformative decision. (We will return to this in a moment.)

In summary, it can be said that the question of transformation is always present, and that action therefore always involves decision-making. There is no need to resort to the concept of "free will" here; instead, we can define autonomy in sociological terms as a feature of sociality. The crucial factor is the structure of interaction. We may not be aware that we are constantly making decisions, sometimes in the blink of an eye; indeed it would hardly be possible to be aware of this, because paying attention to these decisions would distract us from our main business – action. It would also be almost unbearable for us, because, under these conditions, everything would become a crisis. But in actuality we react to exhortations to action, and to the requirements of situations, we choose certain forms of utterance and reject others, we react – once again in great detail, in a series of individual decisions – to the reaction of the other person, but also to our own actions, etc. When Searle (2011) states that we always operate in a sea of institutional facts (see Chapter 3), then it can be said that in doing so we always follow a trail of interaction structures, which is perhaps no less complex than our DNA. But unlike DNA, the structures of interaction do not belong only to us as individuals, but are part of social relationships that are reproduced and transformed in interactions. They are therefore more dynamic than DNA. And like it or not, we have a share in this dynamism.

Decision-making is the condition for something new/ for innovation. And the potential for decision-making is inherent in the sequential organization of interaction. Our leeway in decision-making is established interactively and cannot be circumvented. We must react to every interactive move, and it is impossible to conceive of such a reaction as having no alternatives (cf. Chapter 2).

We position ourselves with our reaction, and this positioning, in turn, opens up follow-on options that must be filled. Thus the decision-making situation is an omnipresent element in the structure of interaction, and the same therefore applies to life practice. But what are the components of "practice?"

Life practice is not an entity that "invents" – or rather, it does so only in the moment of decision-making itself. In fact, a large number of determining elements go into every concrete decision. But these can only be recognized as such after the event, i.e. after the decision has been made, by third-party observers – be it by social scientists or by ourselves as actors. What can these determining factors be? They may be standards of rationality that we follow (cf. e.g. Weber 2013 [1922]); they may be environmental influences, which become noticeable when we perceive or fail to perceive options for action, or habitual tendencies that can be ascribed to class affiliation (cf. e.g. Bourdieu 1984). They may be dispositions that are linked with our family origins, and mainly take effect in couple and family relationships (e.g. the *Triebschicksal* of psychoanalysis (variously translated as "instinctual vicissitudes," "drive-destiny" and "fate of the drives"), or the "attachment styles" of attachment theory). Social patterns of interpretation can also play a part in the perception of decision-making situations (cf. Oevermann 2001a/b). The final factors to be mentioned here are the many "socio-structural conditions" (which are only relevant here): endowment with financial or cultural capital, experiences of power or powerlessness, of recognition or disregard. This list includes several key aspects, but makes no claim to completeness. The important thing is that all these things can be combined, can overlap, and can contradict each other – always with regard to specific situations in interactions. And the way that they take effect depends on the life practices involved.

FOOD FOR THOUGHT

Refer to your transcript of the café scene from *As Good As It Gets*. There are at least two situations of crisis: when Melvin refuses Carol's thank-you note, and when Melvin more or less dismisses Frank from the table. What decisions do Carol and Frank make here in terms of life practice? And what is the problem with these decisions? Both of them are able to make an adequate assessment of the situation. (How do they see Melvin?) But what is the nature of their conflict?

Notes

1 "Dyadic" is meant analytically here: of course more than two actors may be involved, and these actors themselves may consist of several people, e.g. the individual may be part of the collective of a community, a soccer team, or a nation state. At the same time, this is always about interlocutors or counterparts who have an equal standing in terms of the interaction structure. And the third element should not be confused

with the third person or third member who, in the microsociology of Georg Simmel (1968), breaks up the logic of dyadic interaction. The structural parameters we are referring to here are also present in dyadic interactions, and to some extent in the "monologic" actions of individuals.

2 Cf., in lieu of many others: Coleman (1990); Esser (1993).

3 To be more precise, it is assumed that when contemplating our own (marital) situation we will choose a general model to define the situation, a model which is then linked with various possible actions (scripts). This model is not based on Goffman's (1986 [1974]) frame analysis (which we can already see from the fact that in Goffman's work, frames are not "chosen," but provide generally valid categories, over which the individual initially has no influence), but makes use of psychological models. However detailed this model of decision-making processes is, in the end (and in empirical analysis) the complex model dwindles into a mere subjective evaluation of our own situation – since situational definitions such as "happy marriage," "loose partnership" or "divorce," as generally shared "patterns of intellectual cultural models and of 'collective representations'" (Esser 2002, p. 34, tr. by N.B.), can neither be more exactly defined in conceptual terms (as patterns of interpretation? as typifications?), nor clarified in material terms (what are the actual characteristics of a "loose partnership"?).

4 This has consequences for the sociological method, because it gives methodological primacy to a reconstructive process. Models of decision-making such as those found in RC theory, which do not (or cannot) take into account the difference between ex ante and ex post (before and after the event), operate on similarly uncertain terrain to the actors in this phase of action themselves. Even for third-party observers, a rational explanation or justification is only available after the event.

5 Incidentally, a further reason to talk about "being obligated to justify" rather than "being forced to justify" can be added here. This is that the pressure to search for a rationale will vary considerably, depending on whether the decision actually made has proven successful or not; stories of success can afford to have "gaps."

6 There is no space here to explore the questions this raises about the relationship between event and structure, and between specific interaction and general validity. Here we can only point to studies on social history which examine these questions by analyzing specific examples: Duby (1973); Furet (1981); Meier (2000 [1993]).

References

Mead, George Herbert (1964). *Selected Writings*. Andrew J. Reck (Ed.). Chicago, IL: University of Chicago Press. See especially: The Definition of the Psychical, pp. 25–59.

Mead, George Herbert (1992 [1934]). *Mind, Self, and Society*. Charles Morris (Ed.). Chicago, IL: University of Chicago Press.

Oevermann, Ulrich (1991). Genetischer Strukturalismus und das sozialwissenschaftliche Problem der Erklärung der Entstehung des Neuen. In Stefan Müller-Doohm (Ed.), *Jenseits der Utopie* (pp. 267–335). Frankfurt a. M., Germany: Suhrkamp.

Oevermann, Ulrich (2005). Natural Utopianism in Everyday Life Practice: An Elementary Theoretical Model. In Jörn Rüsen (Ed.), *Thinking Utopia. Steps into Other Worlds* (pp. 136–148). New York/Oxford: Berghahn Books.

Further reading

Bourdieu, Pierre (1984). *Distinction. A Social Critique of the Judgement of Taste*. Cambridge, MA: Harvard University Press.

Coleman, George (1990). *Foundations of Social Theory.* Cambridge, UK: Belknap Press.

Duby, Georges (1973). *Le Dimanche de Bouvines: 27 Juillet 1214.* Paris, France: Editions Gallimard.

Durkheim, Emile (1961 [1905]). *Moral Education. A Study in the Theory & Application of the Sociology of Education.* New York: The Free Press.

Esser, Hartmut (1993). *Soziologie. Allgemeine Grundlagen.* Frankfurt a. M., Germany: Campus.

Esser, Hartmut (2002). In guten wie in schlechten Tagen? Das Framing der Ehe und das Risiko zur Scheidung. Eine Anwendung und ein Test des Modells der Frame-Selektion. *Kölner Zeitschrift für Soziologie und Sozialpsychologie, 54/1,* 27–63.

Furet, Francois (1981). *Interpreting the French Revolution.* Cambridge, UK: Cambridge University Press.

Garz, Detlef, & Raven, Uwe (2015). *Theorie der Lebenspraxis. Einführung in das Werk Ulrich Oevermanns.* Wiesbaden, Germany: Springer VS.

Hegel, Georg Friedrich Wilhelm (2008 [1821]). *Outlines of the Philosophy of Right.* Oxford, UK: Oxford University Press.

Meier, Christian (2000 [1993]). *Athens. A Portrait of the City in its Golden Age.* Bournemouth, UK: Pimlico.

Oevermann, Ulrich (2001a [1973]). Zur Analyse der Struktur von sozialen Deutungsmustern. Sozialer Sinn, *2001/1,* 3–33.

Oevermann, Ulrich (2001b). Die Struktur sozialer Deutungsmuster – Versuch einer Aktualisierung. *Sozialer Sinn, 2001/1,* 35–81.

Parsons, Talcott (1956). Family Structure and the Socialization of the Child. In Talcott Parsons & Robert F. Bale (Eds.), *Family. Socialization and Interaction Process* (pp. 35–131). London, UK: Routledge & Kegan Paul.

Searle, John R. (2001). *Rationality in Action.* Cambridge, MA: The MIT Press.

Searle, John R. (2011). *Making the Social World. The Structure of Human Civilization.* Oxford, UK: Oxford University Press.

Simmel, Georg (1968 [1908]). *Soziologie.* Berlin, Germany: Duncker & Humblot.

Weber, Max (2013 [1922]). *Economy and Society.* Berkeley, CA: University of California Press.

EPILOGUE

Structure and method

In the last 12 chapters, we have presented those aspects that we see as constitutive of structure formation in interactions. In other words, they always play a part in interactions. Without them, interaction as a process cannot take place. Even the smallest segments of interaction are unthinkable without the mechanisms of addressing, allocation of participation status and sequentiality, without the automatic reference to institutions (as semantic content) and to ways of framing the situation, without the rules of reciprocity, which allow cooperation and without the mechanisms of perspective-taking. As we interact, we always refer to pre-established patterns of relationship organization (roles) and to socially preferred patterns of action (norms). We fall back on typifications of the people we interact with, we react to the material facts of the situation, we allow our emotions to become relevant or not – and sometimes we face the fact that we have done both these things too much or too little. And lastly, we must constantly make decisions, either selecting from the socially predefined options or creating something new with reference to this range of possibilities.

These aspects are not only indispensable for interaction from an observer perspective, they also constitute unavoidable requirements from a participant perspective. "Whether we like it or not" is, in a sense, the subtitle of every chapter, and at various points we have explicitly used this or a similar phrase to make it clear that we cannot get by without these requirements. These are constitutive components of the social order of interaction. But is there not more to it than this? Are there not many other things without which interaction would be unthinkable? What about, for example, gender differentiation, identity, social patterns of interpretation, recognition, power, conflict? Do these things not always play a role in interactions too? "Empirically," this will probably be the case. It is difficult to imagine interactions that do not involve gender differences, identity formation and social patterns of interpretation which guide actions; and it is also likely that interactions will always involve questions of recognition and disregard, power and symmetry, conflict and harmony. At the same time, we believe these are not elementary components of interaction, but structural phenomena which develop *in* interactions. Or in other words: the aspects we have dealt with are needed in order to describe these structural phenomena. The converse does not apply.

But before we move on, let us consider power and conflict. If one tries, as we have done, to explicate elements of a social order, there is always a suspicion that a falsely harmonious image of the world is being propagated: as if all actors always let each other finish their sentences, always followed rules of reciprocity or norms, never embarrassed each other, always adapted their typifications to reality, etc. Of course, this is not the case. Social reality is full of violations of rules and norms, and sometimes they occur in order to assert positions of power. And of course there are conflicts, for example about the claim to validity of social norms, and there is racism, homophobia and misogyny. Indeed we have taken pains to discuss such phenomena in the individual chapters. However, our aim here has always been to identify and explore the crucial point: that these phenomena, from an analytical perspective, do not call into question the significance of the different aspects of order in interactions, but always occur on the basis of this social order. They are not "the other" of this order, but are a part of it themselves. Even if they may constitute serious problems for the relevant social practice – not only in interactions, but also on the macro level of social communities – they are not problematic from a more distant, analytical perspective.

Another potential objection might be that we are too demanding when it comes to the assumed competencies of our actors. Do we not always assume fully socialized actors, who have a complete grasp of all the rules, and are familiar with all role expectations and social typifications? Should we not take more account of the various misunderstandings and interpretive conflicts that are empirically expected? The answer is "yes" to the first question, and "no" to the second. We do indeed base our assumptions on a normal level of competency, i.e. we assume adult, socialized members of society, with no physical or mental limitations which would prevent them from implementing the mechanisms of co-presence, "nextness", perspective-taking or decision-making pressure, from having emotions, or from mastering the arsenal of rule complexes discussed previously. In other words, we assume the existence of subjects who are capable of action, and have internalized the requisite competencies as part of an implicit, action-generating stock of knowledge. We also assume that these competencies are, to a large extent, evenly distributed among the actors. These are not particularly "idealistic" assumptions; empirical linguistics, for example, works with them as a matter of course – and with good results. Individual and structural differences are located, on the one hand, on the level of performance (Chomsky 1972 [1965]), i.e. they concern the practical and situational *implementation* of the competencies. For example, the ability to express oneself well linguistically is quite unequally distributed, while the ability to adequately understand what has been said, and to distinguish grammatical from ungrammatical usages, is not. On the other hand, there are differences on the level of *explicit* stocks of knowledge. Thus there are roles and social typifications which reflect a specific knowledge, and cannot be regarded as part of the "social store of knowledge" (Schütz) that is arguably accessible to every socialized member of society. These differences, however, are of no great importance for the aspects we have dealt with here, as they mainly lie on the level of implicit knowledge. All other misunderstandings and interpretive conflicts ultimately concern the problem of *cultural differences*, i.e. the varying range of validity of rule systems. The fact that these can exist, and that an "intercultural interaction" of this kind can lead to its own misunderstandings and interpretive conflicts, was discussed in Chapter 8, as well as elsewhere. At this point, there is no need to explore the related translation problems in any greater depth. It is sufficient to point out that they are not insurmountable, as there are always shared rule systems we can refer to when dealing with them.

But what is "structure"? And what is to be understood by "structure formation"? Are the elements discussed not also (already) "structure?" Firstly, we have to bear in mind that there is no alternative, in sociology, to the concept of structure. Claude Lévi-Strauss encapsulated this in the following remark: "If these concepts have a meaning at all, they mean, first, that the notion of structure has a structure" (Lévi-Strauss 1964 [1953], p. 278). Everything that we define, in sociology, as general patterns beyond the particular or accidental is structure. Furthermore, even the particular or accidental cannot be defined without recourse to structure (more on this later). Given this unavoidability of the concept of structure, all that remains is for us to specify what *kind* of structure and what *level* of structure formation we are looking at in each case. Regardless of their heterogeneity, the aspects dealt with here are, as elementary components of interaction, also part of its structure. When we talk of structure *formation*, however, this always implies that the structure does not yet exist (in this form) and that it only emerges with the interaction. Surely this cannot apply to the "building blocks" of interaction since they exist prior to every concrete interaction – or can it?

Before we go on, it makes sense to insert a brief remark on terminology here. At first glance, the terminology we have used in this book to describe the components of interaction seems inconsistent. Sometimes we have spoken of "mechanisms," sometimes of "rules," and at other times of "structures." The reason for this, however, is the heterogeneity of the components; this does not fit into any unified terminology. It seems obvious to refer to co-presence and its consequences, "nextness," perspective-taking and the pressure to act as "mechanisms" (which are already heterogeneous in themselves), because they cannot linguistically be formulated as rules and because it is not possible to deviate from them in any way. At most, we can deny them by making someone who is co-present interactively "invisible" (Honneth 2001), or by trying to convince others that not acting relieves us of responsibility. This then leads to structures of neglect or irresponsibility, making the structure-forming power of the mechanisms involved especially clear. In contrast, norms, role expectations, frames and other non-linguistic or linguistic institutions (as understood by Searle) constitute complexes of rules which can be presented linguistically as regulative or constitutive rules. We take our bearings from them, either manifestly (norms, roles) or latently (institutions), we follow them or deviate from them, sometimes we dispute their claim to validity (norms). And all of this has consequences for the structure of the interaction. On the other hand, structural problems of action, which arise from the material contexts of interactions (see Chapter 10), can be the starting point for complexes of rules (our example of the elevator), but cannot be described as such themselves. Instead, they constitute a different kind of structural parameter for interactions. The crucial point for the present context is that from a broader perspective, regardless of their internal heterogeneity and the different terms used for them because of this, all components of interaction – including mechanisms and rule complexes – are structural phenomena, since they themselves constitute patterns that lead to other patterns.

But can we also now say that even these structural phenomena not only have the power to form structure, but that they themselves are "formed" in interactions? In a way, yes. This mainly applies to the rule complexes dealt with here. Strictly speaking, they are not "produced" in specific interactions, but precede them analytically, as mentioned several times above. Yet, on the other hand, their validity is up for negotiation in every interaction. This is explicitly the case for norms and role expectations. The question in every concrete interaction is whether they will be reproduced or transformed. But even in the case of the more fundamental varieties of social institutions, it can at least be said that their validity is bound to their use in interactions. In this context, John Searle talks about the primacy of action, or the primacy of the process – in our terminology this would be the primacy of interaction – over the (social) object, i.e. institutions such as marriage, money, property or universities: "The priority of process over product [...] explains why [...] institutions are not worn out by continued use, but each use of the institution is in a sense a renewal of that institution" (Searle 1995, p. 57). If we say that the interactive use of non-linguistic and linguistic institutions "renews" or reinforces them in their validity, then we can refer to interaction in general as the place where institutional facts are "ratified." This would offer at least one starting point for explaining institutional change: for example, the shift from a formal "Good morning" to a casual "Hi," and from "Mr. Smith" to "Jack" in institutional contexts could then be examined by studying how these linguistic institutions are introduced and processed in interactions.

But in actual fact, when talking about "structure formation in interactions," we have mainly been concerned with other phenomena: structures that only form in interactions, and that cannot be adequately defined without a microsociological perspective. These structures are as diverse as social reality itself. They have to do with our relationship to ourselves (biography, identity) and to others. This is about patterns that characterize relationships between couples, family members, friends, neighbors or colleagues, or that can be found in interactions between market participants and in political debates. This is about general and formal patterns for the structuring of interactions, "forms of talk," communicative genres such as gossip, jokes or sermons. These structures have to do with the particular and the general simultaneously: the structure of the specific couple relationship always points to the way couple relationships are structured in general; the structure of the specific organization points to the way organizations are structured. They extend to the general structures of conflict resolution, and of the social organization of labor and economic exchange. They encompass the generic issues of power and domination (or the absence thereof), conflict and harmony, recognition or disregard, equality and inequality. All these things can – and this is the weaker assumption of our approach – be analyzed in microsociological terms in the process of interaction, on the basis of the components presented.

In itself, the attempt undertaken in this book – to define microsociology in terms of interaction theory – is not especially original. Herbert Blumer, Erving Goffman, Niklas Luhmann and, following on from these authors, André Kieserling, have tried to define "interaction" as an independent level of structuring of the social. Our project goes beyond these attempts, especially in two respects. On the one hand, we have expanded the inventory of terms for describing interaction to include various elements, some of which would not readily be assigned to the micro level in standard sociological practice. Norms, roles, social typifications, frames and in particular the broad field of social institutions are not only aspects that exist prior to any concrete interaction, but they can also be assigned to the macro area of the social, due to their *generally valid* nature.[1] In this respect, we have taken further steps along a path which Goffman embarked on, particularly in his *Frame Analysis* (Goffman 1986 [1974]). If we study the structure of interactions, we cannot help but notice that some of the aspects relevant here are, according to the common understanding, neither "big" nor "small." Even if actors may sometimes succeed, by virtue of their actions, in "defining" the situation of interaction[2] they are in, we normally find ourselves in situations whose framing qualities already exist, and can only be discovered or accessed by us. In short, every interaction operates within a "casing" of generally valid rules. The "interaction system" always includes an "order of interaction", comprising elements that exist prior to any concrete interaction. "Interaction" is therefore not just a specific combination of actions, but always includes the mechanisms, rules and structures that allow such a combination in the first place – and this means that, strictly speaking, we can no longer talk about a combination of individual actions, or at least not if we think of them as isolated actions.

On the other hand – and connected with this – by making interaction theory the basis for our approach to microsociology, we are attributing a particularly important position to interaction. According to our understanding, interaction is not simply one level of structuring alongside others: there is not "interaction" and then – independent of it – "organization" and "society" (in the terminology of systems theory). Instead, organization and society are always, in part, realized in interactions. And nor can microsociology, according to this understanding, be reduced to a lower aggregate level of the social, "above" which the meso and macro levels then lie. Microsociology is neither "big" nor "small." Instead – and this is the stronger assumption of our approach – all the structures that affect different aggregate levels of society must have their foundation in interactions. The special importance ascribed to interaction can thus be formulated as follows: the central social "location" of structure is interaction.

This does not mean that we wish to dispute the independence of macro-phenomena such as milieu, legal parameters, social patterns of interpretation, risks of poverty and divorce, unequal distribution of educational opportunities, etc. At the same time, it can be said, in light of this, that these phenomena only develop their meaning on the level of interaction. Or in other words: if they have no meaning on this level, then they are meaningless. It must be possible to identify them in concrete interactions. Analyses of social structure that work with aggregate data should, therefore, be asking one key question: how do these phenomena enter into interactions? As an expectation of normality, which actors bring to interactions? As a quality of the structure of a relationship, which develops interactively? As a decision-making option which is not taken into account in interactions, or is seen as having no alternative? This is something that cannot be determined purely on the basis of the patterns identified by means of aggregate data. We cannot draw conclusions about the microstructure from the description of the macrostructure. In contrast, the macrostructure is always present in the microstructure.

These reflections bring us to the question of what consequences the approach presented – the choice of interaction theory as a basis for microsociology – has for the *methods* used to examine social reality. This approach is not an explicit methodology, but it does have methodological consequences. While we cannot deal with these in detail here, we would like to at least address some general aspects for orientation purposes. The first aspect is the heuristic quality of the concepts presented. We assume that they can be used as a suitable conceptual toolbox for the examination of social reality. This is certainly not an especially risky assumption, given that at least some of them (role, norm, typification, emotion, institution) are established basic concepts of general sociology, even if our understanding of them differs in some respects from the usual understanding. The consequences become more specific when it comes to the idea of a unity of structure and process, associated with the talk of "structure formation." The crucial insight here is the fundamental importance of sequentiality for interaction: generally speaking, interaction does not only unfold in a temporal succession of interaction turns, but in their systematic relatedness to one another. Every turn can be presented as a choice, made in the moment, from a range of possibilities, which is marked out by the preceding turn and by structural parameters that are broader than this particular interaction; each turn, therefore, opens up a new range of possible subsequent actions. "Structure" thus presents itself as a selective, gradually unfolding combination of interaction turns. This insight was first formulated in the context of conversation analysis (see Chapter 2), then further elaborated, most notably in the methodology of objective hermeneutics (e.g. Oevermann 2000, Wernet 2014, Maiwald 2005). Against this background, it is no surprise that this approach is associated with a preference for *reconstructive* research methods, i.e. methods that attempt to retrace the formation of structure in specific interactions.

Lastly, given the central role of the concept of meaning for a microsociology based on interaction theory, it follows that such approaches should simultaneously be *interpretive*. In this respect too, the methodology of objective hermeneutics is a key point of reference. We explored the concept of meaning mainly in the chapters on institutions and perspective-taking. Here it should have become clear that, in interaction analyses, we are always dealing simultaneously with two different levels of meaning: the meaning that the significant elements of an interaction turn *have*, on the basis of generally valid rules, and the meaning that these elements *acquire* from being used at a specific point in a sequence. This latter meaning marks the structure of the interaction as a specific relationship between interaction partners. An interpretive process has the potential to gain epistemic objectivity by referring to the generally valid structures of meaning, and it gains relevance for the social structures under examination by being able to identify the particular selectivity with which elements of meaning are used at the different points in the sequence.

We would like to conclude by discussing a matter that has been foreshadowed in these methodological remarks. It can be regarded as a commonplace that we, as sociologists, are always part of the subject area we are studying. What this really means only becomes apparent in its full drama from a microsociological perspective: "structure" is not only inescapable for distanced social science observers, but also in a participant perspective. It does not take place in segments, once every few hours, as it were, but occurs at every point of every sequence of our lives. Nothing about our interactions with others, but also nothing about our "solitary" actions is without structure. There are no "blank spaces," no "quiet zones" in which structure is absent. We are constantly (co-)producing it. And not only in the actions that we are fully committed to, not only in situations where we are aware that we are interacting. We do not only participate in those structures toward which we have an explicit "attitude," or in those which appear to us, in our actions, as "available."[3] Instead, we are constantly reproducing (mostly) or transforming (fairly seldom) structures about which we usually know very little. Admittedly, this does not match our everyday experience. Nor can it do so, because if we were aware of the abundance of options for action which we are constantly choosing between in interaction processes, and of the structural consequences that our decisions have for the interaction process, we would, in fact, be incapable of action. Seen in terms of interaction theory, structure is not only ubiquitous, it is also (evidently as a matter of necessity) largely latent, i.e. it takes place beyond the threshold of consciousness.

Thus there is an inevitable tension between what our actions (potentially) say about us, right down to the smallest gestures, and what we are able to say about ourselves; our individual and collective self-images. But these self-images are, as it were, the "working basis" of our interactions, a basis which we cling to and are only prepared to revise in the painful processes of experience – i.e. under conditions of the manifest failure of our convictions. This means that, as "ordinary people," we do not have an especially friendly attitude towards sociological critique, which must call into question these very self-images, with reference to latent structures of meaning. For us as ordinary people, sociological investigation is not a source of pleasure. It always has considerable potential for causing offence as it identifies latent structures of social practice (cf. Wernet 2018). This is a burden which the discipline must learn to expect. There is no short-term prospect of a Nobel Prize (or anything of the kind) for sociology. Understood in this way, sociological investigation is only a source of pleasure (intellectual pleasure at least) if we have learnt how to make a break with everyday experience and to adopt a distanced attitude toward it, without believing that we are outside of the analysis.

Notes

1 This is true even if we concede that the *scope* of this general validity does not necessarily have to extend to a "whole society" (or beyond), but can be restricted to a particular social milieu, subculture or even – in individual elements – a family.
2 Why did we not place the concept of the situation in the center of our analysis? Could one not say that "situation" has the same significance for the micro level of the social as "society" has for the macro level? This is in fact the case, but the same problem applies to both "situation" and "society:" the terms are indispensable, but it seems impossible to define them satisfactorily.
3 For this and the following see Wernet (2018). The reflections presented there are focused on objective hermeneutics or on reconstructive educational research analyzing latent case structures. Here we transfer them to a microsociology based on interaction theory.

References

Chomsky, Noam (1965). *Aspects of the Theory of Syntax*. Cambridge, MA: The MIT Press.

Goffman, Erving (1986 [1974]). *Frame Analysis. An Essay on the Organization of Experience.* Lebanon, NH: Northeastern University Press.

Honneth, Axel (2001). Invisibility: On the Epistemology of "Recognition." *Aristotelian Society Supplementary Volume, 75/1,* 111–126.

Lévi-Strauss, Claude (1974 [1953]). *Structural Anthropology*. New York: Basic Books. See especially: Social Structure, pp. 277–323.

Maiwald, Kai-Olaf (2005). Competence and Praxis: Sequential Analysis in German Sociology. *Forum: Qualitative Social Research, 6,* 3, Art. 31 (www.qualitative-research. net/index.php/fqs/article/view/21/46).

Oevermann, Ulrich (2000). Die Methode der Fallrekonstruktion in der Grundlagenforschung sowie der klinischen und pädagogischen Praxis. In Klaus Kraimer (Ed.), *Die Fallrekonstruktion. Sinnverstehen in der sozialwissenschaftlichen Forschung* (pp. 58–156). Frankfurt a. M., Germany: Suhrkamp.

Searle, John (1995). *The Construction of Social Reality*. New York: The Free Press.

Wernet, Andreas (2014). Hermeneutics and Objective Hermeneutics. In Uwe Flick (Ed.), *The SAGE Handbook of Qualitative Data Analysis* (pp. 234–246). Los Angeles, CA: Sage.

Wernet, Andreas (2018). Über das spezifische Erkenntnisinteresse einer auf die Rekonstruktion latenter Sinnstrukturen zielenden Bildungsforschung. In Martin Heinrich & Andreas Wernet (Eds.), *Rekonstruktive Bildungsforschung: Zugänge und Methoden* (pp. 125–140). Wiesbaden, Germany: Springer VS.

INDEX